D1283061

The 'Danzig Trilogy' of Günter Grass

The 'Danzig Trilogy' of Günter Grass

❀ ❀ ❀

A Study of
The Tin Drum, Cat and Mouse and Dog Years

❀

JOHN REDDICK

A Helen and Kurt Wolff Book
Harcourt Brace Jovanovich
NEW YORK AND LONDON

Copyright © 1974 by John Reddick

All rights reserved. No part of this publication may be reproduced or transmitted in any form or by any means, electronic or mechanical, including photocopy, recording, or any information storage and retrieval system, without permission in writing from the publisher.

Printed in Great Britain

Quotations from *The Tin Drum* by Günter Grass, translated by Ralph Manheim, are reprinted by permission of Pantheon Books, English translation copyright © 1961, 1962 by Pantheon Books, a Division of Random House, Inc. Those from *Cat and Mouse* by Günter Grass, translated by Ralph Manheim, English translation © 1963 by Harcourt Brace Jovanovich, Inc. and Martin Secker & Warburg Limited, and from *Dog Years* by Günter Grass, translated by Ralph Manheim, English translation © 1965 by Harcourt Brace Jovanovich, Inc. and Martin Secker & Warburg Limited, and from *Selected Poems* by Günter Grass, translated by Michael Hamburger and Christopher Middleton, English translation copyright © 1966 by Martin Secker & Warburg Limited are reprinted by permission of Harcourt Brace Jovanovich, Inc.

Library of Congress Cataloging in Publication Data
Reddick, John.
  The 'Danzig trilogy' of Günter Grass.
  "A Helen and Kurt Wolff book."
  Bibliography : p. 287
    1. Grass, Günter, 1927–   —Criticism and interpretation. I. Title.
  PT2613.R338Z78 1975   833'.9'14   74–11027
  ISBN 0–15–123815–4

First American edition 1975

B C D E

for Gill, Kate and Adam

Acknowledgments

I happily acknowledge my special indebtedness to Günter Grass, who has not only met my years of pestering with patience and sceptical good humour, but has also gone out of his way to be helpful. It is a debt I cannot easily repay.

More generally, I should like to record my lasting gratitude towards Gilbert McKay, of St Peter's College, Oxford, without whose teaching this book – and much else besides – might not have come about.

I am also grateful to Elisabeth Stopp and Jill Mann, both of Girton College, Cambridge, and to Michael Butler, of Birmingham University, who checked through the manuscript and made many valuable suggestions.

John Reddick
Cambridge, August 1972

Note on Translations

English-language quotations from the 'trilogy' are taken from the official translations by Ralph Manheim, to whom all credit is due, with amendments where appropriate for extra clarity.

In the case of other translated matter, the translations are by the author unless otherwise indicated.

Contents

Preface

If it seems odd to devote a critical study to just three out of the ever increasing mass of writings by Günter Grass (the fullest bibliography to date lists no fewer than one hundred and twenty-nine items), there is a simple explanation, and one that is already implicit in the title of this book: *The Tin Drum*, *Cat and Mouse* and *Dog Years* form a natural focus of attention not merely for the incidental reason that they are the best known of Grass's works so far, but because they belong together as a kind of trilogy – 'a single whole complex' ('Gesamtkomplex'), to borrow Grass's own description.[1]

To say that the books belong together is not to say that they are simply variations on the same theme, or that they are dependent parts of a single utterance (indeed I will argue that there were crucial shifts in Grass's perspective between the separate books, completed and published at precise two-year intervals in 1959, 1961 and 1963; and it certainly makes little sense to allege, as Walter Jens and others have done,[2] that *Dog Years* is really little more than a rehash of the earlier books). It is rather that they are deeply and organically related to one another – different in many important respects, maybe, but all inspired as it were by the same muse. This is apparent if one takes even the hastiest of glances at *Local Anaesthetic*, which followed a full six years later (1969), and bears the stamp of a very different sort of muse. It shows itself equally clearly when one compares the three books themselves, for their common features – characters, episodes, settings of time and place, themes, mood, style, etc. – are immediately obvious. But it shows itself most decisively of all when one looks at the genetic evidence – for there is palpable proof that the three books have origins in common.

That *Cat and Mouse* started out, not as a separate creation, but as an integral part of *Dog Years*, is commonly known.[3] What is less well appreciated is that many of the major elements of *Dog*

xi

Years were themselves already well established in Grass's imagination before *The Tin Drum* had even been published. The figure of Walter Matern, the histrionic, teeth-grinding antagonist of the later novel, is a particular case in point, for he was not only imagined at the same time as *The Tin Drum*, but actually found his way into the novel as published. It is true that he occurs in only one episode ('In the Onion Cellar') and is nameless – but he does appear under the two appellations that are to type him in *Dog Years*, namely as 'the Grinder' and 'the Actor', and his violent bearing in the Onion Cellar is a clear anticipation of later things, with Grass depicting him furiously grinding his teeth, and first savaging, then half devouring, an errant brassière.[4]

Walter Matern may be the only prime element of *Dog Years* to have already appeared in *The Tin Drum* as published, but there is no shortage of external evidence to prove the genetic inter-relatedness of the three books. For one thing, Grass himself has said that by the time he went back to Berlin from Paris in late 1959, soon after the publication of *The Tin Drum*, the Scarecrow, Mound of Bones and Snow Miracle ideas – all central to *Dog Years* – were already worked out in considerable detail.[5] We also know that Grass's ballet *Remnants (Stoffreste)*, a first version of the scarecrow ballet in *Dog Years*, was staged by Marcel Luipart as early as 1957, and had therefore conceivably been finished before the manuscript work on *The Tin Drum* had even been started in late 1956. And we know that the radio play *Thirty-Two Teeth (Zweiunddreissig Zähne)*, with its anticipation of the *Dog Years* motif of Eduard Amsel's knocked-out teeth, was first broadcast in 1959. Most important of all, there is direct evidence from Grass's own hand. He has always made great use of wall-plans in working out material for his books, plans which he says he tends to destroy once they have served their purpose. Certainly I have been able myself to unearth only a few (all relating to what we know as *Dog Years*) – but although Grass disparages them as footling and unrepresentative, even these few offer some remarkable insights into his creative process; more to the point, they constitute firm proof that much of the substance later fashioned into *Dog Years* did not merely exist in Grass's mind before the publication of *The Tin Drum*, but had already reached the stage of being provisionally shaped and organised. Thus we find one plan dating from November 1959, and headed '*The Grinder* or *Scarecrows*', which, with great colourfulness and graphic effect, shapes into four-book-novel form the broad pattern of episodes that we now associate with the Third Book of *Dog Years*. While another November 1959 plan graphically and verbally projects a scheme for a seemingly quite different novel, entitled '*Tulla* or *Ice-warehouse and Mound of Bones*', which in the event was to go to make the section of *Dog Years* from the finding of Jenny Brunies (represented here as 'Halina Lattkau') to almost the end of the Second Book. This plan is highly specific and detailed (albeit in an often cryptic way), and includes prefigurations of virtually every episode of importance to appear in the relevant part of the novel as published. What the plan also crucially does is to make reference to 'Grinder, Amsel, Dog' – that is to say, to the two protagonists and the eponymous dog of the later novel.[6] And on looking back at the 'Grinder or Scarecrows' plan, we find that these same key personas are intensively figured throughout by means of the colour-code system peculiar to the plan. Then again, on the earliest of all the wall-plans that I have been able to see, a tabular one dating from September 1959, and headed 'The Grinder – Part One', we find the same three figures in an even more marked form : a column labelled 'Theme', though numbered all the way down to thirty-three, in fact has entries in only the first three spaces – and these entries are '1 Dog', '2 Amsel', '3 Grinder'.

The plans will come more into their own later on, but their value at this stage is clear : they join with the rest of the evidence in showing beyond serious doubt that *The Tin Drum*, *Cat and Mouse* and *Dog Years* do indeed amount to a distinctive complex. And the aim of this study is to throw more light on that complex by considering each of the books in turn, both in itself and also in its relationship to the others.

PART ONE

The Tin Drum

Now we're on the run and our luggage with us.
All half-empty paper bags, every crater in our beer,
cast-off coats, clocks that have stopped,
graves paid for by other people,
and women very short of time,
for a while we fill them.

GRASS, *'Music for Brass'*
translated by
Christopher Middleton

CHAPTER I

Introduction

The extraordinary éclat of Günter Grass's first novel, which began when he won the 1958 prize of the *Gruppe 47* with his still incomplete manuscript,[1] and which has since resounded through half the countries of the world, has by now become a literary commonplace – though without for that losing much of its force: *The Tin Drum* is still being avidly read (by March 1972 total printings in German alone had reached nearly one and a half million, while printings in other languages are officially reckoned at a third of a million), and the novel has clearly established itself in the general literary consciousness as one of the monumental reference points of post-war writing. Thus Hans Egon Holthusen, for instance, could assert in 1964: 'The Tin Drum re-establishes the form of the novel, perhaps not once and for all, but certainly for this once';[2] and it was the same writer-critic who declared that 'Oskar Matzerath has found general favour as no hero of the German novel has done since Thomas Mann's Hans Castorp and Döblin's Franz Biberkopf.'[3]

But as its very fervour suggests, the reaction to the novel was a complex and passionate affair, particularly in the decisive early stages in Germany, with the Bremen uproar of December 1959– January 1960 dramatically displaying the stormy course of things: the official jury, which included Benno von Wiese and Rolf Schroers, chose Grass *nem. con.* for the annual Bremen City Prize for Literature, but the City Government rejected their recommendation in hedged but symptomatic terms: to award *The Tin Drum* an official government accolade, they declared, would be to provoke 'a public discussion which would not criticise the undisputed literary quality of the book, but would assuredly criticise large areas of its contents from non-artistic points of view'.[4]

Ironically but inevitably, the government's attempt to forestall

3

trouble proved in fact to have a contrary effect. As for the true feelings welling beneath the diplomatic bromide, they were perhaps best revealed by the local author Manfred Hausmann, the single member of the prize jury who abstained from the final vote; in his view, *The Tin Drum* was one of those works 'which do not serve to shake people up and give them a jolt, but rather serve to endanger, if not to destroy, the human soul and mind'.[5] The force of such convictions may be gauged from the fact that altogether some forty legal actions have been started in German courts against the novel and against its successor *Cat and Mouse* – all of them in vain; while in 1965 *The Tin Drum* was prominent amongst a number of books publicly burnt in Düsseldorf by a religious youth organisation[6] – an event not without precedent in German history. Walter Höllerer (whose periodical *Akzente* had been the first to publish Grass, and who became his close friend during the writing of *The Tin Drum* in Paris) well described the fervid irrationality of the phenomenon when he wrote in December 1959:

> Why is it that Grass's novel gets people worked up? Just because of his motifs? Hardly. It is rather that he has probed a hidden, neuralgic web of nerve-fibres that lies entangled in the deepest recesses of our society, and to which all of us, whether we like it or not, are connected.[7]

The furore would be well worth studying in its own right – especially if taken together with the inverted situation in the cultural crisis of Germany in the early 1970s, with Grass having ironically become in turn the *bête noire* of the radical and not-so-radical left, who despise him as too conventionally moral and *scheissliberal*, too much a lapdog of the capitalist, bourgeois establishment. But what matters for our purposes is that the strident, passionate nature of the initial response to *The Tin Drum* and its author seems to have had the effect of reducing the scope for a dispassionate, open-minded approach to the book. Philip Toynbee, at the start of his *Observer* review of the English edition in 1962, echoed the problem in exemplary fashion – before going on to find the book 'inhuman', 'shocking', 'most gravely boring' and afflicted by 'some kind of fanatical and blinded *avant-garde* obsession':

4

This is a book which has arrived with a loud bang – the reverberation of praise and obloquy in France and its native Germany. *Encounter* published a passage from it; it has been described, so the blurb tells us, as 'a barbaric counterpart to Thomas Mann's *Felix Krull* and Goethe's *Wilhelm Meister* on a tin drum'. *The Tin Drum* is now appearing simultaneously in London and New York, and two days ago I received an invitation to hear Grass reading from the book at the German Institute.

This is 'the treatment' with a vengeance, and in face of it the reviewer must try to keep his hackles down and review the book as if it had stolen upon the senses like the scent of violets. Good books have been ballyhooed as well as bad ones.[8]

What appears to have happened is that a sorely inadequate kind of Oskar myth came into being from the earliest stages and tended to thwart the development of other, more rationally based views. The *Times Literary Supplement* reviewer, in a long middle-page article with the symptomatic title 'Drum of Neutrality', showed every sign of standing in the shadow of this myth when he wrote that 'amoral gusto and abandon' characterise the novel, and when he interpreted Oskar Matzerath's perpetual infant state in the novel's first two Books as a device for attaining 'freedom from moral convention', and as being marked by 'freedom, freshness and impishness'. More revealing still is the reviewer's judgement that 'the work seems more like some weird sport of nature than of art'.[9] An article in *Der Spiegel* betrayed the same affinities in characterising the novel's general perspective as a 'Giftzwergperspektive' (*'runt's-eye view'*).[10] In the same vein, Holthusen described Oskar as 'a monster, a grotesque bastard born of a union of surrealist wit and priapically vulgar lust for life'.[11]

More strikingly, there is a passage in Holthusen that demonstrates an assumption about the novel that is almost universal (see the *TLS* review) and which is at the very heart of the 'Oskar myth'; the assumption concerns freedom, Holthusen maintaining of Oskar:

he embodies the principle of an infinite freedom over the circumstances of time and place into which he is born; the freedom of imagination over the ponderous laws of physical reality, and the freedom of mind to revolt at the outrageous state of social reality.[12]

Günter Grass may well be said to display some similar 'freedom' in the sovereign way that he manages his material as author – but it is unquestionably a basic error to infer such grand freedom *within* the narrative, and it is particularly mistaken to regard Oskar Matzerath himself as an 'embodiment of freedom',[13] for the truth is much more complex. Such an interpretation implies a view of *The Tin Drum* as being something essentially linear and picaresque, a string of episodes with Oskar as a swashbuckling, sovereign link-man; indeed Holthusen explicitly describes the book as 'a strange and exciting succession of picaresque tales'.[14] It seems to have been these twin assumptions of freedom and linearity which, more than anything else, have vitiated so much criticism of the novel. It is not that the arguments based on them are necessarily wrong in themselves; it is rather that they leave out of account many of the most essential elements of Grass's fiction. I shall offer a different view. What I shall try to show, among other things, is that Oskar is *not* free : that he is first and last a desperate Victim; and that the book as a whole, the expression of *his* fictive being, is as plural and non-linear in its structure as it is moral and passionate in its intent.

CHAPTER II

Patterns – Images – Motifs

...*egg, chicken, egg*...

'How shall I begin?'; 'who will supply me with a good ending?': these questions, one from the opening paragraphs of *The Tin Drum*, the other from the closing paragraphs of *Cat and Mouse*, have nothing whatever to do with aesthetics, with Grass's own problems as author: Oskar's query comes after Grass has already brilliantly begun his novel; Pilenz's in *Cat and Mouse* prefaces a quiet but scarcely less effective conclusion to the novella. Rather, the significance of both questions is that they reflect the pattern of existence that Grass is concerned with in both books, though more insistently in *The Tin Drum*, a pattern that has nothing within it of centricity or meaningful organisation, that knows no comforting growth from notable beginnings to manifest conclusions; a pattern that is evoked with rare directness in the first pages of the novel, when Oskar refers to his readers as 'all you who have to live a life of confusion outside this mental hospital'.

The 'chicken-and-egg' image, one of the most striking in Grass's early work generally, recurs time and again as a figuration of this process that is random and infinite, and hence unfathomable and potentially menacing. The prose-poem 'Fünf Vögel' (*'Five Birds'*) is typical when it speaks of 'die grosse Reise, die dauernde Wandlung, welche am Ende das Ei meint' (*'The great journey, the endless transformation, which at the last means and is meant by the egg'*);[15] typical, too, are the opening lines of 'Zwischen Marathon und Athen' (*'Between Marathon and Athens'*):

> Die Henne wohnt auf leisen Eiern
> Und brütet über Start und Ziel.[16]

> The chicken dwells on quiet eggs
> And broods over start and end.

And *The Tin Drum* itself speaks of 'Cackling hens symbolising immortality with and through their eggs' (199; 167).[17] Much the most powerful use of the egg image in Grass's work, though, is in the poem 'Im Ei' ('*In the Egg*'), probably written soon after the completion of *The Tin Drum* manuscript in February 1959:

> Wir leben im Ei.
> Die Innenseite der Schale
> haben wir mit unanständigen Zeichnungen[18]
> und den Vornamen unserer Feinde bekritzelt.
> Wir werden gebrütet.
>
> ...
>
> Wir nehmen an, dass wir gebrütet werden....
>
> ...
>
> Und wenn wir nun nicht gebrütet werden?
> Wenn diese Schale niemals ein Loch bekommt?
> Wenn unser Horizont nur der Horizont
> unserer Kritzeleien ist und auch bleiben wird?
> Wir hoffen, dass wir gebrütet werden.
>
> Wenn wir auch nur noch vom Brüten reden,
> bleibt doch zu befürchten, dass jemand,
> ausserhalb unserer Schale, Hunger verspürt,
> uns in die Pfanne haut und mit Salz bestreut. –
> Was machen wir dann, ihr Brüder im Ei?[19]

> *We live in the egg.*
> *We have covered the inside wall*
> *of the shell with dirty drawings*[18]
> *and the Christian names of our enemies.*
> *We are being hatched.*
>
> ...
>
> *We assume that we're being hatched....*

And what if we're not being hatched?
If this shell will never break?
If our horizon is only that
of our scribbles, and always will be?
We hope that we're being hatched.

Even if we only talk of hatching
There remains the fear that someone
outside our shell will feel hungry
and crack us into the frying pan with a pinch of salt.
What shall we do then, my brethren inside the egg?[20]

One distinctive feature of this grim-comic poem is its progressive undermining of a situation initially presented as fixed and reliable. At the beginning: a sordid, confined but certain reality, coupled with a clear future; at the end: nothing but questions and uncertainty, together with a sardonic sense of vulnerability. In this degenerative respect, 'Im Ei' echoes *The Tin Drum*: at the beginning of both the steadily converging Oskar time-scales of the book – that is, at the beginning of his act of narration, and at the time of his birth – he is safe and confident, if in very different degrees; the process whereby the hero's position thereafter degenerates remorselessly into one of ultimate fear, impotence and desperate vulnerability, is something that will claim particular attention.

... egg, chicken, egg, chicken, egg ... : the image not only undermines all teleological confidence as to origin and purpose, 'Start und Ziel'; it may also imply a cycle of existence so desolate that little value and absolutely no uniqueness can be ascribed to any of its separate elements, indeed these elements may be said to have no existence of their own at all but to be merely functions of what precedes and causes of what follows. It is in just such a sense that the image and its analogues recur persistently in *The Tin Drum*, and it is characteristic indeed that in his very first use of the idea, Grass should parody the Bible and so throw doubt on the opposite, benign tenets of Christianity: the poetic, driving paragraph on the disappearance of Joseph Koljaiczek extends over a single sentence of thirty-three lines, and closes then with one short sentence:

9

Und musste tauchen wegen Barkassen und unten bleiben wegen Barkassen, und das Floss schob sich über ihn und wollte nicht mehr aufhören, gebar immer ein neues Floss: Floss von deinem Floss, in alle Ewigkeit: Floss. (35)

But he has to dive on account of the launches and he has to stay under on account of the launches, and the raft passes over him and it won't stop, one raft engenders another: raft of thy raft, for all eternity: raft. (36)

This parody[21] is echoed later at the height of one of the novel's most critical sequences: during the burial service for his mother, Oskar is convinced that her vomitings have still not finished, that her corpse will still spew forth one last thing –

ein Stückchen Aal meine ich, ... Karfreitagsaal, Aal aus dem Haupte des Rosses entsprungen, womöglich Aal aus ihrem Vater Joseph Koljaiczek, der unters Floss geriet und den Aalen anheimfiel, Aal von deinem Aal, denn Aal wird zu Aal ... (194-5)

a little chunk of eel ..., Good Friday eel, eel from that horse's head, possibly eel from her father Joseph Koljaiczek who ended under the raft, a prey to the eels, eel of thine eel, for eel thou art, to eel returnest ... (163-4)

The cycle is bleak indeed in this passage, with its suggestion that Agnes Matzerath may have eaten of her own father's flesh (see also below, pp. 25-6, 99-100!) The content of both these death-centred passages is arresting enough; but their particular threnodic impact arises from their form: in both, the language departs from its normal narrative tone and becomes rhythmic, concentrated, emphatic. Such shifts of tone are of the essence in Grass (Grass himself in 1970: 'Everything I've so far written has its origin and impulse in the lyrical'[22]); and they not only reflect the poet in him, they almost always manifest the humanism that is one of the strongest influences throughout all his work, that 'old-fashioned' humanism as in Donne's *Devotions*: 'any man's death diminishes me, because I am involved in mankind; And therefore never send to know for whom the bell tolls; It tolls for thee.'

It is by no means just in these two passages that the egg-chicken-egg motif is used by Grass in the context of death. Indeed

10

one may say that it is the persistent coupling of the motif to the motifs of death, persecution and suffering that makes it so effective in reinforcing the ever more pervasive impression that, where there *is* any identifiable pattern in the otherwise random course of existence, it is a sinister one. It is typical, for instance, that Grass should have Oskar describe ships as beginning to perish the moment they are launched (38; 38). Particularly motto-like and characteristic is Oskar's remark that the sight of buildings under construction makes him think of buildings being demolished: '[ich] — der ich beim Anblick von Baugerüsten immer an Abbrucharbeiten denken muss' (301; 247). A much more substantial case in point, however, occurs early on in one of the novel's most graphic passages: as the tug carries Wranka-Koljaiczek to his (presumable) death, the landscape to either side of the Vistula is described, associations take over, and suddenly this landscape appears as 'geschaffen für Kavallerieattacken ... für die Schlacht, die schon dagewesen, die immer wieder kommt' (28; *made for cavalry attacks ... for the battle that was and will always recur'*, *30*), and there follows a 'painting' ('Gemälde') that is magnificent for its rhythmic vitality and its historical span from Tartars to tanks, but above all for its oblique lament at the perpetual round of destruction:

Tataren flach, Dragoner aufbäumend, Schwertritter stürzend, Hochmeister färbend den Ordensmantel, dem Kürass kein Knöpfchen fehlt, bis auf einen, den abhaut Masoviens Herzog, und Pferde, kein Zirkus hat solche Schimmel, nervös, voller Troddeln, die Sehnen peinlich genau und die Nüstern gebläht, karminrot, draus Wölkchen, durchstochen von Lanzen, bewimpelt, gesenkt und den Himmel, das Abendrot teilend, die Säbel und dort, im Hintergrund – denn jedes Gemälde hat einen Hintergrund – fest auf dem Horizont klebend, schmauchend ein Dörfchen friedlich zwischen den Hinterbeinen des Rappen, geduckte Katen, bemoost, strohgedeckt; und in den Katen, das konserviert sich, die hübschen, vom kommenden Tage träumenden Panzer, da auch sie ins Bild hinausdürfen auf die Ebene hinter den Weichseldeichen, gleich leichten Fohlen zwischen der schweren Kavallerie. (28-9)

Tartars flat against the necks of their horses, dragoons rearing, knights in armour falling, grand masters in blood-spattered mantles, not a button missing from their cuirasses, all but one, struck off by the Duke of Mazowsze; and horses, whiter than in any circus, bedecked with tassels, sinews delineated with precision, nostrils dilated, carmine red, sending up little clouds and the clouds are pierced by lowered lances hung with pennants, sabres part the sky and the sunset, and there in the background – for every painting has a background – pasted firmly against the horizon, a little village with peacefully smoking chimneys between the hind legs of the black stallion, little squat cottages with moss-covered walls and thatched roofs; and in the cottages the pretty little tanks – they keep well – dreaming of the day to come when they too will sally forth into the picture behind the Vistula dikes, like light foals amid the heavy cavalry. (30-1)

There is a similar conspectus of history much later, at the opening of the chapter 'Should I or Shouldn't I?', this time concerning the vicissitudes of Danzig, and again focussing on the senseless round of death and destruction. Typically, there is a murder at the outset, the martyring of Adalbert of Prague in 997;[23] there follows the description of a first phase of ruination at the hands of a succession of enemies, and this is followed in turn by a description of a second phase that figures the eternal cyclic principle by means of a depreciative image typical of the early Grass: history as a grotesque children's game:

For several centuries the game of destroying and rebuilding the city was played in turn by the dukes of Pomerelia, the grand masters of the Teutonic Order, the kings and antikings of Poland, the counts of Brandenburg, and the bishops of Wloclawek. (491; 395)

A few of these 'Baumeister und Abbruchunternehmer' ('*builders and wreckers*') are then enumerated – and a few pages earlier we find the same resonant device, concerning the razing of Danzig in 1945:

Yet this was not the first fire to descend on the city of Danzig. For centuries Pomerelians, Brandenburgers, Teutonic Knights, Poles, Swedes, and a second time Swedes, Frenchmen, Prussians, and Russians, even Saxons, had made history by deciding every few years that the city of Danzig was worth burning. And now it was Russians, Poles, Germans, and Englishmen all at once who were burning the city's Gothic bricks for the hundredth time. (483; 389-90)

So much for the past and present; but the future, too, is envisaged in similar terms. Thus for instance Rokossovski, the Soviet Commander, is described as finding Danzig intact in 1945, whereupon he copied his predecessors, shot it to bits, and so gave his successors plenty to do, namely, put the city together again – and so on *ad infinitum* (494; 397). But the most striking of such anticipations of the future is undoubtedly the paragraph on Poland that Grass uses to end the chapter 'The Stockturm. Long-Distance Song Effects': while present-day Germans bewail the past misfortunes of the Poles and lay regretful wreaths at the site of the Warsaw ghetto, they are at the same time, we read, busily preparing the next partitioning, the next invasion (126; 107-8); and so Oskar finally goes in search of Poland on his drum – 'und trommelt: Verloren, noch nicht verloren, schon wieder verloren, an wen verloren, bald verloren, bereits verloren, Polen verloren, alles verloren, noch ist Polen nicht verloren.' ('*and drums: lost, not yet lost, lost again, lost to whom, lost soon, already lost, Poland is lost, all is lost, Poland still is not quite lost.*')[24] This sad, sardonic passage is interesting for other reasons too. It was written in the depth of the Adenauer cold-war era; but Grass could still echo its sentiments in the bitter conclusion to his Georg Büchner Prize speech, just after the failure of Willy Brandt and the Social-Democratic Party in the general election of 1965:

the occasion of this speech allowed me to do honour to Georg Büchner and with him to all German émigrés ... If, as is today the case, we must fear yet again that our spirit and our art will emigrate, as so often before, then it will soon be time to warn our neighbours: beware, you Czechs, Poles, Dutch and French! the Germans need to be feared again![25]

But it is an irony as well as an accurate reflection of how much both Grass's own position and the atmosphere of German *Ostpolitik* have meanwhile altered, that Grass was one of the special guests invited to go with Brandt on his historic journey to Poland

13

in 1970; a journey that included laying regretful wreaths at the site of the Warsaw ghetto.

The Merry-go-round

It is perhaps fair to say that all the evocations in *The Tin Drum* of remorseless '... egg, chicken, egg ...' absurdity are crowned by one grand figuration: the 'merry-go-round' passage in the chapter 'Disinfectant'. Again here, senseless death is the point of focus (the death by exposure of four thousand refugee children by the Vistula towards the end of World War II); and again, the plangent tone of these lines makes plain the humanism that otherwise usually stays disguised behind the picaresque front of Oskar's narrative:

Da sah und hörte ich allerlei unterm Fieber, da sass ich in einem Karussell, wollte aussteigen, durfte aber nicht. Mit vielen Kleinkindern sass ich in Feuerwehrautos, ausgehöhlten Schwänen, auf Hunden, Katzen, Säuen und Hirschen, fuhr, fuhr, fuhr, wollte aussteigen, durfte aber nicht. Da weinten alle die Kleinkinderchen, wollten gleich mir aus den Feuer-wehrautos, ausgehöhlten Schwänen heraus, herunter von den Katzen, Hunden, Hirschen und Säuen, wollten nicht mehr Karussell fahren, durften aber nicht. Da stand nämlich der himmlische Vater neben dem Karussellbesitzer und bezahlte für uns immer noch eine Runde. Und wir beteten: 'Ach, Vaterunser, wir wissen ja, dass Du viel Kleingeld hast, dass Du uns gerne Karussell fahren lässt, dass es Dir Spass macht, uns das Runde dieser Welt zu beweisen. Steck bitte Deine Börse ein, sag stop, halt, fertig, Feierabend, basta, aussteigen, Ladenschluss, stoi – es schwindelt uns armen Kinderchen, man hat uns, viertausend, nach Käsemark an die Weichsel gebracht, doch wir kommen nicht rüber, weil Dein Karussell, Dein Karussell ...'
Aber der liebe Gott, Vaterunser, Karussellbesitzer lächelte, wie es im Buche steht, liess abermals eine Münze aus seiner Börse hüpfen, damit es die viertausend Kleinkinderchen, mittenmang Oskar, in Feuerwehrautos und ausgehöhlten

Schwänen, auf Katzen, Hunden, Säuen und Hirschen im Kreise
herumtrug ... (511-12)

I saw and heard all sorts of things in my fever; I was riding
a merry-go-round, I wanted to get off but I wasn't allowed to.
I was one of many little children sitting in fire engines and
hollowed-out swans, on dogs, cats, pigs, and stags, riding round
and round. I wanted to get off but I wasn't allowed to. All the
little children were crying, like me they wanted to get out of
the fire engines and hollowed-out swans, down from the backs
of the cats, dogs, pigs, and stags, they didn't want to ride on
the merry-go-round any more, but they weren't allowed to
get off. The Heavenly Father was standing beside the merry-
go-round owner and every time it stopped, he paid for another
turn. And we prayed: 'Oh, our Father who art in heaven, we
know you have lots of loose change, we know you like to
treat us to rides on the merry-go-round, we know you like to
prove to us that this world is round. Please put your money
away, say stop, finished, fertig, basta, stoi, closing time, all
change – we poor little children are dizzy, they've brought
us, four thousand of us, to Käsemark on the Vistula, but we
can't get across, because your merry-go-round, your merry-go-
round ...'

But God our Father, the merry-go-round owner, smiled in his
most benevolent manner and another coin came sailing out of
his purse to make the merry-go-round keep on turning, carry-
ing four thousand children with Oskar in their midst, in fire
engines and hollowed-out swans, on cats, dogs, pigs, and stags,
round and round in a circle ... (411-12)

The parodying of Christian assumptions, and the ironic depiction
of human existence as a game for the amusement of capricious
superior forces: these are elements that we have found Grass
using to effect elsewhere, but separately and on a far smaller
scale, and it is thus no wonder that their combined impact
throughout this extensive passage is that much greater. But there
is another factor too: the tell-tale rhythmic drive that replaces
the normal narrative tone throughout, and whose power derives
from Grass's constant use of the simple language, rhythms and
repetitions of nursery lore. What chiefly marks the passage out,
though, is that it puts across a single, sustained metaphor, and so

gives shape to the existential view that is normally left inexplicit through most of the book: existence as a roundabout, as movement 'im Kreise', the whole governed by a principle expressed through the figure of 'God our Father the roundabout-owner' who delights in confronting his creatures, however much they may writhe, with the proof of their world's vanity, of 'das Runde dieser Welt'.

A most important characteristic of Grass's style is demonstrated in this passage: a radical unsentimentality. No haze of false pathos distorts the sharp delineations of the image or lulls the reader into a beguiling sensation of sorrow. Here as almost always in Grass, *ironic contrast* is the means for achieving this deliberate 'coolness': the gross disproportion between the cheery nursery style and the horrible senselessness of the children's death. And this device of ironic, relativising contrast governs every detail: on the one hand, the death of the children; on the other, the ostensibly gay trappings of the fairground, the apostrophisation of God in one breath as both 'dear God, our Father' and 'roundabout-owner', the presentation of the whole as merely a hallucination of the fevered Oskar, the parodistic tone at the end when Fajngold rescues Oskar from his vision – and at the same time dismantles the imagery piece by piece:

Herr Fajngold beugte sich und stoppte das Karussell. Feuerwehr, Schwan und Hirsch stellte er ab, entwertete die Münzen des Rasputin, schickte Goethe hinab zu den Müttern, liess viertausend schwindlige Kleinkinderchen davonwehen, nach Käsemark über die Weichsel ins Himmelreich – (512)

Mr Fajngold bent over me and stopped the merry-go-round. He stopped the fire engines, the swan, and the stag, devaluated Rasputin's coins, sent Goethe back to the Mothers, sent four thousand dizzy little children floating off to Käsemark, across the Vistula, to the kingdom of heaven – (412)

False pathos is kept at bay throughout, the imagery is ironically dismantled at the end – but it would be wrong to imagine that the passage is for that 'unfeeling', to see it in 'amoral-gusto-and-abandon' terms. It is in essence a poetic lament of great intensity, and with its fairground trappings it shows a characteristic of the early Grass with unusual clarity: his use of that compelling

16

irony whereby clownish caricature may serve to communicate
sorrow more poignantly than tears might do.[26]

'Faith Hope Love'

The bitter ironisation of Christian assumptions in Grass's cal-
culatedly irreverent representation of the deity as a cheapjack
merry-go-round owner, is no isolated phenomenon: equally
caustic treatments of Christianity, and particularly of Grass's
own former faith, Catholicism, are to be found throughout the
novel, from the 'raft of thy raft' parody (above, p. 10) to Oskar's
introduction of himself to the Interpol agents towards the close
of the novel: 'first in German: "ich bin Jesus", then ... in
French, and finally in English: "I am Jesus" ' (732; 587). But there
is one particular sequence in the novel – the chapter 'Faith Hope
Love' concluding Book One – that directly parallels the merry-
go-round passage inasmuch as it, too, both depicts a violent,
senseless order of existence, and also savagely unmasks Christian
conventional assumptions as a mockery, at any rate so far as
the given reality is concerned. The chapter is one of the bleakest
and most plangent in the novel. And nothing shows more clearly
than these few pages do how unlikely is the view that 'Grass's
book is entirely in line with Catholic theology', and that 'Implicit
in the whole apparently passionless description of the German
scene [in *The Tin Drum*] is the possibility of Christian redemption':[27] not only does the whole regressive development of the
novel indicate the opposite of Christian redemption, but it is
also the case that Grass's stance is constantly a humanistic, never
a theological, metaphysical one. As Grass himself has said (in
1966): 'My concern as an author is with reality. This reality
bears the stamp of a variety of religions. In our part of the world
they are Christian in kind. When I compare the claims of these
religions with reality, there's little in Christianity that stands the
comparison.'[28]

The ironic intent behind the chapter's Pauline title is rapidly
confirmed in the second paragraph: the real matter of the
chapter is the utterly unchristian 'disaster' of National Socialism,
a catastrophe whose approach was clearly visible – 'there were

plenty of omens' – and which was so insidious that everyone necessarily partook of it:

Doch man kann das Unglück nicht einkellern. Mit den Abwässern findet es durch die Kanalisation, es teilt sich den Gasleitungen mit, kommt allen Haushaltungen zu, und niemand, der da sein Suppentöpfchen auf die bläulichen Flammen stellt, ahnt, dass da das Unglück seinen Frass zum Kochen bringt. (236)

But you can't lock up disaster in a cellar. It drains into the sewer pipes, spreads to the gas pipes, and gets into every household with the gas. And no one who sets his pot of soup on the bluish flame suspects that disaster is bringing his supper to the boil. (197)

The 'disaster' and its grotesque distortion of norms and standards are glaringly demonstrated in the subsequent paragraphs: on the one hand the *Kristallnacht* pogrom of 9-10 November 1938 – Sigismund Markus's suicide and the brutish destruction of his toyshop being its symbol in Grass's fiction; on the other hand the expulsion of Meyn from the SA for 'dishonourable conduct' and 'inhuman cruelty to animals' (241; 201), and because his cruelty to cats is 'damaging to the reputation of the Party' (241; 201) – a crime compensated for not even by the fact that he showed 'conspicuous bravery' in the rampage against the synagogues and property of the defenceless Jews (241; 201). Grass again sharply fixes the spirit of this gross distortion of values in his picture of Matzerath by the bonfire of sacred objects from the synagogue: 'Der Berg wurde in Brand gesteckt, und der Kolonialwarenhändler benutzte die Gelegenheit und wärmte seine Finger und seine Gefühle über dem öffentlichen Feuer.' (242; '*The mound was set on fire and the grocer took advantage of the opportunity to warm his fingers and his feelings over the public blaze.*', 201).

It is only after eight pages of the chapter that the Pauline title comes into its own through the grotesque image of the group of 'pious women and shivering ugly girls' that Oskar sees on his way from the *Kristallnacht* and Markus's shop, with 'Faith – Hope – Love' across their banner. Then, in the paragraphs that follow, each of the three grand concepts is dealt with in turn and

18

revealed as a meaningless delusion within the given context of reality.

'Hope', the last-considered of the three, is dismissed as just so much unsaleable tat ('der dritte Ladenhüter des Korinther-briefes: die Hoffnung', 245; 204), and is typically pictured in terms of a senseless round: 'for in this country the end is always the beginning and there is hope in every, even the most final, end. And so too is it written: As long as man hopes, he will keep on starting hopeful finales' (etc.). As for 'Love', Grass has Oskar figure it not as *agape* but as thrusting, hungry *eros*: 'And from sheer love they called each other radishes, they loved radishes, they bit into each other, from sheer love each radish bit the other, from sheer love each radish bit the other's radish off.' And this eros is insistently egotistical: 'oh, I love you. Do you love yourself too?', 'do you really love me? I love myself too.', 'say, do you love me? I love myself too.' (245; 204).

Mordant though the 'Hope' and 'Love' paragraphs are, it is undoubtedly the preceding passage on 'Faith' that has the greatest significance: it is here that the 'gas' image of the chapter's beginning is further elaborated and so made a powerful analogue to the later symbols of the merry-go-round and the dubious deity that owns it. After the picture of the religious females and their banner, a volley of puns is first triggered off, deflating and neutralising all three words of the Pauline canon (244; 203), but the prose then fixes on the prime constituent of 'Faith' – and at once, in an emphatic rhythm quite different from before, establishes the crass distinction between beliefs and reality: 'Ein ganzes leichtgläubiges Volk glaubte an den Weih-nachtsmann. Aber der Weihnachtsmann war in Wirklichkeit der Gasmann.' ('*A whole credulous nation believed . . . in Santa Claus. But Santa Claus was really the gasman.*') The sentences that follow both heighten this distinction, and at the same time further intensify the metaphor of gas: 'Ich glaube, dass es nach Nüssen riecht und nach Mandeln. Aber es roch nach Gas.' ('*I believe it smells of nuts and almonds. But it smelled of gas.*') The striking shift of tense is a neat device for setting illusion against reality, and Grass uses it to equal effect in the opening of the paragraph that immediately follows: 'Er kommt! Er kommt! Wer kam denn? Das Christkindchen, der Heiland? Oder kam der himmlische Gasmann mit der Gasuhr unter dem Arm, die immer ticktick macht?' ('*He's*

coming, he's coming! Who came? The Christ Child, the Saviour?
Or was it the heavenly gasman that came with the gas meter
under his arm that always goes ticktick?')

'The heavenly gasman' and God as 'merry-go-round owner': the
similarity between these deathly figures is plain, but the two passages work nevertheless in different ways and have different reference points. Whereas the merry-go-round passage is direct and
poetic in style, and concerned with the absurd, offensive round of
things in general, the 'gasman' passage is more oblique in manner
but at the same time much more specific in its subject-matter:
it evokes nothing more nor less than the gullible acceptance by
the Germans of the deadly blandishments of National Socialism.
In Grass's extended, complex metaphor: whilst the Germans
in the *Kristallnacht* days still fondly believed that all was essentially the same, and participated in the spirit prevailing at Advent
or Christmas as if it were just as benign and cosy as ever it had
been, they had in reality become blind devotees of the 'heavenly
gasman' and so contributed willy-nilly to the 'disaster that pulled
on ever bigger boots, made ever bigger steps with its ever bigger
boots, and was intent on spreading disaster' (236; *197*). The main
force of the gas imagery lies in the fact that it immediately brings
to mind the grossest part of National Socialist savagery: the
systematic annihilation of the Jews. But it has a more general
meaning as well: it shows that the outcome was disastrous, too,
for the conniving, gullible masses, that the effect on them was
not just intoxicating but toxic, and that they were left as wrecks
by the twelve-year millennium, by the supposed epiphany of the
New Age, with only those surviving for whom there had been
insufficient poisonous enticements – 'the sole survivors were
those for whom not enough almonds or nuts were left' (244;
203-4). What is implied here is not just physical but also spiritual
survival: one thing that has remained pre-eminent throughout
all Grass's work has been his belief (in common with the tradition
of enlightened humanism) in the concept of wholeness and
integrity; and in all three books of the 'trilogy' he shows not only
the sufferings of the explicit victims of National Socialism, but
also the distortions and disintegrations suffered by all the participants, connivers included. (It is for precisely this reason that all
three books – in sharp contradistinction to *Local Anaesthetic* –
are as it were progressively disintegrative.) The pattern of things
in *Dog Years* will prove particularly interesting: whereas in *The*

20

Tin Drum there is fragmentation everywhere and a kind of generalised break-down of identity, regardless of who did or suffered what, the later novel systematically shows the brutal, oppressive Matern faring far worse than the brutally persecuted half-Jew Eddi Amsel.

It is altogether characteristic of *The Tin Drum* that 'Faith Hope Love' figures the deluded masses, the 'entire credulous nation', but no deluders, no individual manipulators. Specific causation and the particular actions of Hitler or whoever, do not come within the orbit of the book; instead, Grass reflects existence in terms of a dynamic, almost animated historical process, his most striking device being that of personification: the 'merry-go-round owner', the 'heavenly gasman', the figure of 'disaster pulling on its boots' (compare the sinister figurations of death, sexuality and the 'Schwarze Köchin' – '*Black Witch*'![29]) It follows that no blame is apportioned to anyone for duping and corrupting the masses – but equally, no blame is attached to people, either, for letting themselves be 'poisoned'. The presentation of Meyn is a fine case in point; there is no hint of moral indictment of him or his actions; though at the same time Grass does use him to symbolise the deadening *effects* of National Socialism and its grotesque 'sobriety' and 'orderedness': Meyn 'played the trumpet too beautifully for words' (236; *196*) – but only until he joined the band of the Mounted SA, when he began to play 'much more impeccably, it's true, but no longer too beautifully for words ... because ... from then on his playing was loud and sober, nothing more' (237; *198*). All this does not mean that concepts of blame and guilt are alien to the novel; on the contrary, they are central to it by being central to the persona of Oskar Matzerath. The important thing is that they too, like the forces determining existence in general, are figured in non-specific, supra-personal terms. It thus comes as no surprise to find that Oskar's consuming sense of guilt and his increasing fixation on the 'Schwarze Köchin' finally come together into one motif at the end of the novel. In these respects, again, *Dog Years* shows a striking shift of attitude on Grass's part: the focus there is not on 'existence in general' but 'Germany in particular'; personifications of universal processes are quite absent; and guilt is conceived in far sharper and more specific terms. Whereas *The Tin Drum* presents the masses as having not realised the nature of their reality, and as having 'turned on the gas' in all innocence, *Dog Years* will depict them as behaving *as if* they had not realised – an altogether different matter (see below, p. 184).

The House of Cards

Oskar's remark, already quoted, that he can't help thinking of demolition works whenever he sees buildings under construction (301; 247), appropriately appears in the context of one of the novel's most forceful images: the house of cards that Jan Bronski builds as the defence of the Polish Post Office steadily crumbles around him during the course of the novel's first practical demonstration of the 'Schlacht, die schon dagewesen, die immer wieder kommt' (*'the battle that was and will always recur'*; see above, p. 11). The whole sequence is effective, but the lead-in to the image is particularly well contrived: the comic, grotesque picture of the candle-lit skat-game amongst the baskets heavy with mail and corpses, and with one of the players himself more dead than alive and only reviving sporadically just enough to make his bid or play his hand – an unforgettable instance of that kind of irony, fundamental to *The Tin Drum*, through which a reality, too gross to be meaningfully evoked by direct means, is indirectly mirrored through an almost caricatural rendering of its periphery.

There is sharp irony, too, in the paragraph with which the house-of-cards image is first created (296; 243-4). The main body of the paragraph is almost idyllic in mood: in the peaceful letter depository – 'windstill und sonntäglich' (*'still and Sunday-like'*) as though far removed from the destruction and dying around it – Jan Bronski, deliriously gay and happy, builds his airy, delicate house to seem like a symbol validating faith and hope; in Grass's poetic description:

das Gebäude [fiel] nicht etwa zusammen; nein, luftig stand es, empfindsam, leicht atmend in jenem Raum voller atemloser Toter und Lebendiger, die den Atem anhielten, und erlaubte uns, die Hände zusammenzulegen, liess den skeptischen Oskar ... den beizenden Qualm und Gestank vergessen, der sparsam

22

und gewunden durch die Türritzen des Briefraumes schlich ...

the edifice did not collapse; no, airy it stood and delicate,
breathing softly in that room full of the dead that breathed
no more and the living who held their breath, and enabled us
to put our hands together, let Oskar for all his scepticism ...
forget the acrid smoke and stench that crept in tiny wisps and
coils through the cracks around the door ...

Such is the appearance, and such is Jan Bronski's oblivious conviction — for him, indeed, the airy edifice with its crowning
storey of the king and queen of hearts[30] is the glorious image of
his relationship with Agnes Matzerath, a relationship which he
imagines to have been rich and passionate, but which, as the
reader well knows by this stage, was in reality mechanical, mean
and dismal. However, this blissful appearance is also sharply
relativised within the paragraph itself. To begin the paragraph,
Grass depicts Jan switching suddenly from abject weeping and
despair to carefree laughter — and by this point the motifs of
laughter and tears are well established as indicators of a crisis
in a character's relationship to his existence. But more: the
description of Jan's shift from despair to gaiety implies that his
relationship to reality is disrupted even to the point of dementia:
'Something funny must have happened in Jan's little head to
make him start laughing in the midst of his tears'; and the reader
is all the more ready to recognise this implication since Jan has
already been shown as so deranged in his cognition that he regis-
tered Oskar and the half-dead Kobyella as Alfred Matzerath and
Agnes, the other set characters in the desultory tragicomedy of
his existence (292 f.; 240 f.). At the close of the paragraph, the
ironisation of Jan's seemingly stable, seemingly auspicious con-
struct is sharper still: Oskar may be swayed for a moment into
suspending his disbelief — but Grass has him describe himself all
the same as 'the sceptical Oskar, who saw through the house of
cards in every way', and then has him go on to figure the true
setting of the apparently idyllic little room in terms of the apter
imagery of hell: the wisps of smoke and stench, says Oskar,
'made it seem as though the little room with the card house in
it were right next door and wall to wall with hell'. The irony is
further intensified in the paragraphs that follow: as Jan was
building his blissful house, the Germans were already flushing

23

out the last few defenders with flame-throwers; and a whole
short paragraph laconically points the contrast between the
reality of the doomed captives and Jan's consummation of his
blithe illusion:

Die anderen aber ... die standen schon an der Mauer, dem
Seitenportal gegenüber, als Jan gerade die Herz Königin gegen
den Herz König lehnte und beglückt seine Hände zurück-
zog. (297)

The others however ... were already standing against the
wall across from the side entrance when Jan leaned the
queen of hearts against the king of hearts and, thoroughly
blissful, took his hands away. (245)

Whereupon, in the opening lines of the succeeding paragraph,
the house of cards bears out its inner reality by collapsing utterly
on the invaders' violent arrival in Jan's illusory haven.

The chapter ends shortly afterwards, but early in the next
chapter Grass follows it up with an emphatic paragraph which
not only extends the ironic pattern of the preceding pages by
again contrasting Jan's demented technicolour romanticisation
and Oskar's all too percipient insight, but also increases the force
of the house-of-cards image by representing the entire world of
human constructs as having the same frail and ephemeral character as Jan Bronski's airy edifice:

Während sich Jan schon im ewigen Reich der Kartenhäuser
befand ... standen wir, die Heimwehrleute und ich ... zwischen Ziegelmauern, auf gefliesten Korridorfussböden, unter
Decken mit Stuckgesimsen, die mit Wänden und Zwischen-
wänden derart ineinander verkrampft waren, dass man das
Schlimmste für jenen Tag befürchten musste, da all die Kle-
bearbeit, die wir Architektur nennen, diesen oder jenen
Umständen gehorchend, den Zusammenhalt aufgeben wird.
(301)

Already Jan had gone off to the eternal realm of card houses
... whereas the Home Guard and I ... stood amid brick walls,
in stone corridors, beneath ceilings with plaster cornices, all
so intricately interlocked with walls and partitions that the

24

*worst was to be feared for the day when, in response to one
set of circumstances or another, all this patchwork we call
architecture would lose its cohesion. (247)*

It is precisely at this point that Grass has Oskar drop his classic
remark about building works always reminding him of demolition works – a remark that comes only as a parenthesis in the
final and bleakest figuration of the house of cards as the proper
metaphor of human life: 'I was no stranger to the belief that
houses of cards are the only dwellings worthy of mankind.' And
here, as so often, the grim perspective of the novel comes
through all the more strongly for being couched in language
and rhythms that are pert, detached, seemingly playful. There
is no warm wallowing in *Weltschmerz* or any such thing; as
though incidentally, the bare notion is conveyed that dislocation is the paramount principle of existence, that the inception of
anything at all of an integrated nature is at once the omen of
its disintegration.

The Horse's Head

The horse's head episode in the chapter 'Good Friday Fare' is
the most penetrating evocation of vileness in the novel, and
has accordingly earned Grass more calumny than anything else,
largely from those like Günter Blöcker who consider it gratuitous
filth.[31] It is of course the very opposite of gratuitous: at the
symbolic level, it is one of the most eloquent passages of the
novel; at the level of plot, it leads directly to the death of one
of the main characters, Agnes Matzerath, which in turn leads
directly to a severe crisis for the hero and thereby gives a first
major impetus to the process of his own steady dislocation.

The tenor of the episode is first established when Grass describes the screaming seagulls snatching up the tasty morsel of the
old fisherman's spittle bobbing in the sea (176; *149*). Two pages
later, the image is reinforced when the seagulls pounce on the
mess of egg, bread, coffee and 'greenish slime' sicked up by
Agnes Matzerath. In both these sordid incidents one creature
feeds off another's excretions,[32] and extra point is thus given to

25

the episode's central symbol: the bleak process whereby eels are caught for human consumption by the lure of a feast of horse's brain (and are killed by being made to squirm to death in a sack of salt); and these eels, we hear, have quite likely become fat for human eating through eating humans – for they not only scavenge such things as horse's brain, but human corpses too ('in menschliche Leichen gehen sie auch', 180; *152*). And the symbolism will be given its final edge in the following chapter, when Oskar says that he was sure that the corpse of his dead mother would spew forth one final thing: a bit of an eel that perhaps had eaten of her own father's flesh (above, page 10).

It is not that there is anything unheard-of about the events depicted in the horse's head episode; as Matzerath says when telling Agnes to stop making a fuss: 'You've always known that eels go for that sort of thing and you've always eaten them just the same, even fresh ones' (181; *153*). It is rather that such events are normally conveniently forgotton, whereas here they are sharply illuminated in silent mockery of that view of existence that is false for ignoring them – a mockery that is finely pointed up when the old fisherman only spits and grins when Agnes flippantly asks him what he is doing, and above all when Grass depicts the carrion horse's head as seeming to laugh (176, 178; *149*, *150*; both things are expressly repeated in the re-narration of the sequence much later in the book, 613 f.; *494* f.).

It is not only the actual events of the episode that are significant, but equally the reactions to them of the various characters – above all, Agnes Matzerath. The significant response of her husband and her lover is that neither really responds at all, since nothing, however stark, is capable of unseating them from their hobby-horses: they show minimal responses at the time, and straight afterwards Matzerath compulsively haggles for a few of the eels in order to indulge his solitary passion of cooking, while Jan Bronski gets back to groping underneath Agnes's clothes. Agnes's reaction, on the other hand, is a radical, if gradual one. Whereas at first she wants to leave (176; *149*), it is a measure of her involvement that soon Jan cannot even turn her head away (178; *150*) – and it is shortly after this that her mental response is physically signalled by the way she vomits and retches until nothing is left but 'green slime'.

26

Once they have left the shore, Agnes for the time being returns more or less to normal. She does swear never to touch fish and especially eels again, but, most importantly, her sexuality rapidly re-asserts itself : she replies to Jan's advances on the way to the tram-stop by putting her hand into his trouser-pocket, and no sooner are the couple alone in the sitting-room at home (except for Oskar) than they revert to the indulgence of their lust. The whole aftermath of the events by the waterside is pointed above all in the way that it displays more clearly than ever the deadness and lack of fulfilment of the Matzerath-Agnes-Bronski triangle : husband and wife fight out the same old battles over the same old terrain, and the provisional end of the business is the customary session of skat. Grass expresses it – typically and trenchantly – as just one more performance of an unchanging piece of theatre, an empty and meaningless ritual : 'Mama started shouting ... Matzerath answered back. They knew their parts. Jan intervened. Without him there could be no performance. Then Act Two; ... Act Three : ...' (186-7; 157-8).[33]

It is only in the following chapter that Agnes's reaction comes to its full maturity and shows itself outwardly through her sudden and total addiction to the sea-food for which the events at the shore two weeks earlier had filled her with equally absolute repulsion. Her new behaviour, which causes her to vomit 'several times a day' (190; 160), is presented as being quite different in kind from her involuntary nausea by the sea : she is explicitly stated to act 'aus freien Stücken und von einem rätselhaften Willen besessen' (190; *quite of her own accord and possessed of a mysterious resolve*', 159-60). In line with a constant principle in Grass's work generally, any impression of authorial omniscience is carefully avoided : Agnes's resolve is described precisely as 'rätselhaft' ('*mysterious*'). A variety of possible explanations is mooted : Agnes is perhaps pregnant, says Matzerath (190; 160) – and this indeed turns out to be so; it is also suggested that it may have been her intention to dissolve the triangle in such a way as to inflict guilt feelings on Matzerath and allow Jan to believe she had died for his sake (192; 161-2); or again, she may have died to escape Oskar and his eternal banging on the drum (204, 207; 171, 174). But beyond all this, Grass indicates a much more fundamental explanation : that Agnes is led by the horse's head experience to recognise a deadness in existence, and especially her own existence, that is too much for

27

her to bear. This is not distinctly spelt out until far later in the novel, in the chapter 'In the Clothes Cupboard' towards the middle of Book Three:

> Meine arme Mama jedoch ... hatte genug.... wollte auch anfangs keinen Fisch mehr essen, fing aber eines schönen Tages an, so viel und so fetten Fisch zu essen, bis sie nicht mehr konnte, nein, wollte, genug hatte, nicht nur vom Aal, auch vom Leben, besonders von den Männern, vielleicht auch von Oskar, jedenfalls wurde sie, die sonst auf nichts verzichten konnte, plötzlich genügsam, enthaltsam, und liess sich in Brenntau beerdigen. (615)

> *But my poor Mama ... had had enough.... at first she wouldn't eat any more fish, but one fine day she began to eat so much fish, such big fish and fat fish, until one day she couldn't manage, no, didn't want any more, she had had enough, not only of eels but also of life, especially of men, perhaps also of Oskar, in any case she, who had never been able to forego anything, became frugal and abstemious and had herself buried in Brenntau. (496)*

The earlier chapter, on the other hand, offers more oblique indications: Agnes, it is said, dies in order to find 'peace' (195; 164); her face is described as reflecting 'repulsion' ('ihr angeekeltes, im Ekel mich manchmal anlächelndes ... Gesicht', 191-2; 161), and again, when she is already a corpse: 'das gleichviel entschlossene wie angewiderte Gesicht meiner armen Mama' (195; 'my poor Mama's resolute, nauseated face', 164). This motif of nausea is strongly conveyed, too, in the key paragraphs where Oskar recounts his conviction that the dead Agnes would regurgitate a last bit of eel, 'perhaps eel from her father Joseph Koljaiczek'. The existential tenor of the whole sequence is particularly clear in this passage, as it is a few pages earlier when Oskar relates how his mother 'jumped up, clutched me, lifted me, squeezed me, and revealed an abyss that apparently nothing could fill, not even countless quantities of fried, boiled, preserved and smoked fish' (191; 160).[34]

This existential tenor is greatly emphasised by the fact that the horse's head episode is related not just once, but altogether three times: a second time in the penultimate paragraph of

28

'Good Friday Fare' (188-9; *159*), and again, much more extensively, in the post-war chapter 'In the Clothes Cupboard' (613 f.; *494* f.). These repetitions certainly serve to emphasise the situation concerning Agnes: that her experience inflicted an insight on her that was as fundamental as it was deadly. But they also serve another, more crucial purpose: they indicate that the events by the shore are equally a factor in the gradual but total dislocation suffered by the hero himself. This is particularly clear in the 'Clothes Cupboard' passage in that Grass has Oskar heighten his re-narration with mention of the 'Schwarze Köchin' and the motif of his consuming fear (613; *494*), the implication being that whereas the events and Agnes's response to them did Oskar no harm at the time, they did give him his first sight of the 'abyss' that later gapes as widely for him as it had done for his mother, and so represent a first station on the road to his 'present' state as a disoriented, impotent, fear-stricken inmate of a lunatic asylum, vainly seeking refuge in solitude and his past. And this 'Stations of the Cross' image is by no means far-fetched on my part: Grass's narrator represents things in just such terms in the lapidary close to 'Good Friday Fare': 'Zwar war der Karfreitag für Oskar zu Ende, aber die Passionszeit sollte erst nach Ostern beginnen' (189; '*Good Friday was over for Oskar, but it was not until after Easter that his Passiontide was to begin*', *159*). Joachim Mahlke and Eduard Amsel will later be figured as sufferers in almost identical ways; and it can hardly be said too often that in this threnodic mode we have one of the most powerful and cohesive elements of the 'trilogy'.[35] As for Oskar himself: we shall see later how desperate are the beginnings of his Passion once his Mama has 'dropped him in it' ('Mama hatte mich reingelegt', 207; *173*).

Death and War

In an epic novel covering a period of fifty-five years, including the two most devastating wars of history, death is bound to play a part. But this natural order of things does not begin to explain the position in *The Tin Drum*, for death figures so prominently and insistently in Grass's first novel (in sharp contradistinction to

29

Dog Years) that it acquires the dimension of a major symbol – all the more so since birth is as arrestingly underplayed in the book as death is emphasised: apart from the paragraphs on the birth of Oskar himself, births are only ever mentioned passingly and factually, if at all, whilst the various individual deaths and burials of the narrative account on their own for little less than forty pages.

In this respect as in respect of the ...egg-chicken-egg... motif generally, the consistent slant of the novel is that death and disintegration are the decisive element in the cycle, and that any particular individual's death is a barely reckonable quantity in the gross infinitude of the cycle as a whole. This is most tellingly emphasised in the pages on Matzerath's death, by means of the ant image that Grass makes a leitmotif of the whole episode, and whose importance is signalled by the chapter's title: 'The Ant Trail'. The image is established in the paragraph recounting the Russian invaders' descent into the Matzeraths' cellar: Oskar concentrates on an army of ants that move resolutely on a path between winter potatoes and a sack of sugar, and remain quite unconcerned by the momentous arrival of the soldiers ('die Ameisen [liessen sich] durch den Auftritt der russischen Armee nicht beeinflussen', 486; 392). In due course, Matzerath is machine-gunned, and his body falls across the ants' trail; but they merely make the necessary adjustment and carry on as before – and the effect of the metaphor is heightened by the fact that Grass characteristically closes the chapter with it:

Die Ameisen fanden eine veränderte Situation vor, scheuten aber den Umweg nicht, bauten ihre Heerstrasse um den gekrümmten Matzerath herum; denn jener aus dem geplatzten Sack rieselnde Zucker hatte während der Besetzung der Stadt Danzig durch die Armee Marschall Rokossowskis nichts von seiner Süsse verloren. (490)

The ants found themselves facing a new situation but, undismayed by the detour, soon built a new highway round the doubled-up Matzerath; for the sugar that trickled out of the burst sack had lost nothing of its sweetness while Marshal Rokossovski was occupying the city of Danzig. (394-5)

In this we have yet another evocation of that bleak vision whereby the whole is dismally repetitive ('die dauernde Wandlung, welche am Ende das Ei meint', see above, p. 7), the parts just fleeting and insignificant, whether it be the death of Matzerath or even the invasion of Danzig.

Quite apart from the various individual deaths in all their meanness and banality, we are never permitted to forget the historical reality of the years in which the novel is set. Like *Simplicius Simplicissimus* or *Candide*, *The Tin Drum* confronts its readers ceaselessly with the brutality distinctive of an era, and so also with death on a monstrous scale – though of course there is sharp emphasis on the ultimate triviality even of major events of the Second World War (itself just another phase of the 'Schlacht, die schon dagewesen, die immer wieder kommt'), an emphasis that is chiefly effected by the device of coupling such major events with particularly banal private events in Oskar's family life. Thus for instance the decisive defeat at Stalingrad is dismissed with the statement: 'I was far less interested in the fate of the Sixth Army than in Maria, who had a touch of flu at the time' (392; *318*); and on the same page we read: 'Kurt's whooping cough and the Afrika Korps came to an end together'. But the chief emphasis is always on the wanton destructiveness of the war, which annihilates a whole host of named characters, not to mention the masses of anonymous corpses that are strewn among the wartime pages. Such is the end of Sigismund Markus; of Greff's favourite boy scout, Horst Donath; of Nuchi Eyke, Harry Schlager and Hans Kollin; of the boys of the 'Stäuberbande' ('*Dusters*'); of Stephan Bronski and Fritz Truczinski; of the nuns on the Normandy coast; of Roswitha; and of Jan Bronski and Matzerath.

The novel's most intense evocation of death through war has already been discussed: the merry-go-round sequence on the death of the four thousand evacuee children. But the same phase of the narrative also includes another most penetrating depiction of wartime suffering and slaughter: the passages on the concentration camps. The first of these passages is coupled with the death of Matzerath: Herr Fajngold sees the corpse in the cellar, and

Seine ganze Familie ... rief er in den Keller, und sicherlich sah er alle kommen, denn er nannte sie beim Namen ... erklärte gleich darauf uns, dass alle, die er soeben gerufen habe,

31

auch so dalagen, bevor sie in die Öfen von Treblinka kamen, dazu noch seine Schwägerin und der Schwägerin Schwester-mann, der fünf Kinderchen hatte, und alle lagen, nur er, der Herr Fajngold, lag nicht, weil er Chlor streuen musste. (494-5)

He called ... his whole family into the cellar, and no doubt he saw them all coming, for he called them by name ... and went on to tell us that all those he had just summoned as well as his sister-in-law and her other brother-in-law who had five children had lain in the same way, before being taken to the crematoria of Treblinka, and the whole lot of them had been lying there — except for him because he had had to strew lime. (398)

Later, a page-long outline of Treblinka follows (including a picture of the famous revolt of captives that prefaced its end), and it is begun and finished with images of the dominant feature of Treblinka and the concentration camps in general: mass extermination. The closing sentence is especially mordant in expressing the cruel order of things:

Lysol ist wichtiger als das Leben! Und Herr Fajngold konnte das nur bestätigen; denn er hatte ja Tote, nicht einen Toten, nein Tote, was soll ich eine Zahl sagen, Tote, sag ich, gab es, die er mit Lysol besprenkelt hatte. Und Namen wusste er, dass es langweilig wurde, dass mir, der ich im Lysol schwamm, die Frage nach Leben oder Tod von hunderttausend Namen nicht so wichtig war wie die Frage, ob man das Leben, und wenn nicht das Leben, dann den Tod mit Herrn Fajngolds Desinfek-tionsmitteln auch rechtzeitig und ausreichend desinfiziert hatte. (513-4)

Lysol is more important than life. This Mr Fajngold could corroborate, for he had sprinkled the dead, not one corpse but many, why bother with figures; he had sprinkled dead men and women with Lysol and that was that. And he knew names, so many that it became tedious, that to me who was also swim-ming in Lysol the question of the life and death of a hundred thousand names became less important than the question of whether life and, if not life, then death, had been disinfected adequately and on time with Mr Fajngold's disinfectants. (413-414)

There is in both these passages – as in the corresponding and crucial 'mound of bones' sequence of *Dog Years* later on – a particularly striking feature: evaluative language and concepts are meticulously avoided, there is no parade of passionate condemnation. This is one part of Grass's answer to a problem that has beset all attempts in German literature to write about the concentration camps: the problem of how to cope adequately with a reality that lies beyond the scope of normal concepts and of traditional categories of understanding and evaluation, a reality that is so monstrous as to be immune against direct verbal assault. Grass's approach is an indirect and much more effective one: beyond the seeming neutrality of the actual words he generates a subtle but powerful emotional intensity that lights up the horror of the object at the same time that it is the means of lamenting it; in Theodor Wieser's phrase: 'hell is reflected by the most indirect means and yet with shattering effect'.[36] A small instance of this process is the ironical device of Oskar's visible assumption of a mask of indifference in the second passage (his alleged boredom at all the names of the dead, his alleged preoccupation with abstract irrelevancies): the scale of values professed here is so patently not a felt one that it automatically suggests its opposite which thus finds expression independently of direct statement. But the decisive factor is the way both passages are conceived poetically in patterns of rhythms, repeats and enumerations which depart completely from the normal narrative tone: in the first passage, the roll-call of Fajngold's exterminated family together with 'seine Schwägerin und der Schwägerin Schwestermann, der fünf Kinderchen hatte', the succession of four forms of the verb 'liegen', the sequence of third-person, past-tense verbs, the strongly rhythmic flow of accented syllables; similar features likewise mark the second passage, and in the excerpt quoted there is above all the insistent repetition of 'Tote': four times within thirteen words. And in a sense these passages may be reckoned an epitome of the whole style of the novel, with its persistent combination of seeming neutrality on the surface, and profound commitment and concern beneath it.

One of the main aspects of the novel's death theme is the gradually developed pattern of Oskar's own attitudes on the subject. It is his mother's death that triggers this off, and it is here that the beginnings of his characteristic attachment to the paraphernalia of death are projected: the shape of coffins appeals to him for the first time at his mother's burial place (195; *164*), and the point is underlined through a rhetorical question: 'Is there any other form in this world so admirably suited to the proportions of the human body?' (196; *164*). The clear implication is that the pattern of human existence has its most perfect reflection in coffins and their shape, that coffins are the most undeceiving measure of existence, and that the whole of life is played out in effect beneath their sign. This is elaborated with unusual directness:

> Hätten die Betten doch diesen Schwund zum Fussende hin! Möchten sich doch all unsere gewohnten und gelegentlichen Liegen so eindeutig zum Fussende hin verjüngen. Denn, mögen wir uns noch so spreizen, endlich ist es doch nur diese schmale Basis, die unseren Füssen zukommt, die sich vom breiten Aufwand, den Kopf, Schultern und Rumpf beanspruchen, zum Fussende hin verjüngt. (196)

> *If only beds had that narrowing at the foot end! If only all our habitual and occasional resting-places could taper off so unambiguously towards the foot end. For strut and struggle as we may, it is after all the ultimate lot of our feet to be confined to that meagre area that narrows down from the more generous space taken up by head, shoulders and torso. (164-5)*

Death as 'unambiguous': Grass later has Oskar use the same word in glossing his fondness for cemeteries with the remark that they are 'unambiguous, logical' (543; *438*), and it is precisely this unambiguousness of death that attracts Oskar, for it means that death is for him the one reliable certainty in an ever worsening plethora of ambiguity and insecurity. As the same commentary on cemeteries puts it: 'Cemeteries have always had a lure for me.... In cemeteries life takes on distinct contours ... and if you will, a meaning.'

In the first two Books of the novel, covering Oskar's childhood and youth, he is repeatedly drawn to seeking refuge beneath his grandmother's skirts, a place that is strongly associated in the narrative with birth (cf. 17 f., 201, 432 f.; *22 f., 169, 348 f.*). In the Third Book, on the other hand, when he has lost all he previously had, including his family and his proper physical shape,

34

he is drawn equally strongly to places associated with death. He thus spends hours at a time over a period of months gazing through the fence at Korneff's gravestone business, and it is there that he ultimately takes a job. His remark apropos of Korneff's initial refusal to take him along on professional trips to cemeteries, is characteristic: 'Time and time again I unsuccessfully offered my help for cemetery work; cemeteries after all held a great attraction for me' (551; 445). Again, the same propensity is shown when he quits the household of Kurt and Maria to live on his own: the room he chooses looks out onto an undertaker's yard, and 'I was often enough to find the coffin-store worth looking at from my window' (591; 476-7); and his first conversation with his fellow-tenant Klepp, ironic and parodistic though it is, makes the point yet again: 'Did he believe that all men were doomed to die? Yes, he felt certain that all men would ultimately have to die, but he was much less sure that all men had to be born' (625; 503).

Korneff's gravestone business, and then cemeteries, are made the scene of much of the first two chapters of Book III, and this setting in itself assures the constant presence of death as a theme, even when it is not in the narrative foreground. With Oskar's first professional visit to a cemetery, however, death and decay become the predominant theme, this predominance being signalled through a magnificently executed – and then magnificently ironised – metaphor: 'Oktober, Friedhofsalleen, der Welt fallen die Haare und Zähne aus, ich meine, immerzu schaukeln gelbe Blätter von oben nach unten.' (552; *October, cemetery paths, the world losing its hair and teeth, which is to say that yellow leaves kept falling from the trees.*, 446). And the paragraph introduced by this metaphor is notable, too, for the fact that it clearly demonstrates the process of disintegration going on within Oskar himself: he day-dreams, and in his fantasy sees the washed-up corpse of Luzie Rennwand,[37] the prototype for him of the 'Schwarze Köchin', and as such a prime agent of the dislocation which he suffers. Oskar's sense of his predicament is most plainly shown by the last part of this day-dream: his discovery of Luzie's heart in the form of a small, cold gravestone bearing the legend 'Here lies Oskar – Here lies Oskar – Here lies Oskar ...' (553; 446); no other passage indicates more strongly the extent to which Oskar's activity as Korneff's apprentice is meant as a reflection of his inner state of being.

The primacy of the death theme is further emphasised in the paragraph that follows, for Grass uses personification to invest the theme with a kind of epic breadth and presence: the newly opened section of the cemetery is described as lying 'flat and hungry', and the nearby protestant burial is consistently personified: 'Coming from Section Seven, a Protestant funeral crawled through Section Eight to Section Nine', 'Meanwhile the funeral had reached Section Nine, where it arranged itself and gave forth the pastor's voice, rising and falling', 'the funeral in Section Nine dispersed' (554-5; 447-8). This personification of the burial contributes greatly to the markedly grotesque tone of the passage, for it has the effect of inverting the normal order of things: the fact of death, customarily disguised by the euphemistic ritual of Christian burial, is greatly emphasised, while the accompanying human beings, normally tending, in all their fulness of life, to dominate the ritual, are reduced to almost comic insignificance – as epitomised in the depiction of the chief mourner as 'eine kleine, schwarze, schiefe Frau' ('*a lopsided little woman in black*'). The other thing that chiefly makes for the grotesque tone is the fact that the depiction of the funeral is interspersed throughout with a detailed account of Oskar's evacuation of Korneff's large, ripe boils: the rapid switches of focus from burial to boils and back again relativise the goings-on of the funeral even further, and reduce the individual death in question to something completely banal and insignificant. At the same time, the Christian element of the funeral is sharply ironised too, in that it is the Paternoster that is taken up, its truncated phrases then being alternated with the descriptions of Oskar's ministrations to Korneff's purulent neck (a purposefully scurrilous device that will be echoed later in *Cat and Mouse*; see below p. 160-1).

Undoubtedly the most radical treatment of death in these first two chapters of Book III is the depiction of the exhumation in 'Fortuna North', for the reader is confronted here not just with dying but with the reality of decomposition. In the funeral of the previous chapter, as in funerals generally, the physical reality of death was veiled by the coffin, the mourners, the ceremonial. In 'Fortuna North', however, these things are absent: there is nothing but the decomposed, disintegrated corpse that has to be 'persuaded piece by piece' to change graves (567; 457). The tone is grotesquely playful and ironic: 'I don't think she felt cold in the proverbially chilly March air, in particular since she still had plenty of skin, which, though laddered and full of holes, bore compensating quantities of hair and fragments of cloth, the former still permanently waved – ' (567; 458). This sardonic tone, the various switches to the other, quite unrelated subjects (Cardinal Frings, the dismantling of industrial plant, etc.), and the repeated emphasis on the fragmented state of the remains,[38] have the effect once again of entirely diminishing and dehumanising the woman and her death, and the Hamlet-Yorick scene that is soon afterwards introduced supplies an effective contrast, for Grass's treatment of the exhumation is quite without that warm solace of emotion that characterises Shakespeare's famous scene.

To say there is a cold, dehumanising effect in these cemetery pages, is to come up against a profound ambivalence concerning the death theme – an ambivalence which in turn has to do with the novel's central areas of meaning. The two faces of this ambivalence are easily seen when one compares the different ways in which death is treated in the case of the merry-go-round passage and in the case of the personified burial in Book III. On the latter occasion, there is a carefully established mood of non-involvement; the text avoids almost all mention of the dead person, the attendant group is reduced to insignificant, almost lifeless adjuncts, and it is the sheer reality of burial that is writ large and rendered animate; an objective, universal generality is so forcefully displayed that the other sphere – the sphere of the individual, subjective, time-bound – appears by implication almost comically pretentious. In the merry-go-round passage, on the other hand, there is quite the opposite perspective: the pervasive spirit there is one of compassionate involvement, and implies the conviction that individual human lives have their own full value, subjective though it may be, and that their loss is worthy of sorrow. On the face of it, these ambivalent attitudes might appear to amount to a contradiction. In reality, though, they are two complementary perspectives on to a single phenomenon, and may perhaps be best character-ised as a 'bird's-eye view' and a 'worm's-eye view'. In the latter case, the focus is on the subjective reality of human beings despite all their creatural limitations; it is the reality of their suffering and their loss which is made to fill the screen, and which is thus not invalidated by comparisons with the endless

37

pattern of all existence. This subjective, worm's-eye view plainly presupposes a sense in the viewer of identity with his subject, however inexplicit it may be; it is just that sense of humanist involvement voiced in the lines of Donne already quoted. There is a striking reflection of this even in the structure of the two different passages: in the merry-go-round figure, Grass makes Oskar an actual participant in the events he relates; in the burial passage, however, Oskar's role is that of a cold, distant observer. Here, as with the bird's-eye view generally, it is the measureless, all-engulfing cycle of existence that is focussed on, so that individual elements of the cycle appear as nothing.

This bird's-eye perspective is expressed with remarkable clarity at one point in the novel. During the story of the 'Stäuberbande' trial ('*The Dusters*'), Grass develops the image of a high diving-board and empty swimming-pool to depict the ignominious end of Oskar's accomplices, but then extends this in a way that clearly echoes the writer who has always held the greatest fascination for Grass: Jean Paul. With Oskar on the high-board in his turn (and describing himself as 'Jesus'), Grass has him see just the same kind of chilling, all-encompassing vision of the world as did the dead Christ in the 'Rede des todten Christus vom Weltgebäude herab, dass kein Gott sei' in Jean Paul's *Siebenkäs* ('*The Dead Christ's Speech from the Top of the World Declaring that There Is No God*').[39] The motive device of Grass's passage comes as no surprise: the deliberate coupling of events that are totally unconnected and – on a worm's-eye view – vastly different in importance, the furious paroxysms of the Second World War being persistently twinned with trivialities and domestic banalities – the sewing on of buttons, the frying of eggs, the burning of milk, etc.[40] Mountbatten's war in Burma and the training of a parrot in Peru may seem grossly different when considered normally and in themselves; but on a bird's-eye view such differences shrink to insignificance, become just elements in the relentless, value-free cycle of being, the 'Faden des Zeitgeschehens' (477; '*thread of events*', 385), that differentiates in no way between murdering someone and cleaning one's teeth:

Auch fiel mir auf, dass Tätigkeiten wie: Daumendrehen, Stirnrunzeln, Köpfchensenken, Händeschütteln, Kinder-machen, Falschgeldprägen, Lichtausknipsen, Zähneputzen, Totschiessen und Trockenlegen überall, wenn auch nicht gleichmässig geschickt, geübt wurden. (477)

I also saw that activities such as thumb-twiddling, frowning, looking up and down, handshaking, making babies, counterfeiting, turning out the light, brushing teeth, shooting people, and changing nappies were being practised all over the world, though not always with the same skill. (385)

But whilst this bird's-eye view and the awareness that goes with it might be fine for a witless bird or an all-witting divinity, they amount to a real threat to the equilibrium of ordinary humans, who cannot dispense with relativity and the subjective, centric pattern which it makes possible; it is thus unsurprising that Grass should have his hero break off the vision with the remark: 'I was thrown into confusion by all these purposeful actions' (477; 385). For it is indeed just such a cold, inescapable awareness that is one of the most disruptive factors in the predicament of Oskar in the narrative present, this would-be hermit who seeks refuge within refuge, and who is reduced to seeing a white-painted asylum bed as his one 'yardstick' and 'solace', his 'goal attained at last' (9; 15).

Sexuality

Sex notoriously constitutes one of *The Tin Drum*'s most forceful elements, and one straightforward reason for this is that sex is a part of life and Grass sees no cause to leave it out. As he was once reported as saying, people making love is for him just as proper a subject as people eating lunch.[41] It is this openness, then, which accounts for quite a number of the novel's sexual allusions and depictions, such things as Greff's taste for boy scouts, the 'minor orgy' at Oskar's birthday-party, the sex games of Susi Kater and co., Oskar's studious activities with the bed-ridden Lina Greff, the Russian soldiers' shiftwork on the same woman later on, the pair of lesbians at the Düsseldorf *Künstlerfest*, Oskar's winter of titillation with the telephonist Hannelore.

39

Most often, however, sex is not merely included as just one among many neutral aspects of reality, but is turned instead to such powerful metaphoric use that it becomes one of the book's most expressive motifs, the aptness of which was well put by the critic K. A. Horst: 'How often is it not true that the more intimate half of the body below the navel tells us more than the empty gesturing of the upper half.'[42] It turns out indeed that even the seemingly neutral and incidental depictions of sex are figurative in a general sense, in that they all amount to a tacit denial of the Lawrentian, Novalis kind of philosophy in which sex is reckoned a supreme expression of love and beauty, an unsurpassable symbol of humanness and human communion. For Grass (or, rather, for the Grass of *The Tin Drum*), the manifestation of a man's sexuality is the sharpest demonstration of his lack of wholeness, of his inherent lack of autonomy, of the unbridgeable distance that separates him from others. An oblique indication of this is the way that loving affection and sex are constantly kept separate in the novel. Oskar has love for his grandmother, his mother, Mutter Truczinski, Herbert Truczinski perhaps; he does not appear to have such feelings towards Maria any more than towards Lina Greff or the Düsseldorf telephonist (Roswitha, as one of the 'little people', seems a case apart). Similarly, there is little love and certainly no spirit of giving in the Matzerath-Agnes-Jan Bronski triangle or in the later relationship between Matzerath and Maria. The idealist view of sex is refuted with unusual explicitness at one point in the book, apropos of the first stirrings of Oskar's own sexuality:

> Merkwürdigerweise erwartete ich von der Literatur mehr Anregungen als vom nackten, tatsächlichen Leben.... Obgleich ich wusste, dieses abwechselnd aus Mama und Jan oder Matzerath und Mama bestehende, seufzende, angestrengte, endlich ermattet ächzende, Fäden ziehend auseinanderfallende Knäuel bedeutet Liebe, wollte Oskar dennoch nicht glauben, dass Liebe Liebe war, und suchte aus Liebe andere Liebe und kam doch immer wieder auf die Knäuelliebe und hasste diese Liebe, bevor er sie als Liebe exerzierte und als einzig wahre und mögliche Liebe sich selbst gegenüber verteidigen musste. (341)

> *Strange to say, I expected more inspiration from literature*

than from real, naked life.... Although I knew that this
tangle, consisting by turns of Mama and Jan or Matzerath
and Mama, this knot which sighed, exerted itself, moaned
with fatigue, and at last fell stickily apart, meant love, Oskar
was still unwilling to believe that love was love; love itself
made him cast about for some other love, and yet time and
again he came back to tangled love, which he hated until
the day when he practised it as love, and was obliged to
defend it in his own eyes as the only true and feasible love.
(278-9)

Grass's own view is particularly evident in the case of Agnes.
At first it appears as though her sexuality were just a neutral
aspect of character; but the more we learn of her indefatigable
cavortings with Jan Bronski – 'Jan, der vom Fleisch meiner
Mama lebte' (156; '*Jan, who lived off my Mama's flesh*', 132)
– the more this impression of neutrality recedes. For one thing,
their goings-on are always so depicted that they consistently
appear inordinate and compulsive – their irrepressible petting
at the least opportunity, Jan's foot between Agnes's thighs
whenever they are at the skat table, their regular coitus in a
rented room. But the narrative also makes this excessiveness
and uncontrollability quite explicit: at a very early stage,
Grass has Oskar describe their passion as 'raging blindly'
('blindwütige Leidenschaft', 62; 56) and as 'reeking of extrava-
gance and surfeit' ('da riecht es nach ... Verstiegenheit, die
zum Überdruss wird, Überdruss der Verstiegenheit mit sich
bringt', 61-2; 56). There is a particularly important remark later
on when Oskar, relating how Sigismund Markus longed for
some crumbs left over by Agnes and her sex partner, adds:
'Mama und Jan Bronski liessen kein Krümelchen übrig. Die
assen alles selbst auf. Die hatten den grossen Appetit, der nie
aufhört, der sich selbst in den Schwanz beisst.' (118; '*Mama and
Jan Bronski left no crumbs. Not a one. They ate everything
themselves. They had the ravenous appetite that never dies
down, that bites its own tail.*', 101); this not only points up the
gross insatiability of their lust, but is also the novel's first
explicit indication that it tends to self-destructiveness.
    It is surely in the light of these things that Agnes Matzerath's
subsequent 'passion' and death are chiefly to be understood
(even though, as I have suggested, there are other more general

factors too; see above, page 27); when the horse's head events inflict insight on her and confront her with an 'unfillable abyss', we may infer that what she sees above all is the deadness of her own life, ravaged as it is by an uncontrollable drive. It is not by chance that sequences of sexuality are prominent amongst the events depicted in the period between her nausea and renunciation of fish, and her subsequent fatal return to fish: first the mutual stimulation between Jan and herself on the way from the mole, then their cuddling on the living-room couch, and finally Jan's way of consoling her by masturbating her on the Matzerath's marriage bed. The implication is clear: the fact that not even so traumatic an experience as Agnes's on the sea-front can inhibit their furious sexuality is a final demonstration of its excessiveness and autonomy, its complete governance of Agnes's being. And it is impossible not to associate this with the 'abyss' that then opens up before Agnes's eyes. Extra indications of a link between her sexuality and her 'mysterious will' to die, may readily be seen in the fact that she is pregnant, and in the fact that her sexual apathy, once she is possessed of her strange resolve, is apparently so marked as to bring Jan Bronski to tears (191; *160*).

Other, more fleeting instances of sex depicted along similar lines are the episode of Herbert Truczinski's death (234-5; *195-196*) and the episode in Book III with the young nun Schwester Agneta – her own sexuality drives her willy-nilly into the bunker with Lankes, and she draws the consequences afterwards by apparently drowning herself (680 f.; *547 f.*). This helplessness of Schwester Agneta's is beautifully described in the much earlier chapter with the nuns in Book II: she moves towards the soldiers and their bunker, is told to come away by her Superior, and replies: 'Ich kann ja nicht! Das läuft von alleine!' (423; *'I can't! It's stronger than I am!'*, *341*). Another short but intense figuration of sex in the same kind of terms is, of course, the 'love' paragraph in 'Faith Hope Love' (see above, p. 19). But there is certainly nothing fleeting about the depiction of sexuality in Oskar's case: Grass uses it as an insistent motif that demonstrates over and over again the hero's lack of personal autonomy. A first hint of this comes with his automatic erection on fondling the naked Christ statue (168; *141-2*), and we are told elsewhere that it was this that first made him aware of his genitals – which, he remarks, he still

42

carries around with him 'like a capricious monument to my powerlessness and limited possibilities' (213; *179*). It is not until much later, though, that Oskar is made thoroughly aware of sexuality: at the sight of Maria's naked body in the swimming-pool cubicle he again experiences an involuntary erection, and suddenly recognises – with 'rage, shame, indignation, disap-pointment' (329; *269*) – that, whether he likes it or not, Maria is to him what Agnes was to Matzerath and Bronski. But this is not all he becomes aware of: his later preoccupation with death is strongly prefigured in that his first proper experience of sex simultaneously afflicts him with an ineradicable know-ledge of mortality: he bites desperately into Maria's genitals, and 'only when this earthy smell that Maria concealed behind the vanilla nailed the mouldering body of Jan Bronski to my brow and contaminated me for all time with the taste of mortality – only then did I let go.' (329; *269*).[43] The seriousness of this experience is then conclusively indicated by the fact that Oskar ends up by crying, something which is infrequent in the novel and always a sign of his deepest responses.

In the following chapter, when Oskar is in bed with Maria – whose bottom half participates while her top half sleeps ('Maria, die oben schlief und unten dabei war', 343; *280*) – Grass includes an emphatic, almost programmatic passage on the autonomy of the sex urge, Oskar's own sexuality even being figured here as a quite separate personality:

[Maria wollte nicht den,] den ja auch ich nicht wollte, der sich selbständig gemacht hatte, der den eigenen Kopf bewies, der etwas von sich gab, was ich ihm nicht eingegeben, der aufstand, als ich mich legte, der andere Träume hatte als ich, der weder lesen noch schreiben konnte, der dennoch für mich unterschrieb, der heute noch seinen eigenen Weg geht, der sich an jenem Tage schon von mir trennte, da ich ihn erstmals wahrnahm, der mein Feind ist, mit dem ich mich immer wieder verbünden muss, der mich verrät und im Stich lässt,[44] den ich verraten und verkaufen möchte, dessen ich mich schäme, der meiner überdrüssig ist, den ich wasche, der mich beschmutzt, der nichts sieht und alles wittert, der mir so fremd ist, dass ich ihn siezen möchte, der ein ganz anderes Gedächtnis als Oskar hat: denn wenn heute Maria mein Zimmer betritt ... erkennt er Maria nicht wieder, will nicht, kann nicht... (343)

> [*Maria didn't want*] *this little gentleman whom I didn't want either, who had made himself independent, who knew his own mind, who gave forth something that didn't come from me, who stood up when I lay down, who had different dreams from mine, who could neither read nor write but nevertheless signed for me, who goes his own way to this very day, who broke with me on the very day I first became aware of his existence, who is my enemy with whom I have to ally myself time and again, who betrays me and leaves me in the lurch,*[44] *whom I should like to betray and doublecross, of whom I am ashamed, who is sick of me, whom I wash, who befouls me, who sees nothing and senses everything, who is completely alien to me, whose memory is quite different from Oskar's: for today when Maria comes into the room ... he no longer recognises Maria, he won't, he can't ... (280)*

Nothing could illustrate more pointedly than this passage does the crucial significance of sexuality as a theme in the novel – and nothing, incidentally, refutes more eloquently the denigrations of such as Günter Blöcker who castigated *The Tin Drum*'s author as a purveyor of gratuitous obscenities.

It is by no means only Oskar's own sexuality which demonstrates his lack of wholeness and personal sovereignty: the sexuality of others may do so equally vividly, and this is certainly the case in the episode where Oskar surprises Matzerath and Maria in the middle of copulation (350 f.; 285 f.) – a passage that is also marvellously expressive at a more general level, for it reflects the novel's whole sexual perspective in the way that it points up the grotesquely cold and mechanical banality of the couple's 'work' ('Arbeit'); indeed there is no other scene that so sharply evokes the spirit of deadness and inadequacy that attaches throughout to the novel's presentation of sexuality. The effect of this experience on Oskar is profound, and is once again characteristically indicated by the turbulence of his reactions: he leaps on to Matzerath's back, tries later to win Maria back with fizz-powder, earning only blows and insults, punches her in the genitals, bites her at the same 'accursed place', and is finally overcome by a tell-tale spasm

44

of crying, much as he was when first compelled to recognise his own sexuality earlier on. This pattern of reactions is continued in the following chapter, with Oskar making two forcible attempts to provoke the abortion of Maria's foetus (365-7; 297-9); but the culmination comes at the end of the chapter with an image which in Grass is always an indicator of crisis: Oskar is overcome by nausea and vomits up all he has eaten at the baptism feast for Kurt, his new-born brother/son. The key word here is 'Ohnmacht' ('impotence', in the general sense): as emphasised in the final sentence of the previous chapter, it was Oskar's recognition of his utter helplessness, his 'bleierne Ohnmacht', that accounted for his frenzy of tears (357; 291); here, the word 'Ohnmacht' (already present in the chapter's title) is repeated not just once but four times in the closing four lines. The broken pattern of Oskar's outward relationships is thus conveyed through sexuality just as distinctly as is the fractured state within himself; and in this way there is a progressive illumination of what lies behind the 'present' complete isolation of the memoir-writing asylum-patient that is emphasised from the very first words of the novel.

CHAPTER III

Dislocation and Ambiguity

There is a distinctive Lewis Carroll-ish kind of effect in Grass's first novel: instead of things becoming clearer the further you penetrate into the book, they in fact appear to take on an ever more dislocated and obscure aspect. This does not mean that the book in itself is bitty or confused – it is very much the reverse. What it does turn out to mean is that *The Tin Drum* points with almost the whole of its huge apparatus of metaphor to an order of reality whose workings are random, inorganic and deeply ambiguous (and therewith ultimately terrifying for those, exemplified by Oskar, who are aware of being especially exposed to them). In talking about some of the decisive structures of form and imagery in the novel, we have already touched at several points on this central area of meaning; but the whole of the rest of this First Part will be directly concerned with it, first in the shape of various separate motifs, then in the shape of the novel's paramount metaphor: the persona of Oskar Matzerath himself.

Theatre and Role-playing

There can be little doubt that in any reasonable list of half a dozen characteristic elements of Grass's narrative writing so far, theatrical imagery would be likely to figure. It is fundamental, for instance, in *Local Anaesthetic*, with Starusch inveterately posturing and imagining whole strings of roles and television sequences; and it is equally important in *The Tin Drum*, if somewhat more diffusely.

The description of the Bronski-Agnes-Matzerath triangle in terms of 'Theater', with a first act, second act and third act, is a typical case in point. As suggested earlier (above, p. 27), the function of this is to show how the relationships of the three are devoid of any vital reality, of any genuine responsiveness; the whole pattern of their behaviour is shown as a drab, unchanging stereotype: 'They knew their parts', and their adopted roles have usurped whatever richer identity they may have had. But it does not stop there. For Grass most importantly represents his characters as living more than one false role. In particular, he repeatedly depicts a severe duality as between people's actual practice, and their professed attitudes and their image of themselves. Jan and Agnes are thus described as showing much calculating cunning ('Berechnung') in creating opportunities to indulge their lust – whilst at the same time evincing 'just as much talent for romancing' (192; 162). This is true of Agnes generally: upstairs in the flat she likes to cultivate a mood that drips with romantic sentimentality ('Mama liess sich gerne rühren', 128; 109), as when she plays the slow movements of Beethoven sonatas slower than marked so that they come trickling sweetly out ('dahintropfen', 136; 115); down in the shop, on the other hand, sentiment is no part of her life. The very same pattern is mirrored later in Maria: when not working, she indulges her escapist fancies on her mouth-organ – 'But Maria never took out her "Hohner" during business hours. Even when there were no customers about, she refrained from music and wrote price tags and inventories ...' (321; 263). Indeed the existence of the whole Matzerath circle is constantly projected in terms of this same kind of schizophrenic duality of attitudes – a duality epitomised in the detail that pictures of Beethoven and Hitler glare direfully at one another from opposite sides of the Matzeraths' living room (a symbolic confrontation that Grass recreates in variant forms throughout the trilogy).[45]

Undoubtedly the most crucial aspect of all this is that there is just as deep an ambivalence in moral attitudes as in everything else. This is always implicit, but the narrative often points it up with particular sharpness: Greff, who is partial to scouts and ultimately attracts the attentions of the vice-squad, finds Scheffler's lip-licking habit 'indecent' (63; 58); Agnes and Gretchen Scheffler enjoy a joint orgasm over the Rasputin book,

47

but then, after a pause filled with rich cream-cakes, they wax indignant at the 'immorality' of Rasputin's Russia (109; 94); Maria's reaction to the 'lewd' 'Madonna 49' painting of Ulla and Oskar in the Third Book is described thus:

> Sie ... begegnete mir als nunmehr im Westen guteingebür-gerte Person, war kein Schwarzhandel treibender Ostflücht-ling mehr und konnte mich deshalb mit ziemlicher Über-zeugungskraft ein Ferkel, einen Hurenbock, ein verkommenes Subjekt nennen, schrie auch, sie wolle das Saugeld, das ich mit der Schweinerei verdiene, nicht mehr sehen, auch mich wolle sie nicht mehr sehen. (587)

> *She ... now confronted me in the guise of an established citizen of West Germany, was a blackmarketing refugee from the East no longer, and so could with a certain conviction call me a pig, a pimp and a degenerate, as well as shouting that she wanted no more of the filthy money I made with my filthy occupations, nor of me for that matter. (474)*

And the sentence that follows remarks that within a fortnight Maria was again taking a sizeable portion of the same 'filthy money'.

The importance of this theme of moral dislocation is best pinned down if one turns again to the 'Faith Hope Love' sequence, for this most intense of chapters includes amongst its imagery the novel's keenest demonstration of perverted stan-dards: Meyn is fined and expelled from the SA just after the *Kristallnacht* for his 'inhuman' actions and 'unworthy' behaviour; but his offence is cruelty to cats, not cruelty to humans; and his zealous participation in the brutality of the *Kristallnacht*, far from being considered inhuman or unworthy, is counted as an extenuating factor, though insufficient to compensate for his crime against the cats and against the 'good name' of the Party (Grass will later echo this directly in Mahlke's expulsion from the Conradinum and Matern's expulsion from the SA). As with the Matzerath circle, only more starkly, Grass presents us here with the spectacle of a sentimentality that is warped and false, above all because it is so grotesquely at odds with the actual practice of those indulging in it. And the suggestion is clear: that the vast institutionalised distortedness of National Socialist

48

Germany was essentially an expression of the fractured consciousness and behaviour of the countless mass of Matzeraths, Greffs and Schefflers. Grass's own remarks in a 1966 interview are relevant indeed :

> He consciously restricted his choice of subject matter, says Günter Grass, to the confined world of the petty bourgeoisie ... In the course of working on his novels it became clear that large areas that are normally considered unpolitical are really close adjuncts of politics, for instance the 'fug' of the constricted petty bourgeois world with its falsely idyllic family festivities etc.... In *The Tin Drum*, he says, he attempted to show 'how latently political petty bourgeois classes were as carriers of a world-view like that of the National Socialist regime'.[46]

Just as the Bronski-Agnes-Matzerath triangle was represented in stage terms, so, too, is the new Matzerath-Maria-Oskar situation : Grass has Oskar describe it with typical irony as a miscast tragedy in which he is conceded only a superfluous bit-part instead of the lead to which he feels entitled (353; 287). And this theatre perspective is reintroduced time and again for ironic effect. Viktor Weluhn declaims and gestures 'as on the stage' (287; 236); Greff's face as he hangs dead in his fantastic machine is 'theatrically posed' (388; 315); the Russian soldiers' arrival in Matzerath's cellar is 'Fate making its entrance' (489; 394); nature 'acts the part' of Spring, and a storm gives a 'longish performance' (543, 145; 438, 123). In the 'Inspection of Concrete' chapter, not only is the imminent invasion figured as a 'Gala performance' for which the defence forces are 'adequately rehearsed' (412; 334), but no less than fourteen pages are written in stage form complete with dialogue, stage directions and 'noises off'[47] – the effect of this being to put maximum distance between reader and events by entirely confounding the illusion of spontaneity and reality (an illusion that is never given much of a foothold in the novel at the best of times). It is this passage, incidentally, which more than any other reflects Grass's original intention of casting the whole novel in dialogue form; and it has to be remembered that Grass would anyway much prefer to have succeeded in drama than in prose, and indeed was allegedly only driven to writing *The Tin Drum* by his irritation at the way he felt he had been treated as a dramatist.[48]

49

Film imagery is also frequently used in the novel in the same debunking sort of way, with the pattern being set at an early stage when Oskar explains in detail how the Koljaiczek-Dückerhoff story might conceivably have ended with a romantic splurge of heroism and reconciliation, adding:

Wir kennen diese Szene aus betörend gut fotografierten Filmen, wenn es den Regisseuren einfällt, famos schauspielernde, feindliche Brüder zu fortan durch dick und dünn gehenden, noch tausend Abenteuer bestehenden Spiessgesellen zu machen. (31)

We know the scene from the films: the reconciliation between two enemy brothers, brilliantly performed, brilliantly photographed, from this day onward comrades forever, through thick and thin and a thousand adventures. (32)

By implication, this demonstrates exactly the sort of writing that Grass is *not* interested in: the false, easy sentimentality that aims to satisfy (and profit from) the needs of escapism. For him, such a facile perspective could only mean a dereliction of responsibility; his concern is to create 'first and foremost a realistic novel', to catch hold of a 'reality that needs to be exactly pinned down and described'[49] – and he is all too aware of the problems involved: 'I know I'm doing a rope-walking act, but you just can't write "simply" any more if you want your work to have more than sheer entertainment value.'[50] And it goes almost without saying that the sham sentimentality parodied here and in later film pastiches,[51] is very much of a piece with the dangerously vapid romanticism of the Matzerath circle.

'Falseness' is one keynote, too, of the other main aspect of theatricality in the novel: the repeated emphasis on role-playing. Again, no time is lost in establishing this characteristic motif: the fifth paragraph of the book conveys the strong impression that Oskar's visitors are thoroughly ungenuine, that the attitudes they affect towards him are a mere game ('Then these people come ... whom it amuses to love me', etc). And as the narrative progresses it becomes apparent that even the dramatic first sentence had to do with role-playing: the question as to whether Oskar is truly mad, or only pretending to be mad, remains one of the ultimate ambiguities of the fiction. Almost the whole of the

50

novel accords with this beginning: except in the case of a very few characters such as Anna Bronski and Herbert Truczinski, the impression is consistently given that people do not behave genuinely and organically, but instead act out a false role of one kind or another. The description of the photographs in Oskar's album is especially pointed in this respect: everyone concerned – even Anna Bronski! – is shown as striking a pose (57 f.; 53 f.). So too, though in a different way, is the description of the Onion Cellar, whose cultivated, outré artificiality conforms to a whimsical escapist stereotype – and which, like the equally outré Morgue Restaurant of *Dog Years*, is meant as an image of postwar German society, 'that society that developed after the currency reform – fairly rapidly in Düsseldorf, more slowly but equally surely elsewhere.' (648; 521). The particularly chilling thing about this is that it is only by means of the Onion Cellar's gross artificiality that its habitués can achieve expression of their most vital and real feelings.

Grass's emphasis on role-playing has another key function, too, in that it adds to the general impression of ambiguity. This is most importantly the case with Oskar, as we shall see, but it is also true with his grandfather, for instance, who is shown as undergoing a complete switch of personality:

[Koljaiczek kroch] zuerst in Wrankas Joppe, sodann in dessen amtlich papierene, nicht vorbestrafte Haut, gewöhnte sich die Pfeife ab, verlegte sich auf Kautabak, übernahm sogar vom Wranka das Persönlichste, dessen Sprachfehler und gab in den folgenden Jahren einen braven, sparsamen, leicht stotternden Flösser ab ... (26)

Koljaiczek ... *crept first into Wranka's jacket, then into his irreproachable official skin, gave up pipe-smoking, took to chewing tobacco, and even adopted Wranka's most personal and characteristic trait, his speech defect. In the years that followed he played the part of a hard-working, thrifty raftsman with a slight stutter ... (28)*

Koljaiczek was an intrepid fire-raiser, but Wranka-Koljaiczek is afraid even of the sight of matches, and later becomes a devoted fireman; Gunner Koljaiczek was notoriously bad in his military service, but Corporal Wranka-Koljaiczek is notably successful in his. Where then lies the 'truth' of Koljaiczek's identity? And who is he now, assuming he is alive: is he Goljaczek a Pole, Koljaiczek a Kashubian, or Joe Colchic an American (38; 37)? Similar ambiguities are later depicted in the cases of Klepp and Meyn. Thus Klepp is not 'really' Klepp but Egon Münzer (624; 503); and so long as he is in bed he is a devoted royalist, but he no sooner abandons his bed than he becomes a card-carrying communist (632; 508-9). As for Meyn, he had been in a communist youth group and then in the 'Red Falcons' (237; 198), but come National Socialism and he switches to the SA (a pattern that will be re-created on a large scale with Walter Matern later on). The change is brilliantly high-lighted from another angle: the one Meyn gets incessantly drunk on *Machandel* and plays his trumpet magnificently, while the other Meyn rejects drink entirely and loses his touch on the trumpet; and it is not as if the change were permanent: Grass describes Meyn as fluctuating periodically between the two contrary states of being.

One revealing variant of this aspect of the role motif occurs in connection with Oskar's post-war phase as an artists' model (573 ff.; 462 ff.). Professor 'Kuchen' and his students fail entirely to catch a true image of Oskar's reality: they are so role-defined by their black preconceptions that they see only his 'Rasputinian' hump-back and are blind to his 'Goethean' blue eyes and the colour of his hair; they try in their drawings to force him into the roles of darkly symbolic 'gypsy', 'refugee' and 'prisoner' – and misrepresent him completely. The sculptors and painters in their turn fail for similar reasons. But 'Ziege' and 'Raskolnikoff' do succeed, the reason being that they are unimpeded by pre-conceptions and are able to let the multiple reality of their subject and their own unfettered imagination interact to produce cogent, appealing works – 'now in colour, then in superior shades of grey, now touched in with a fine brush, then smashed on with a spatula in the true style of genius' (584; 471). The fascinating thing about this is that it amounts to a description of Grass's own style in *The Tin Drum*, with its plural structure, its endless alternation of colour, tone and intensity, its constantly shifting pattern of comedy, parody, tragedy, lament, description, protest, ambivalence, irony and so on, a pattern that occurs partly because Grass so obviously revels in it – but also because it is felt to be the only tentative means of staking out a reality so amorphous and multiple that any attempt to grasp it at one fell swoop cannot but end in travesty, *vide* the efforts of 'Kuchen' and company. And it is one eloquent measure of Grass's critically changed perspective in *Dog Years* that in this later novel both its actual structure and the reflections on aesthetic cogency which it contains (in connection with Amsel's art) prove to be signally different from those in *The Tin Drum*.

One of the main functions of Grass's theatre motif, I have suggested, is to demonstrate falseness, especially false, escapist indulgence in sentimentality and empty gesturing, and this is nowhere more pointedly emphasised than in the novel's most explicit theatrical passage: the *Hamlet* parody cued in by the woman's exhumation in 'Fortuna North' (568 f.; 458 f.).

The essence of the passage is an extended and sharp contrasting of two opposite responses to reality, a grandly 'tragical' response that is rejected, and an anti-tragical one that is endorsed (all this being anticipated some twenty pages earlier in a neat satire on the cocooning pretence and complacent emotionalism of post-war German theatre, 540-1; 436-7). The 'grandiose' perspective is finely established as soon as Oskar and Korneff reach the scene of the exhumation: the power-station in the plain below is depicted in an epic, Zola-esque kind of vein, it becomes a heaving, almost animate thing; at the climax it is unrecognisable as just any prosaic bit of industrial plant, but has become instead 'Welt, Knotenpunkt' (566; *'hub of the world'*, 457). The narrative then changes focus and mood entirely; the evocation of the reeking, fragmented corpse is powerful precisely because of its quiet touching-in of detail, its juxtaposing of disparates, its avoidance of any kind of easy emotionalism and big-screen effects. Grass then begins to make his point quite clear by having Oskar explicitly prefer the one response to the other: he finds the woman's dismembered head and finger 'closer to me, and more human, than the beauty of the power-station' (568; 458); the grand pathos of the industrial landscape may have appealed to him, he concedes, just as Gustaf Gründgens' theatrical antics once had done, but he remains 'mistrustful of such superficial kinds of beauty'; and whilst the pulsating high-voltage wires imbue him, like Goethe's *Tasso*, with a grand sense of universality ('Weltgefühl'), he is more intimately, more inwardly touched by the dead woman's fingers ('the woman's fingers touched my heart').

It is here that the *Hamlet* parody is introduced – with a characteristic twist: instead of the woman's corpse being figured as Yorick's, and Oskar adopting the guise of Hamlet, the roles are reversed: Hamlet is relegated to the grave, while the Fool becomes the 'hero'. And instead of Yorick having to lend out his skull 'so that some Gründgens or Sir Laurence Olivier in the role of Hamlet may ponder over it', it is 'Hamlet's' finger – i.e. the dead woman's – that has to serve the equivalent purpose. The parody is magnificently set up, as here for instance, when Oskar-Yorick establishes his pseudo-tragical perspective:

[ich] machte den dörflichen Friedhof zum Mittelpunkt der Welt, das Kraftwerk Fortuna Nord zu meinem imponierenden halbgöttlichen Gegenüber, die Äcker waren Dänemarks Äcker, die Erft war mein Belt, was hier faulte, das faulte mir im Reich der Dänen – (568-9)

I made this village graveyard the centre of the world and made Fortuna North my imposing demi-god antagonist, the fields were Denmark's fields, the Erft was my Belt, what rotted here was to me rotten in the state of Denmark – (459)

Soon after this, however, the tragical bubble is unceremoniously burst in a passage that offers a brilliant conspectus of the novel's pattern, and in so doing reflects with precision the characteristic anti-tragical perspective of the book:

[ich] liess, dritter Aufzug, den Gründgens in erster Szene nach Sein oder Nichtsein fragen, verwarf diese törichte Fragestellung, hielt vielmehr Konkretes nebeneinander: so meinen Sohn und meines Sohnes Feuersteine, meine mutmasslichen irdischen und himmlischen Väter, die vier Röcke meiner Grossmutter, die auf Fotos unsterbliche Schönheit meiner armen Mama, den narbigen Irrgarten auf Herbert Truczinskis Rücken, die blutaufsaugenden Briefkörbe der Polnischen Post, Amerika – ach, was ist Amerika gegen die Strassenbahnlinie neun, die nach Brösen fuhr ... (569)

I had Gründgens, Act III, Scene i, ask his question about being or not being, rejected this foolish enquiry and instead kept hold of concrete things, things like my son and my son's flints, my presumptive earthly and heavenly fathers, the four skirts

54

of my grandmother, my poor Mama's beauty, immortalised
in photographs, the maze of scars on Herbert Truczinski's
back, the blood-absorbing mail-baskets of the Polish Post
Office, America – but oh, what is America compared to tram-
way number nine that went to Brösen ... (459-60)

Nowhere else in the novel are Grass's own stance as author and
his thorough disregard for complacent, sham emotionalism more
pungently expressed than in these few pages. And if one is in any
doubt about the importance of all this to Grass, one need only
remember that it is precisely these two contrary attitudes to
reality that Grass incorporates later on in Eduard Amsel and
Walter Matern; as for the Hamlet passage itself : we shall find
that it is echoed in a quite startling way in the episode in *Dog
Years* involving Amsel, Matern and the subterranean skeleton
(see below, pp. 225 f., 240).

The Reader-'Reality' Relationship

When Grass has Oskar describe Agnes's will to die as 'puzzling',
and proffer not one but several explanations for it, this is just
one among many devices in the novel that bring alive its fundamental notion of dislocation and ambiguity by communicating a
sense of insecurity even to the reader himself, who is prevented
from settling back comfortably in the assumption that The
Narrator Knows All. The account of Koljaiczek's disappearance
towards the beginning of the book is a typical case in point:
Oskar first claims to believe that his grandfather died beneath
the logs, then cites three other different versions ('Versionen'),
and finally gives another version (alleging that his grandfather
reached America) which is ostentatiously rejected at the time
but frequently adduced later on (35 f.; 36 f.). A similar sense
of uncertainty is produced over the fate of the ship being
launched at the time of Koljaiczek's disappearance : was it subsequently sunk or did it sink on its own? was it raised and re-
built? was it renamed or scrapped? or did it just go down and
stay down? Oskar doesn't know, and can only say that he
'believes' that at some stage it sank on its own (38; 38). In the

Third Book, the 'truth' about Schmuh's death remains equally obscure: Oskar recounts Klepp's strange report of it, then remarks: 'You are free to think what you please of Klepp's story; Oskar remains sceptical' (668; 537). And Oskar's explicit scepticism about Klepp's reliability is an oblique reminder to the reader to be sceptical about Oskar's own.

One particularly effective method for inducing doubt and puzzlement in the reader is the practice, most marked in the earlier chapters, of referring quite casually to things that the reader as yet knows nothing whatsoever about. Thus we are given no clue as to why this person is in a mental asylum, why he needs a lawyer, or why he is thought to require 'saving'; we are not told his first name for over two pages, and it is a long time before we hear his surname; we are given no information about Klepp and Vittlar, this strangely named, strangely behaving pair of alleged 'friends' of Oskar's; and Oskar speaks of 'my trial' (39; 38) without a word of further explanation. What was 'fateful' (24; 27) about Jan Bronski's stamp-collecting habit? What is this 'journey in the freight-wagon' (53; 49)? And what is 'that ring finger' (213; 178)? We are given no idea who 'Kurtchen' is (347; 283), and when Maria is mentioned on page 251 (209), we are not told that she is the same person as the Maria named on pages 114 and 210 (98, 176).

It is not just that Grass avoids suspending disbelief – he makes a particular point of cultivating it, thus structuring the whole novel according to the kind of principle expressed in the earlier prose piece 'Fünf Vögel' ('Five Birds') in Die Vorzüge der Windhühner: 'Glaube hin, Glaube her, hier wird gezweifelt.' ('Belief boloney, here doubt is the thing.'); as Klaus Wagenbach has remarked in the same connection: 'Grass's writing is governed by this atmosphere of radical doubt.'[52] In The Tin Drum the traditional straightforward relationship between reader and events is severely dislocated. In place of the conventional illusion that what the reader sees is a direct image of what 'actually happened', Grass substitutes the troubling illusion that the image arrives only after having been refracted through a kind of double prism: can one be sure that Oskar's sheer knowledge and memory do justice to the supposed events? and can one be sure that the desperate predicament behind his flight to the past has no distorting effect? That his memory has its limitations is clearly indicated by the phrase 'I only hope my memory is

56

accurate' (10; *16*). But what is most startling is that the reader is warned within the very first lines of the novel that he is faced with a narrator who is not only an apparent lunatic but also a deliberate liar: Grass has Oskar speak first of giving an account of actual events in his life ('Begebenheiten aus meinem Leben'), then of telling stories ('meine Erzählungen'), and finally of inventing sheer lies ('sobald ich ihm etwas vorgelogen habe').

This matter of the narrator's untrustworthiness will need looking at more closely within the context of Oskar himself. But on a more general level, it will be clear that Grass's whole dislocation of the reader-'reality' relationship is far from gratuitous; it is in fact a structural metaphor that mirrors the supposed obscure complexity of empirical reality itself, that reality to which the readers themselves belong – 'all you who have to live a life of confusion outside this mental asylum' (12; *18*). No wonder Grass spoke of the difficulties of serious writing (see above, p. *50*): he wanted to write a 'realistic novel' about a 'reality that needs to be exactly pinned down and described' – and yet which seemed to him at that stage so multiple and ambiguous that it could not be shown by direct reflection but only by refraction and re-refraction through a succession of prisms.

CHAPTER IV

The Meaning of Oskar

The figure of Oskar Matzerath, combining as it does the two roles of chief protagonist and supposed narrator, is unquestionably paramount in the novel – this much is self-evident. What is less self-evident, but to my mind equally certain, is that Oskar not only combines two outward roles as narrator-cum-protagonist, but is also compounded inwardly of two quite distinct personas – thereby manifesting in a most crucial respect that same principle of duality and dislocation that we have repeatedly come across elsewhere.

Even on a first reading of the novel, in other words even without being especially alive to its characteristic ambivalences, one can scarcely fail to be struck by the fact that Oskar's account implies two quite different kinds of relationship between himself and events. Expressed briefly and provisionally: there is a relationship marked by scepticism, detachment, independence, superiority, the operation of mind; and there is a relationship marked by involvement, dependence, vulnerability and impotence, the operation of feeling. For the most part these separate relationships are not precisely spelt out in the narrative, but there is one vignette which, quite out of the blue, exactly characterises both at once; Oskar, we hear, is enticed into cinemas by Maria Schell's seductively sentimental films – and responds thus:

> Während Oskars Kleinhirn und Grosshirn lachten und Unanständigkeiten am laufenden Band dem Filmstreifen einflochten, weinten Oskars Augen Tränen, ich irrte halbblind in einer Wüste ... (599)

> *While Oskar's brainbox laughed and wove an endless stream of obscenities into the film, Oskar's eyes wept tears, I wandered half-blind in a desert ... (483)*

It is of course the ironic, swashbuckling 'brainbox'-Oskar that is most blatantly paraded in the narrative, and it is this more ostentatious mask that has so often been mistaken for the whole reality, and which has given rise to such misconceptions as those that Oskar is 'free', 'innocent', 'in confident control' etc. The truth is clearly much more complex.

'Brainbox' Oskar

All the external evidence about Oskar suggests that it was the detached, 'brainbox' kind of hero that first presented itself to Grass, and that the 'tears' persona came later in the creative process. Grass himself has described in an interview how he first tried his hand in the early fifties at a long poem-cycle centring on a pillar-dweller, a 'stylite'. He then tried to transfer the same figure to the medium of prose, but found the figure too static. His problem was how to generate movement without sacrificing the distinctively detached perspective of the stylite, and a pint-sized hero was the perfect solution: he has maximum freedom of movement, and yet remains 'ein umgekehrter Säulenheiliger' ('a stylite in reverse') in that his angle of vision from down below is essentially the same as that from up above.[53] In an earlier interview (1959 as opposed to 1962), Grass also offered another, equally revealing explanation:

> At friends of friends about seven years ago I saw a three-year-old boy with a tin drum round his neck, he was supposed to shake hands and say 'good day'. But he ignored the adults, refused to call the day a good day, and attended only to his drum. This little boy's perspective later became Oskar's perspective.[54]

Really the only prime element in Oskar that is missing here is the protective device of his glass-shattering voice.

The great attraction of this kind of persona is clear: it meant that Grass could have a narrator who had watched and even participated in the events of a whole era, and yet remained apparently free of involvement in its otherwise engulfing complexes of guilt, responsibility, self-justification etc., with the result that the narrative itself was freed from the risk of getting bogged down in these same issues (indeed far from getting engulfed by them, the narrative expressively mirrors them – using the other side of Oskar, the 'tears' persona). What is equally clear is that this kind of hero has a long literary lineage: in his outer guise, Oskar Matzerath is a triumphant heir to the picaresque tradition, another addition to that strange family that includes such figures as Simplicius Simplicissimus, Schelmuffsky, Gil Blas, Candide, Roderick Random, Felix Krull.[55]

The picaresque train in the novel is first apparent in Oskar's account of his birth, where there is the same kind of comical detachment from events as we find, say, in Tristram Shandy's depiction of his progeniture, and above all in Schelmuffsky's description of his wondrous birth, which Grass can scarcely not have had in mind. There is one particularly important picaresque element in Reuter's episode which Grass echoes: the device of having the narrator maintain that even as a foetus and infant he possessed a fully formed mind and will. Reuter's Schelmuffsky speaks incessantly of 'willing' and 'thinking' this that and the other; in The Tin Drum, this kind of pattern is almost programmatically announced: 'I may as well come right out with it: I was one of those clair-audient infants whose mental development is already complete at birth and has nothing further to do but assert itself.' (49; 47). Already in the womb, so Oskar claims, he developed his attitudes with complete independence and self-sufficiency, and once born, he listened carefully and critically to his parents' first reactions ('kritisch lauschte ich den ersten spontanen Äusserungen der Eltern'). Again here, the operation of mind and will is carefully stressed: 'And what my ear took in my tiny *brain evaluated*. After *meditating* at some length on what I had heard, I *decided* to do certain things and on no account to do others.' When it comes later on to Oskar's alleged 'decision' to stop growing, we find the same insistent emphasis: 'It was then that I declared, resolved and determined that I would ... remain as I was' (66-7; 60). Being already 'inwardly and outwardly fully developed', 'a three-year-old, but a super-clever one, towered over by grown-ups but superior to all grown-ups' (67; 60-1), he allegedly opts out of all future involvement in the 'normal' world, whose possibilities and standards he fully rejects ('he refused to measure his shadow with theirs').

Certain associated characteristics are not explicitly mentioned until later, such as his scepticism and his complete freedom from principles,[56] but the persona is nonetheless firmly established in all its essentials by the time Oskar's decision has been recounted – and as such it precisely fulfils the traditional picaresque criteria. In the words of Robert Alter: '[the picaroon] does instinctively reject the stale and inapplicable truths accepted by the generality of men', and: 'the picaroon, before all else, is an outsider'.[57] It also fulfils another crucial condition of the picaresque, namely that the hero must have a static character, since his function is not to be in the limelight himself as an exemplum of human development or whatever, but simply to hold up a mirror to the reality around him.

The picaro is thus characteristically a watcher, not a doer, and Oskar's particular form of dissociation from the normal world fits him splendidly for this role:[58] his combination of super-cleverness and apparent retardedness means that he can watch the most intimate goings-on of his family circle without being either involved, or suspected as a Peeping Tom. Equally importantly, it also means that he can get himself into potentially dangerous situations and then extricate himself with little trouble, since no one treats him as a responsible person. Thus he can experience the siege of the Polish Post Office on the losers' side without yet being held to account for it: his 'all-excusing three-year-oldness' (298; 245) ensures that he is at once separated from the doomed prisoners. It is true that he has a close shave in the 'Dusters' episode in that he, too, is put on trial, but he is again the only one to survive.[59] And when Oskar tells of casually walking away from the grandstand after having ruined the Party rally, with the SA and the SS searching everywhere for the culprit, he remarks: 'Who paid any attention to the little boy of three slowly whistling his way along the edge of the Maiwiese ...?' (145; 123). This touches on another important factor, which is that the picaro's observer role, and the detachment that it presupposes, by no means impose complete passivity on him. On the contrary, the picaro's intelligence, versatility and invulnerability traditionally enable him to play along and dupe the given society as much as he pleases. This facet of the picaresque is well represented in The Tin Drum; hence, for instance, Oskar's shattering of the plate-glass in the new civic theatre, or his winter of tempting adults to theft; but the 'grandstand' and

'Dusters' episodes remain the most important cases in point, with Oskar concerned each time to rout the society he abandoned at birth.

One of Oskar's vital means for preserving his indispensable detachment from the normal world is his eponymous drum, which enables him to 'drum up a necessary distance between me and the grown-ups' (71; 64). But this makes his drum a potential weak spot ('for without my drum I am always exposed and helpless'; 345; 281), and it therefore needs protecting, as indeed Oskar himself does in respect of his diminutive physical size – hence the device of the hero's glass-shattering voice, which Grass introduces in the very same sentence as he does the distancing function of the drum (71; 64). The consequent inviolability is essential to the 'brainbox' persona, for Oskar in this guise may not by definition become in any serious sense a victim or sufferer, for that would be to undermine his given superiority, which exists only so long as he coolly surveys events with his sceptical, super-clever *mind* and remains emotionally unaffected. But what happens is that he does prove vulnerable after all, he does suffer and become emotionally engaged, with the result that the Oskar who professedly began life as the confident master of every situation ends up as the beleaguered victim of a Passion, and hence as the asylum patient so dramatically presented in the novel's first phrase.

One of the most notable of the picaro's traditional characteristics is a limitless faculty for role-paying. Being both acutely sensitive to circumstances as they confront him, and quite unfettered by conventional morality, the picaro is by nature a chameleon; indeed his ability to assume any guise at a moment's notice is one of his chief means of keeping on top. In Alter's words:

> Born in – or rather outside of – a hierarchical society where each individual is assigned a fixed place, [the picaro] can envisage for himself the possibility of assuming multiple roles. Life is not for him a cut-and-dried product which the buyer must accept exactly as it is handed to him ... [60]

Considered under this head, Oskar Matzerath's picaresqueness is clearer than ever, especially when one thinks of his account of his birth, on which Alter's words might almost be a commentary.

Matzerath immediately assigns to his newborn son just such a 'fixed role' (49; 47), whereupon Oskar both decides to reject it outright, and promptly adopts a mask calculated to deceive all around him: 'Äusserlich schreiend und einen Säugling blaurot vortäuschend, kam ich zu dem Entschluss, meines Vaters Vorschlag, also alles was das Kolonialwarengeschäft betraf, schlankweg abzulehnen ...' (51; *Outwardly wailing and purplishly impersonating a baby, I made up my mind to reject my father's projects, in short everything connected with the grocery shop, out of hand ...*', 48). This alleged mask is then rigorously maintained throughout his childhood and youth – by means of 'All the deceptions I had been practising for years: my occasional bed-wetting, my childlike babbling of evening prayers, my fear of Santa Claus, whose real name was Greff, my indefatigable asking of droll, typically three-year-old questions such as: Why have cars got wheels?' (255; 212). Similarly, Oskar says that he pretended not to be able to speak, and that he learnt to read without ever letting on ('It was not so easy to learn how to read while playing the ignoramus'; 104; 91). Indeed it is not until the siege of the Polish Post Office that he 'drops all disguises' and behaves genuinely in front of adults – but then only because he knows that they will not live to tell the tale (289 ff.; 238 ff.).

Oskar's guise of infantility, which is only one, albeit the most important, among his many false roles, very well demonstrates his picaresque ability to dupe his society. His proteanism thus confers a great advantage on him. Or rather: it confers an advantage on him just so long as he actually remains a picaro. So long as he remains unprincipled, cerebral and, above all, detached, then he does nothing but profit from his proteanism; but as soon as factors intervene like 'emotion' and the 'urge to be involved', then the position appears radically different, and we find ourselves back in the familiar twilight area of dislocation and ambiguity: once Oskar has become a normal feeling being, how will he be able to discover a 'real' identity amidst all the masks?

The 'Tears' Persona

If it is true that the picaresque Oskar's function is to reflect an image of the social, existential reality of an era, while at the same time keeping the narrative perspective free of problems of guilt, connivance, responsibility, etc., what then can be the point of the additional 'Tears' persona? One commentator has even argued that there cannot be such a dimension in Oskar: comparing Grass's hero and John Wain's in *Master Richard*, L. W. Forster declared: 'Master Richard is tragic; Oskar is grotesque. There are no such [tragic] conflicts in Oskar; if there had been, it would have been impossible to cover the vast canvas which Grass envisaged.'[61] The truth is rather that Grass found it necessary to use *both* these modes that Forster terms 'grotesque' and 'tragic'. The question is: why?

Now the traditional happy confidence and superiority of the picaro, the professional outsider, are by no means a straight reflection of a similar state in the reality he stands up against – quite the reverse: the picaro detaches himself from the generality and establishes an existence centred on himself because he has the wit to recognise that the normal order (or disorder) of things is so gross that he will be lost as a person if he stays within it. In Alter's words:

> The picaro, or to view the question genetically, the pic-
> aresque author, finds himself in a world where the centre
> cannot hold – which is precisely why the picaroon is an in-
> veterate vagabond, turning and turning in a widening gyre.[62]

This implies a progressive dislocation in the particular society concerned: 'The typical social background for the picaresque novel is a world where the old social order is disintegrating, but is still regarded as though it were continuing undisturbed.'[63] In other words, the degree of joyful sovereignty in the picaro is in direct proportion to the degree of incipient chaos in the existence he escapes from; or in more formal terms: the general tone embodied in the picaresque hero is a wholly ironical reflection of the world he confronts. But what if the disintegration is felt to be not just incipient but already far advanced? Can the novelist adequately mirror such a reality just by means of the urbane, ironical smile of the confidence man? Thomas Mann provides a fascinating contrast: *Felix Krull* is vibrant with the spirit of just such a smile, but in *Dr Faustus*, Mann's mimesis of the National Socialist catastrophe and its pathology, the only kind of smile or laughter we come across is the 'devilish laughter', the 'gale of infernal laughter', that ends the first part of Leverkühn's *apocalipsis cum figuris*. Günter Grass, for his part, clearly felt that the picaresque mode of itself *was* inadequate to express reality as he conceived it, and that a sufficient sense of dislocation could be conveyed only by having Oskar *suffer* the reality as well as detachedly mirror it. To borrow the imagery of Kafka's *In the Penal Colony*: it is not enough merely to describe the machine; there must also be an execution.

The beauty of this duality of the ironic and the affective is that, far from producing any damaging contradictions, it involves a delightful economy of means: by the simple addition of personal feeling in Oskar Matzerath, every single one of those characteristics which together make for his picaresque sovereignty is suddenly inverted into a major liability. So long as Oskar is a complete, self-sufficient, static being, so long as he genuinely needs nothing from those he so peremptorily rejects – at least nothing that cannot be his for the intelligent taking – and so long as his inner activity does not go beyond the operation of eye and mind, he is in a supreme position. As soon as he *feels* and *wants*, thus joining after all in the normal order of existence, then the fact that he is a lone outsider with no links to his family works radically to his disadvantage; likewise his permanent mask of infantility and his dwarf proportions, which parade his otherness and preclude any proper emotional relationship; likewise his protean versatility, which means he can achieve no sense of real identity; likewise his ironic insight, which makes him only too aware of the 'potential multiplicity of the nature of things'.[64]

We might note here, too, that even in his picaresque persona, Oskar is made vulnerable by a crucial weak spot: his glass-shattering voice is a perfect defence against property-minded adults, but it is useless against children, who consequently represent a continual menace to Oskar in view of his diminutive size. And in due course he becomes the helpless victim of a brutal children's ritual when he is force-fed with the foul brew cooked up by Susi Kater and her backyard gang (113-15; 97-9) – an experience that produces a strong emotional response, with Oskar first trying to shatter even faraway windows with his voice, and then wishing he could escape from the street, the suburb and the depredations of the 'soup-cooks'. But he does not escape yet, and once again becomes the children's victim when 'Dr' Susi forces him later on to swallow the sperm-'serum' produced by her pubescent playmates (149; *126*). However, much the most marked episode of this kind is the vicious whipping meted out to Oskar by his 'son' Kurt on his third birthday, the date on which, so Oskar had vainly hoped, 'father' and 'son' would at last join forces (435-6; *351-2*). What with the sudden change to poetic rhythms, the appearance of the archetypal Grass symbol of Cain and Abel, and the desperate progression of imagery, there is a moving intensity in this passage, a passage that serves as well as any to show how much Oskar is an abject victim as well as a sovereign picaro.

The point at which Oskar's unpicaresque emotional involvement is first dramatically revealed, is when his mother 'lets him down' by dying ('Mama hatte mich reingelegt', 207; *173*): when she dies he cannot hide his feelings and plays a kind of lament on his drum (193; *162*); when she is buried he desperately wants to join her in the grave (and the intensity of his emotions here is signalled by the customary device of driving poetic rhythms: 197; *165*); and at the burial feast he seeks refuge from his sense of loneliness beneath his grandmother's warm skirts – in the closing words of the chapters: 'I ... was close to my poor Mama's beginnings and as still as she ... in her box tapered at the foot end' (201; *169*). With this, the 'Tears' persona is fully in operation, and Oskar's Passion has truly commenced.

The deep emotional vacuum produced in Oskar by his mother's death is evoked at length in the first part of 'Herbert Truczinski's Back', with the very first sentence declaring the theme: 'Nothing, so they say, can take the place of a mother.' (202; *169*). Bebra's troupe might have been the way out, but even these closest spiritual kin of Oskar fail him, for he cannot (yet) accept Bebra's politic alliance with the prevailing 'Unglück' ('disaster'), and sadly lets them leave without him (206; *172-3*). As a result, he has to take recourse to the one thing faithful to him – and it is a 'thing', not a human being – namely his drum: 'Ich hielt mich an meine Trommel und vereinsamte gänzlich ...' (207; *I resorted to my drum and became utterly lonely ...*, *173*). Previously, Oskar's drum was instrumental in maintaining his picaresque detachment; but here it is quite the opposite: it is a mark of his weakness and isolation.[65]

Oskar manages for a while to latch on to the Truczinskis, especially Herbert, who is specifically described as replacing Oskar's dead mother as the object of his emotions (210; *176*); but this is short-lived, for Oskar is again left stranded by the death of his loved one – a loss that reduces both him and his drum to silence (237; *198*. Bebra's demise is later described as producing the same desperate silence: 695; *558*).

Oskar's next emotional involvement is of course that with Maria, and it is the most revealing one in the novel, for it is Oskar's most elaborate attempt to achieve a relationship with someone of his own age – and he fails miserably and constantly. In the first phase of their relationship, that is, in the Second Book and up to the point where Oskar starts growing again, it is his alleged pretence of infantility that baulks him : it does allow him to sleep in the same bed with Maria and provide her with a modicum of sexual satisfaction, but it quite precludes the development of any genuine mutual relationship between them. What most abundantly demonstrates Oskar's emotional impotence is the liaison between Maria and Alfred Matzerath, and particularly their drab coitus on the chaise longue: yet again, Oskar is critically hurt, his despair being signalled by the violence of his reactions – and we have already seen how strongly the idea of his 'impotence' is emphasised in the narrative (see above, pp. 44-5). Oskar's isolation from 'his' family then becomes increasingly marked in the rest of the Second Book. For one thing, he no longer even lives with them in the same home, since his attempts to induce a miscarriage in Maria lead to his being farmed out to Mutter Truczinski. At first he is meant to stay there only until after Maria's delivery (366; *298*), but two years and several months later he is still there, that is, until he quits Danzig to join Bebra and his troupe; and when he returns a year later, he is promptly lodged with Mutter Truczinski again (430; *347*). His plight is crisply summarised towards the beginning of 'The Dusters':

Es fiel mir leicht, zum Kirchgänger zu werden, da mich zu Hause nichts hielt. Da gab es Maria. Doch Maria hatte den Matzerath. Da gab es meinen Sohn Kurt. Doch der Bengel wurde immer unerträglicher, warf mir Sand in die Augen, kratzte mich, dass seine Fingernägel in meinem väterlichen Fleisch abbrachen. (447)

It was easy for me to become a church-goer, for there was nothing to keep me at home. There was Maria. But Maria had Matzerath. There was my son Kurt. But he was getting more and more insufferable, throwing sand in my eyes and clawing me so ferociously that his fingernails broke off in my paternal flesh. (361)

This unbridgeable gulf between Oskar and Maria is equally in evidence in the Third Book. His position is anomalous from the outset, for while this pint-sized hunchback regards Maria as his contemporary, and Kurt – who is already physically far bigger than he – as his son, they for their part, though happy to take his money, do not in the least think of him as 'one of them'. The measure of his continuing attachment to Maria is given by the fact that he goes to great expense to buy her off from marrying Stenzel; while the futility of their relationship is made plain through Maria's refusal to marry him, and his decision to give up living with her and his 'son', thus reverting in effect to the Danzig situation. And in all this it is clear that Maria and Kurt are quite right, for Oskar *is* an outsider, he *is* different in all respects from them, and in trying to get close to them he is in fact just acting out a role. After all, they are archetypes of that narrow, closeted, commercial existence which he so demonstratively rejected at birth, and if Maria had accepted his marriage offer (which is unthinkable), it would have meant for Oskar the permanent adoption of a single constricting mask.

Were Oskar exclusively a picaro, loneliness would not distress him but merely serve to sharpen his wits, as exemplified in the opening pages of *Lazarillo de Tormes* (the earliest known picaresque novel), when the hero roundly declares: 'It is full time for me to open mine eyes, yea, and to provide and seek mine own advantage, considering that I am alone and without any help.'[66] But Oskar's very yearning for relationships is an expression of how deeply loneliness afflicts him, from the moment of his birth ('Oskar lay lonely and misunderstood beneath the light-bulbs'; 51; *49*) through to the final sequence of his flight, begun as it is by his lonely wanderings with a hired dog to the outskirts of Düsseldorf ('Was aber trieb den Angeklagten vor die Mauern der Stadt Düsseldorf? Ihn trieb, wie er mir später gestand, die Einsamkeit.', 704; 'What motive drove the accused to the outskirts of Düsseldorf? Loneliness, as he later confessed to me.', 565-6). And it is altogether characteristic of the 'Tears' Oskar's plight that he is repeatedly driven to seek refuge from his loneliness in situations that are essentially compensatory. Hence for instance his withdrawal into a relationship just with his drum once his mother has died, this being the only relationship he can still rely on : 'I clung all the more desperately to my much-despised drum; for it did not die as a mother dies ... it stuck to me as I stuck to it.' (207-8; *174*). Similarly, his involvement with the Dusters is a way of escaping from his loneliness vis-à-vis 'his' family : 'Oskar, who was feeling really low and forsaken at the time, wanted to worm his way into a sense of security among this adolescent set' (456; *368*).

More often than not, though, Oskar's sense of loneliness makes him want to seek refuge in anything that recalls the feel of his warm, protected infancy and even the womb. His fixation for nurses is surely to be understood in this light, a fixation that begins with Schwester Inge in the First Book and culminates in his obscure but critical passion for Schwester Dorothea, whom he perhaps never actually sees in daylight, or whom on the other hand he perhaps even murders. For the point about nurses is that they remind Oskar of his mother as she is depicted in his treasured photograph album; as he remarks in the First Book, he only managed to tolerate Dr Hollatz's nasty examinations 'because Sister Inge's lovely white uniform appealed to me greatly even then, reminding me of Mama's wartime nursing as shown in the photo.' (79; *70-1*). Oskar's penchant for cupboards and the underneath of tables is likewise to be understood in this escapist sense. True, it does serve the picaresque observer role as well. But when for instance he shuts himself in the cupboard after the horse's head episode, his one urge is to escape the sordid reality around him, and it is only by chance that he then becomes a witness of Jan's and Agnes's goings-on on the bed (184 f.; *155* f.). And when it comes later on to the chapter actually called 'In the Clothes Cupboard', Oskar's yen for these dark and odorous interiors is described in terms that leave no room for doubt : 'ich beugte mich ins Innere, wehrte mich nicht mehr gegen den immer stärker werdenden Wunsch, dazu gehören zu dürfen, Inhalt des Schrankes zu sein.' (611-12; '*I leant inside it and gave up fighting against my mounting desire to*

69

belong to the cupboard and be contained by it.', *493*).

But it is of course Oskar's untiring urge to withdraw beneath his grandmother's capacious skirts that chiefly characterises his back-to-the-womb response to the world, and the novel's elaborate first depiction of this urge expressively figures his yearning for a kind of mythic, primal, technicolor world in sharp contradistinction to his true reality: 'here our Heavenly Father ... sat beside Oskar, the Devil cleaned his spyglass, and the angels played blindman's buff; beneath my grandmother's skirts it was always summer.' (148-9; *126*) – it is only a few lines later that Oskar is forced to swallow sperm! Grass subsequently uses the image on many occasions, but it is at its most explicit and grandiose in the two-and-a-half-page fantasy in 'The Imitation of Christ', where Oskar imagines himself and Kurt slipping together beneath Anna Koljaiczek's skirts – and entering her womb to meet the waiting company of all their dead relatives ('Erst im Inneren meiner Grossmutter Koljaiczek ... wäre es ... zu einem wahren Familienleben gekommen.', 434; *349*); and the fantasy is then significantly extended: the whole family, the living as well as the dead, are all invited to a special celebration in Anna Koljaiczek's comfortable uterine parlour. But again: this is in total contrast to reality, and within a few lines Oskar is being brutally savaged by none other than Kurt, his imaginary fellow-guest in his grandmother's womb.

If Oskar's plight in the fictive past was bad, at least he *could* find refuge from time to time with his grandmother. In the 'present', on the other hand, he is much worse off. As he laments in recounting his escape beneath Anna's skirts at his mother's burial feast: 'who takes me under her skirts today?' (201; *169*). When he finally breaks towards the end of the novel, he takes flight; but it is a vain flight that will lead him not to a comforting illusion of protectedness and belonging, but only to the minimal and threatened refuge of his madhouse bed. For his one true bolt-hole is gone: he can no longer go east – 'So musste ich also die vier Röcke meiner Grossmutter Anna Koljaiczek ... als Fluchtziel streichen, obgleich ich mir – wenn schon Flucht – die Flucht in Richtung Grossmutters Röcke als einzig aussichtsreiche Flucht nannte.' (720; *'It was not possible to head for my grandmother Anna Koljaiczek's four skirts ..., although I told myself that if flight there must be, my grandmother's skirts were the only worthwhile destination.'*, *577*). He is thus utterly

70

vulnerable in the 'present': he clings to his bed, and to the various representations of his past – the photograph album, the store of old drums, the scribbled narration itself – but bleak reality bears down on him ever more, until at the end he is reduced to impotent silence, crushed as he is by his awareness of the symbolic 'Schwarze Köchin'.

One of the most insistent tokens of the affective Oskar's frail hold on existence is the way he is caught over and over again between two (or more) alternatives without ever knowing which, if any, is the 'true' one. The most obvious case in point is his dubious paternity: he is never sure whether it is Jan Bronski or Alfred Matzerath to whom he owes his origins, he knows only that they and Agnes Matzerath between them were the 'three who brought me into the world' (63; 57); and his uncertainty is finely evoked when Grass has him remark: 'Jan ... who, as to this day I believe and doubt, begot me in Matzerath's name' (156; 132). A comparison with the purely picaresque tradition is instructive here. As Alter has noted, 'the motif of illegitimate birth is one used by many picaresque novelists';[67] but the picaro's bastardy is something that helps him to be where he wants to be, namely outside society, and thus does not trouble him at all; as Gide's Lafcadio exults in Les Caves du Vatican: 'L'avenir appartient aux bâtards!' With Oskar, on the other hand, his dubious paternity is a burden on him, adding, as it does, to his general confusion; and it is made clear that it is for this kind of reason that he contributes to the deaths of both his putative fathers! (cf. 301, 502; 247, 404).

When Oskar describes himself at one point as having 'two souls' (110; 95), this is on the one hand a parody on the traditional German theme of dualism; but Grass characteristically eats his cake and has it too, for Oskar is a strong heir to the very tradition that is parodied. This is particularly clear in the case of Oskar's 'cultural fathers', where he is torn two ways just as much as he is concerning his physical fathers: he can never decide to which of his 'masters' and 'teachers' he owes the greater allegiance – to Goethe? or to Rasputin? – and this is immediately made plain when these two antithetical mentors of Oskar's are first introduced in the narrative:

Bis zum heutigen Tage ... schwanke ich ... zwischen Goethe

und Rasputin, zwischen dem Gesundbeter und dem Alleswisser, zwischen dem Düsteren, der die Frauen bannte, und dem lichten Dichterfürsten, der sich so gern von den Frauen bannen liess. (104)

To this very day ... I ... fluctuate between Rasputin and Goethe, between the faith healer and the man of the Enlightenment, between the dark spirit who cast a spell on women and the luminous poet prince who was so fond of letting women cast a spell on him. (90-1)

Grass creates just the same kind of duality in Oskar's attitude to Catholicism. 'Zwiespältig' (*'divided'*): that is the word that opens 'Good Friday Fare', and which Oskar uses to describe the feelings aroused by his ambivalent experiences in the Herz-Jesu church a few pages earlier; but then, in the second paragraph of 'Good Friday Fare', Oskar takes up the opening word again – and delivers himself of one of the novel's most startling statements of dichotomy: 'Zwiespältig, sage ich. Dieser Bruch blieb, liess sich nicht heilen und klafft heute noch, da ich weder im Sakralen noch im Profanen beheimatet bin, dafür etwas abseits in einer Heil- und Pflegeanstalt hause.' (173; *'Divided, I have said. This split was lasting, I have never been able to heal it, and it still gapes widely today, when I am at home neither in the sacred nor in the profane, but dwell instead somewhat out of things in a mental asylum.', 146*). There is incidentally every reason to believe (though Grass himself vehemently rejects the criticism) that there is a serious imbalance in Grass's treatment of Catholicism, and that it shows all too blatantly that Oskar's dual and overwrought attitude to the faith reflects Grass's own as it then was. The explanation offered by Grass's friend Höllerer would seem to fit the case exactly: in Höllerer's view, Grass, although already entirely free of Catholicism in intellectual terms, was still too viscerally involved in it to be able to write about it with the necessary detachment.[68] Significantly enough, it seems likely that Catholicism was originally to loom even larger in *The Tin Drum* than it does in the final published version, and that Grass tried to cut it down to size – though without sufficient success; for in one early draft of the opening chapter the following appeared as the third sentence – but with the final clause crossed out: 'Täglich, stündlich, fast immer nenne ich mein weisslackiertes

72

Metallbett meine Gewissheit, meinen Trost, Glauben, meine Zuversicht; denn ich bin katholischer Konfession.' (*Daily, hourly, almost incessantly I call my white-lacquered metal bed my certainty, my solace, my belief, my hope; for I am of the Catholic faith.'*) And it is certainly the case that Grass's treatment of Catholicism has changed dramatically from book to book: he used it on a large scale in *Cat and Mouse* – but integrated it fully and with all the necessary detachment; it appeared again in *Dog Years* – but only as a side issue of almost no significance; while in *Local Anaesthetic* it simply did not appear at all.

Oskar's proteanism may confer great advantage on him in his picaresque persona. But as I have suggested, it automatically entails a severe problem of identity for the 'Tears' Oskar. The problem shows signs of becoming a dominant one soon after Oskar's recommencement of growth, which represents the clearest single shift in the novel from the picaresque to the affective. Not two years after his alleged decision to start growing again, Oskar yearns to return to his lost harmonious proportions as a pseudo-three-year-old (541; 437); but he cannot (just as he cannot return to the womb at the start, or escape to his grandmother's skirts at the finish), and he therefore seeks refuge by trying to assume a 'proper' place in the normal order of things, to integrate himself in the same bourgeois social structure which he claimed to have rejected so utterly at birth. He thus goes out with his daily lunch-box to earn a 'decent living', and he tries to dress and behave like everyone else. The final stage in his attempted re-integration is his offer of marriage to Maria – and her refusal demonstrates the futility of the whole venture, which was always bound to fail since Oskar remains irrevocably an outsider, no matter how much he tries to disguise the fact. And this matter of 'disguises' is the real nub: quite apart from the fact that Oskar, dwarfed and distorted as he is, could never be accepted as 'one of them' by normal society as represented by Maria, there is the corresponding fact that he could never be 'normal' and 'bourgeois' anyway in anything but a mask sense. Grass conveys this with brilliant effectiveness even in the language of the would-be normal Oskar: when he first speaks to Korneff, every one of his sentences mirrors banal, normal language patterns that he otherwise never uses: 'Ihre Grabsteine gefallen mir ausserordentlich', 'An sich suchen Sie doch einen Lehrling, oder?', 'Ich meine, würden Sie mich gegebenenfalls als Lehrling einstellen?' – and so on (545, 547, 547; *I find your grave-stones extraordinarily pleasing*', '*You are strictly speaking looking for an apprentice, are you not?*', '*I mean, would you consider taking me on as an apprentice, other things being equal?*', 440, 441, 441-2). Exactly the same artificiality is evident when Oskar does the 'normal' thing of dating Schwester Gertrud: 'Ein wenig Unternehmungsgeist, Schwester Gertrud! Man ist nur einmal jung.' (559; '*A little enterprise, Sister Gertrude! One is only young once.*', 451); and the role quality of his words is then explicitly emphasised: 'den Text begleitend, klopfte ich leicht stilisiert gegen das Tuch vor meiner Brusttasche.' ('*I filled out my part by tapping in a faintly stylised manner against the handkerchief dangling from my breast-pocket*'). This pretence shows itself equally strongly in Oskar's outward appearance: he had previously gone around in a ridiculous-looking converted army uniform (556; 449), but now he sports a dark blue pin-striped suit made to measure in five fittings, waistcoat, braces, black laced boots, elegant shirts and ties, silver tie-pin complete with pearl, leather gloves, pocket-watch and cigarette-holder. The measure of this artificiality is further given once Oskar's attempts to become a 'Bürger' have failed: whereas he had assiduously taken care of his trouser creases and so helped to maintain his image (558; 451), he now displays a contrary image by deliberately making his trousers go baggy (572; 462) and by generally assuming an air of scruffiness once again: 'I gradually wore out my elegant tailor-made suit and began to neglect my appearance' (571; 461). Later, incidentally, when Oskar is rich and renowned as a performer, and so seeming on the outside to be a worthy and integrated member of society, he again wears crisp suits with a silk kerchief in the top pocket and is altogether 'well-dressed' (702; 564) – an appearance that contrasts ironically with his true state of being.

The full theatrical nature of Oskar's attempts at integration is made most patent at their critical juncture: Oskar's offer of marriage to Maria. Characteristically, it is the expansive *Hamlet* parody that forms the narrative background to Oskar's final resolve:

[ich] sagte – da ich langsam zum Entschluss kam und dennoch

74

das Bedürfnis verspürte, vor dem Entschluss eine dem Theater gemässe, Hamlet in Frage stellende, mich, Yorick, als wahren Bürger feiernde Frage zu stellen – zu Korneff sagte ich ... leise und von dem Wunsch bewegt, endlich ein Bürger werden zu dürfen, sprach – leicht Gründgens imitierend, obgleich der kaum einen Yorick spielen könnte – sagte übers Spatenblatt weg: 'Heiraten oder Nichtheiraten, das ist hier die Frage.' (569-70)

I said – my decision was made, but before coming out with it, I felt the need of a theatrical question that would cast doubt on Hamlet and legitimize me, Yorick, as a true citizen – to Korneff ... I said, quietly and stirred by the desire to be admitted as a citizen at last, I said – slightly imitating Gründgens, although he could scarcely have played Yorick – I said across the shovel blade: 'To marry or not to marry, that is the question.' (460)

Oskar then abandons his casual life with the telephone girls, waits a month or so, and pops the question to Maria – who inevitably turns him down. Had he found an entrée to the bourgeois world he might imaginably have carried it off as a picaresque, Yorick-like play-actor ('I would have made a good bourgeois'; 571; 461); but he never stands a chance – and at the end of the day is just a tragic dupe instead: 'And so Yorick did not become a good citizen, but Hamlet, a fool.' (570; 460).

The most significant instance of the 'Tears' Oskar's role-playing, however, is his final flurry of activity before withdrawing to his would-be asylum, namely his 'flight' from Düsseldorf – for the whole thing is a desperate farce from beginning to end. Before he ever sets out on his journey, we read in Vittlar's report that his denunciation of Oskar to the police was 'a game we invented, yet another little way of dispersing and nourishing our boredom and loneliness' (704; 566); and Oskar's Paris escapade is just part of this game: 'You can't have a proper denunciation without a proper flight' (718; 577). This becomes even plainer when Oskar, in the midst of the desperate laughter that resonates throughout the episode,[69] muses on his plan during the taxi-ride into Düsseldorf: 'Voilà, I said to myself, let us flee to Paris, it looks good and sounds good, it would happen in the films, with Gabin smoking his pipe and tracking me down, inexorably but with kindness and understanding. But who will play me? Chaplin? Picasso?' (722-3; 579-80). Once in Paris, he conceives his arrest in equally theatrical terms – and here the grim reality is clearly visible behind the comic mask, for the 'Schwarze Köchin', the true spirit of these final pages, is also included in the scenario : 'it seemed to me that to be arrested at the famous airport of Orly – the Black Witch in the role of stewardess – would have a particularly thrilling and original effect' (725; 582).

The narrative strongly emphasises that for the 'present' hermit-Oskar in his asylum bed, all specific, single directions of activity can be nothing more than so many different roles, acted parts without any full and genuine reality.[70] After narrating how he himself enticed Klepp from his bed, Oskar reviews the empty alternatives open to the bed-dweller who is forced into the world again – and expresses the hope that his own bed will protect him from such misfortune (633 : 'dass es auch mir so ergehe, sei mein Bett vor'; 509). But he hopes in vain : in due course the bad news is joyously brought by his lawyer that he is soon likely to be 'released', i.e. torn away from his 'sweet bed' and thrown out 'on to the cold, exposed street' (721; 578). In the middle of the account of Oskar's ascent of the escalator, there is a detailed review of the various fractional existences that he could step into (729-30; 585); then, two pages later and almost at the end, the catalogue is repeated, but with a more desperate resonance :

> Jetzt habe ich keine Worte mehr, muss aber dennoch über-legen, was Oskar nach seiner unvermeidlichen Entlassung aus der Heil- und Pflegeanstalt zu tun gedenkt. Heiraten? Ledig-bleiben? Auswandern? Modellstehen? Steinbruch kaufen? Jünger sammeln? Sekte gründen?
>
> All die Möglichkeiten, die sich heutzutage einem Dreissig-jährigen bieten, müssen überprüft werden ... (732)

> *I have run out of words, but still I must wonder what Oskar is going to do after his inevitable discharge from the mental hospital. Marry? Stay single? Emigrate? Model? Buy a stone quarry? Gather disciples? Found a sect?*
>
> *All the possibilities that are open nowadays to a man of thirty must be examined ...* (587)

The whole point of Oskar's transient sojourn on the metro

escalator is that it symbolises his crisis of existence. For with its lack of any beginning, middle or end, an escalator exactly reflects that patternless pattern of ...egg-chicken-egg... that Oskar has become so paralysingly aware of; and it is thus a profoundly ironical sense of belonging that is conveyed in Oskar's remark: 'I felt quite at home on that escalator' (731; 586). Already when Oskar walked out of Düsseldorf with his hired dog and 'played' the cable-drum in search of his past, his explicit concern was to get a hold on his own identity and location: 'I ... said to myself: Just wait a minute, Oskar. Let's see now who you are and where you're from.' (697; 559). Now, on the escalator, the same questions are asked, but this time more insistently, more urgently: 'An escalator ride is a good time to reconsider, to reconsider everything: Where are you from? Where are you going? Who are you? What is your real name? What are you after?' (728; 584).[71] But these questions all find no answer, and Oskar's 'questionable existence' (731; 586) remains precisely that to the very last.

I have tried to show that it is the intervention of emotion – Oskar's forlorn attachment to his mother, his vain longing to have his love for Maria returned, and so on – which progressively subverts the hero's supposedly sovereign position as a picaro. But Grass does not leave it at that: he arranges his fiction in such a way that it is likewise emotion, though of a different kind, that increasingly bears in on Oskar in the narrative present and makes him in the end such a desolate wreck: if it is unfulfilled love that first confounds him, it is a consuming sense of *guilt* and *fear* that finally drives him to despair.

So far as guilt is concerned, it is a recurrent motif from the moment that it is emphatically introduced in the opening pages, when Grass has Oskar specify that the kind of paper he wants Münsterberg to buy him is 'unschuldiges Papier' (11; 16), for the word 'unschuldig' not only has its surface meaning of 'virgin', 'untouched', it also of course connotes ideas of purity and taintedness, of guilt and innocence – and the word is used not just once, but altogether four times within fifteen lines.

It is typical of the novel's persistent dualities that guilt, though essentially an urgent and serious issue, is repeatedly parodied and made fun of as just an 'idle game of guilt and innocence' (619; 499). Thus for instance Grass has Vittlar deliver a 'sharply

77

theatrical' declamation in which Oskar, who was more than ten years unborn at the time of his grandfather's disappearance, is ironically accused of his murder (40; 39). The same tone is struck concerning Agnes's death: with Bebra and Roswitha in the café, Oskar theatrically blames himself for her death – but at once remarks: 'I was exaggerating heavily, perhaps I was trying to impress Signora Roswitha. After all, most people blamed Matzerath and especially Jan Bronski for Mama's death.' (204; *171*). Again, in the Third Book, Oskar confesses to Bebra that he is guilty of the murders of Roswitha, Agnes, Jan and Matzerath – and then goes over into an extravagantly histrionic plea for mercy that sends Bebra into an uncontrollable, unearthly spasm of laughter (689; *553*).

As so often, though, Grass manages brilliantly to have it both ways: as with the two-souls dichotomy or the father-son conflict, he burlesques the literary *mea culpa* tradition whilst at the same time making Oskar its serious heir. For Oskar *does* feel the burden of 'grosse Schuld', 'übergrosse Schuld', 'ein unhöfliches, durch nichts aus dem Zimmer zu weisendes Schuldgefühl' (301, 305, 302; *'great guilt', 'enormous guilt', 'an importunate feeling of guilt which nothing can dispel', 247, 250, 248*). And the measure of its crucial importance is given above all by the fact that guilt figures in the novel's very last lines – and is linked directly to the overbearing reality of the 'Schwarze Köchin' and Oskar's desperate fear:

> ... und die Gören auf dem Hof des Mietshauses ... sprachen es aus, sangen, wenn sie die Ziegelmehlsuppe kochten: 'Ist die Schwarze Köchin da? Jajaja! Du bist schuld und du bist schuld und du am allermeisten.' (733)

> *and the brats in the court of our building ... they knew: For what did they sing as they cooked their brickmeal soup: 'Where's the Witch, black as pitch? Here's the black wicked Witch. Ha ha ha! You're to blame, And you are too, You're most to blame, You! you! you!'* (588)

It should perhaps be remembered here that Oskar's double function is highlighted with particular clarity by this ambivalent motif of guilt. On the one hand, it is a chief *raison d'être* of the picaresque perspective that it allows the narrative to refract an

78

image of German National Socialist reality and its aftermath without being itself submerged by the vast and complex issues of guilt and responsibility; but on the other hand Grass ensures by means of the affective Oskar that these very issues are included in the picture after all. We should not forget, too, that Grass goes on to make guilt a decisive factor in both the other books of the 'trilogy': Pilenz and Matern are both hounded by a sense of guilt even more furious than Oskar's (the contrast with *Local Anaesthetic* is startling: in the later novel, the motif of guilt is not only reduced to tiny proportions, but is handled entirely ironically when it does appear).

Like the title Cat and Mouse, the figure of the 'Schwarze Köchin' is borrowed from German children's lore, indeed it is in passing reference to the local children's favourite games that the figure is first introduced into the narrative, as though casually and co-incidentally (71, 74; 64, 66). It is only much later, and notably in the context of the horse's head sequence, that the figure's menacing hold on Oskar's imagination begins to be projected: Oskar in his asylum refuge imagines himself back in the refuge of the Matzeraths' bedroom cupboard, and imagines himself imagining that he is with Schwester Inge in Dr Hollatz's surgery; a flight of fantasy all in reds is triggered by the redness of her nursing badge – but Oskar is not in control of his own imaginings any more than he is master of his pervasive sense of guilt:

> Und wenn ich trotzdem nur rot sage, will rot mich nicht, lässt seinen Mantel wenden: schwarz, die Köchin kommt, schwarz, schreckt mich gelb, trügt mich blau, blau glaub ich nicht, lügt mir nicht, grünt mir nicht: grün ist der Sarg, in dem ich grase, grün deckt mich, grün bin ich mir weiss: das tauft mich schwarz, schwarz schreckt mich gelb (etc.) (185-6)

> *and if I none the less say 'red', red spurns me, turns its coat to black, black comes the Witch, scares me yellow, deceives me blue, blue is a colour that I don't believe, blue doesn't lie to me, blue doesn't green for me: green is the coffin in which I graze, green is all over me, in green am I white: which anoints me black, black scares me yellow (etc.) (156)*

Not only is there the sheer stress on blackness and on the

79

'Schwarze Köchin' herself, but there is also the metaphorically gyrating pattern of language – and the fact that the emphatic third phrase ('lässt seinen Mantel wenden : schwarz') is a direct anticipation of the bleak and strident *envoi* at the novel's close.

The 'Schwarze Köchin' motif is importantly added to later on in the context of the betrayal of the Dusters, in that Grass has his hero suddenly and explicitly identify the hitherto abstract figure with a 'real' person, namely Luzie Rennwand, the gang's denouncer (473; 381). This certainly does give substance to the image, but it also serves to highlight the essential role played by sexuality in Oskar's generalised sense of fear. For when Luzie Rennwand's involvement in the gang is first narrated, she is strongly projected as a kind of juvenile *femme fatale* possessed of murderous sexuality (466-7; 376) – an altogether logical development in view of the novel's treatment of sexuality in general. It is in such terms of devastation, then, that the mental image of Luzie Rennwand/the 'Schwarze Köchin' persecutes Oskar. As Grass has him say at the end of the Dusters episode : he still can't help looking about for an 'unentwegt Männer mordenden Backfisch' (479; *'resolutely man-killing scrap of a girl'*, 386) :

Selbst im Bett meiner Heil- und Pflegeanstalt erschrecke ich, wenn Bruno mir unbekannten Besuch meldet. Mein Entsetzen heisst dann : jetzt kommt Luzie Rennwand und fordert mich als Kinderschreck und Schwarze Köchin letztmals zum Sprung auf.

Even in my bed in the mental hospital I am frightened when Bruno announces an unexpected visitor. My nightmare is that Lucy Rennwand will turn up as a bugbear and Black Witch and for the last time bid me to plunge.

And we have already seen in a different context how Oskar daydreams at the cemetery in the Third Book – and sees Luzie's corpse being washed up on the shore, with the legend 'Here lies Oskar' engraved on the miniature gravestone that the corpse has instead of a heart (see above, p. 35). It scarcely needs to be added that Luzie Rennwand and Susi Kater in *The Tin Drum*, and Tulla Pokriefke in *Cat and Mouse* and *Dog Years*, are all incorporations of the same powerful image in Grass's creative mind – while Vero Lewand in *Local Anaesthetic* is yet another, but

80

much modified, version. And it is intriguing that Grass, himself seemingly almost haunted by the 'murderous young girl' archetype, should have depicted both Oskar and Amsel as being fixated on the same kind of figure, if in very different ways. It seems more clear than usual here how, hidden away in the corners of Grass's 'public' representation of an age, are exits and entrances to an intensely personal, intensely inward world. At the same time, though, the reader is sidetracked from thinking it idiosyncratic by the fact that Grass twice has Oskar drum up the 'Schwarze Köchin' in the presence of 'normal' adults – and each time they are frightened out of their wits (664, 692; 533-4, 555).

It is in the novel's conclusion that the motif of the 'Schwarze Köchin' comes to a head, becoming steadily more dominant in the last ten and a half pages until in the final long paragraph it remorselessly obliterates everything else. Oskar's second cupboard-recapitulation of the horse's head sequence made it explicit that Oskar's fixation on the 'Schwarze Köchin' was largely a matter of *fear* (613; 494), and this is now dramatically re-established in the curt paragraph which in effect prefaces the novel's closing phase:

> Heute bin ich dreissig Jahre alt, habe Flucht und Prozess zwar hinter mir, doch jene Furcht, die ich mir auf der Flucht einredete, ist geblieben. (723)

> *Today I am thirty; flight and trial are behind me, but the fear I talked myself into during my flight is still with me.* (580)

The spectre of the 'Schwarze Köchin' then haunts Oskar at every turn of his pseudo-flight (Matern will likewise be haunted during *his* final flight in *Dog Years* – but by a decidedly different spectre); then, in the final paragraph, it entirely fills the screen : it not only oppresses Oskar in the fictional present, but retrospectively infiltrates the whole of his past whilst simultaneously threatening the whole of his future (732-4; 587-8), and then all is subsumed, past, future and present, in the words of the final *envoi* :

> Schwarz war die Köchin hinter mir immer schon.
> Dass sie mir nun auch entgegenkommt, schwarz.
> . . .
> Ist die Schwarze Köchin da? Ja – Ja – Ja !

Always somewhere behind me, the Black Witch.
Now ahead of me, too, facing me, Black.
. . .
Is the Black Witch there? Yes – Yes – Yes!

How far removed this beleaguered Oskar is from the confident, supreme 'brainbox'-Oskar, 'the super-clever one who was to be so superior to all grown-ups' ! He began, so he would have us believe, as a picaro – and he ends as an exemplary Victim, as a parody Christ-figure who has suffered his Passiontide, not by redeeming himself or anybody else, but by becoming ever more exposed to the forces besetting him, despite all his attempts to escape. And if the deaths of Herbert Truczinski and Bebra struck him temporarily dumb, the odious awareness of what awaits him on his 'release' from the asylum reduces him to complete and permanent silence : page 728 : 'ich bin müde und habe kaum noch Worte' (*'I am tired and words fail me'*, 584); page 732 : 'Jetzt habe ich keine Worte mehr' (*'I have no words left'*, 587); and then in the final few lines: 'Fragt Oskar nicht, wer [die Schwarze Köchin] ist! Er hat keine Worte mehr.' (*'Don't ask Oskar who [the Black Witch] is! He is bereft of words.'*)

A Question of Credibility

So far we have looked at Oskar Matzerath almost exclusively in terms of the role that naturally takes up most space in the novel : his role as an actual participant in the events described. But what about Oskar in his other basic guise as the *narrator* of events? This is clearly a crucial question : it is Oskar as narrator who is interposed between the reader and fictive reality – and who as such bears out the novel's cardinal principles of doubt, ambiguity, dislocation. As I have tried to show, Grass puts the reader on his guard within the very first lines of the book by having the narrator not only confess to being a mental patient, but speak in rapid succession of telling the truth, inventing stories and fabricating lies. And this pattern is in fact continued throughout the novel, with the result that the reader can never approach the narrative with the concrete categories of belief or disbelief, but only with the fluid one of doubt.

Why, for instance, should we believe Oskar's own picture of himself as a child, in particular after the fall down the cellar steps? Oskar claims that his extreme backwardness was just a mask, and that his bed-wetting, his inability to speak, his need to be dressed and his general infantility were all just part of the pretence – but Grass raises the possibility of its not being a mask at all by having virtually everyone else in the novel regard it as a reality. Thus the narrative is strewn with references to the fact that Oskar is considered a 'simpleton' (105; 91), 'a freak, a pathetic midget' (258; 215), 'a ... retarded, pitifully abnormal child' (437; 352). Maria's picture of him (when she wants him sent away for euthanasia) is typical: 'is nich jeworden, wird überall nur rumjestossen und weiss nich zu leben und weiss nich zu sterben!' (448; 'he's come to nothing, he just gets pushed around wherever he goes, he don't know how to live and he don't know how to die', 362).

Strong doubts arise on the critical matter of Oskar's fall down the cellar steps. Oskar claims to have staged the whole thing so that people will have a reason for what they think is his retardedness. But it is equally likely that, in terms of the fiction, he *did* have a bad accident, and that this caused severe brain damage which impeded both his physical and mental development. One thing that nurtures this suspicion is the fact that Grass has Oskar spend a whole month in hospital after the accident – or 'accident'. And is it a statement of fact, an irony or a double irony when Oskar is given to remark in the Third Book: 'An unfortunate accident hampered my growth.' (597; 482)? It is characteristic of the linear view of Oskar, incidentally, that both Theodor Wieser and Klaus Wagenbach (to name only two important critics) blithely accept Oskar's account of the fall and adduce it as evidence of his total 'freedom'.[72]

The question of the effect of the fall on Oskar's mental development is itself a pertinent one, for the reader must wonder – from the opening sentence on – whether Oskar is not perhaps truly deranged. Grass has Maria describe him twice as being off his head and ripe for an asylum (352, 357; 287, 290); on his return from the year with Bebra, there is pressure from the authorities for him to be committed for euthanasia (430; 346-7), and we gather later that this is the course recommended by all the doctors who have examined him (448; 361. After the Dusters trial, Matzerath does in fact sign and post the letter of consent for Oskar's liquidation, but Oskar is saved by the Russian invasion.) When it comes to Oskar's bout of renewed growth, and the severe illness that accompanies it, the doctor diagnoses the trouble as originating in the patient's head (510; 411);[73] and Münsterberg is given to remark that Oskar's head would be too large even for a normal, full-sized adult (532; 428), thus adding substance to the possibility, raised earlier through Maria, that Oskar might be hydrocephalic, a 'Wasserkopp' (514; 414). As for Oskar's 'present' detainment in the asylum: the judges at his trial found him guilty of murder, so the fiction has it, but considered him mentally deficient (721; 579). Strikingly enough, Grass even carries this motif over into the later books, for *Dog Years* includes the passing observation that Oskar is 'not quite right in the head'![74]

The case of Oskar's recommencement of growth is even more conspicuously opaque than is the case with his fall down the cellar steps, for the invitation to scepticism is this time writ large: one account of events is given as the truth, and is then admitted to have been false. In the first version, Oskar claims that he made a deliberate resolve to start growing again, threw his drum into Matzerath's grave, and then began spontaneously to grow, with the result that his nose bled. Four pages later, and in a new chapter, a decisively different version of events is given, with Oskar remarking: 'Ich entschliesse mich also, den Bericht über die Ereignisse auf dem Friedhof zu ergänzen.' (507; *'So I have decided to complete my record of the events at the cemetery.'*, 409). There had previously been no mention of any stone-throwing, but suddenly in this new chapter Oskar comes out with the one-sentence paragraph: 'It was only when that stone hit me ... on the back of the head that I began to grow.' (507; 409). Oskar then also concedes another new detail: that the stone knocked him flying into Matzerath's open grave. But he at once also contradicts himself yet again: he claims that he *did* after all start growing through his own free will before the stone ever hit him – but it is immediately emphasised that both Maria and Fajngold ascribed his new growth to the blow on the head and his heavy fall, and this is supported by the fact that Oskar remains ill – at first 'miserably ill' (509; 410) – for some fourteen months. Oskar's account of things here is patently dis-

84

credited, then – and it is particularly striking that Grass also makes this apply retrospectively to the hero's version of the original fall down the cellar-steps, by having Oskar draw an emphatic and explicit analogy between the two episodes: 'everyone blamed the stone and the fall for my renewed growth [as we, the readers, do!]; but then everyone had always blamed the fall in the cellar for my interrupted growth –' (508-9; *409-10*).

Oskar's accounts of his part in the doom of Jan Bronski and Matzerath are equally important cases in point: on both occasions Grass again has Oskar contradict a version that was previously presented as the truth. In the initial report of the capture of the Polish Post Office, the suggestion is that Oskar behaves like the other captives, and is then sent to hospital because he falls down in a kind of fit. But at the beginning of the following chapter, he blithely admits: 'Oskar's pen ... has managed ... to exaggerate and mislead, if not to lie.' (300; *246*), and it is only then that we hear the details of his 'Judasschauspiel' ('*Judas-like performance*'): his pretence of tears, his accusing gestures, the beating inflicted on the innocent Jan. As for the death of Matzerath: when Oskar first tells of picking up Matzerath's party badge, the implication is that it was already open ('The open pin pricked my hand'; 486; *392*), and he claims that he only palmed it off on Matzerath in order to have his hands free for louse-catching; once again, it is not until the following chapter that Oskar comes out with the fictive truth: that he deliberately opened up the pin and deliberately brought about Matzerath's death (502; *404*).

One of Grass's most telling devices for throwing doubt on Oskar's version of things is his use at one point of Bruno Münsterberg as narrator. The passage ascribed to Münsterberg is full of turns of language that undermine Oskar's credibility – 'Maria Matzerath, whom my patient describes as his former mistress', 'Kurt Matzerath, my patient's alleged son' (522; *420*), 'my patient claims ...' (525, 529; *422, 426*); the verb 'sollen' (which has the force of 'is apparently, allegedly so') is particularly frequent. Münsterberg is even made to remark explicitly that Oskar cannot keep his account of things straight, and that in consequence he, as re-narrator, ought strictly speaking to include 'two or even more versions' (527; *424*) of Oskar's journey to the West.

Towards the end of the book, Grass also makes Vittlar the narrator for a while, and although on the whole this is not

85

directed at further discrediting Oskar, there is strong emphasis on one particularly important area of ambiguity: the question of who killed Dorothea Köngetter. According to Oskar's version of things, he never properly spoke to her, never caught sight of her except during their futile night-time encounter on the coconut runner, and never had any further contact with her once she had left Zeidler's flat. But Vittlar's record of his 'cross-examination' of Oskar concerning the ring-finger plainly suggests that Oskar's relationship with her developed intensely after her departure from Zeidler's flat (708-9; 569; q.v.), and the implication therefore is that Oskar in the Third Book keeps silent over one of his most vital experiences. Why? The close of the cross-examination hints at a compelling reason for this suppression, namely that it *was* indeed Oskar who murdered Schwester Dorothea. There is not the least certainty here, the reader is left in two minds – we are even left in the dark as to whether the woman evoked in the cross-examination is really Schwester Dorothea at all; Grass has Vittlar merely observe that the particulars of the woman given by Oskar, and the particulars of the murdered Dorothea given in court, 'largely coincide with one another' (709; 569). Thus the reader is once more left in the lurch, compelled as he is to experience yet again – in however token a way – that same ambiguity of which Oskar is the desperate, abject victim.[75]

And on this characteristic note of uncertainty and openness, we move now from *The Tin Drum* to the novella that followed two years later, and which will be seen to ring this very same note in its opening words. A novella which indeed is informed in many respects with the same mood and the same attitudes as the earlier novel – and yet which also marks the beginnings of a critical shift in Grass's position and perspective that will go on to have a profound effect on *Dog Years*, and ultimately lead to the new departure represented by *Local Anaesthetic* in 1969.

PART TWO
Cat and Mouse

Savoir se libérer n'est rien;
l'ardu, c'est savoir être libre.

GIDE, *L'Immoraliste*

Note on Editions

The pagination of the British and American editions of *Cat and Mouse* is not identical. The italicised page numbers in the text of this volume relate to the British edition. Page numbers for Parts I to XIII in the two editions are as follows:

British	American		British	American
8 – 24	8 – 24		104 – 117	101 – 115
26 – 39	26 – 39		120 – 134	117 – 131
42 – 51	40 – 49		136 – 145	133 – 141
54 – 65	51 – 63		148 – 156	143 – 152
68 – 74	64 – 71		158 – 170	153 – 166
76 – 86	72 – 83		172 – 191	168 – 189
88 – 102	84 – 99			

Enigma and Paradox: The Narrative Mode

Like the novels *Dog Years* and *Local Anaesthetic* later on (and in contrast to the traditional novella), Günter Grass's *Cat and Mouse* has an opening which, instead of helping the reader to get his bearings, actively disorientates him: '... und einmal, als Mahlke schon schwimmen konnte, lagen wir neben dem Schlag-ballfeld im Gras.' ('... *and once, after Mahlke had learned to swim, we were lying in the grass, in the Schlagball field.*') The three dots and the ensuing uncapitalised 'und' that point back as it were into empty space, the cryptic and seemingly trivial nature of the information that follows: the reader finds himself at once confronted with just the same kind of openness and ambiguity that were so essential to *The Tin Drum*. And again, at the very end of the book, the reader is deliberately left with an open question: did Joachim Mahlke drown or survive when he made his last dive down into the sunken boat? – this final episode in all its uncertainty being almost a repeat performance of the strange disappearance of Joseph Koljaiczek in the earlier book.

But there is a compelling paradox: whereas there is a *theme* of openness right through *Cat and Mouse* from beginning to end, the actual structure and organisation of the novella are astonish-ingly tight and precise. Grass – who is said by Höllerer to have immersed himself in the history of the genre before writing his own novella[1] – could not have stuck more rigorously to such traditional requirements as that a novella be characterised by a single decisive element (the 'red falcon' of Boccaccio), or that it represent some 'singular occurrence' (Goethe's 'unerhörte Bege-benheit'). So punctilious was he indeed that *Cat and Mouse* easily bears comparison in point of formal purity with any other Ger-man example of the genre – a fact that is not a little remarkable when one thinks of the diffuse and epic spread of *The Tin Drum*.

In *Cat and Mouse*, even the title and the image on the dust-jacket (designed, as always, by Grass himself)[2] play an active part in pointing to the book's central configuration: the relationship of cat and mouse, persecutor and victim, Cain and Abel, Pilenz and Mahlke. And while the beginning and the conclusion of the narrative do convey a sense of openness, they none the less also depict the precise beginning and the precise end of that relationship, however disguised this design may be at first sight.

This contrast between theme and structure is far from being contradictory; it is indeed one of the book's most productive and engaging features: Grass achieves the singular feat of exploiting the closed, compressed novella structure in such a way that it illuminates his themes of openness etc. with a clarity and intensity that could never have been attained within the naturally more diffuse framework of a novel. The key to this lies in one of the implications of the compact novella form, namely that the narrative can be just as striking for the things that are omitted as for the things that are included, like a jigsaw puzzle from which some of the main pieces have deliberately been removed. It is in his choice of narrative perspective that Grass exploits this possibility – as might be expected after *The Tin Drum*, in which the narrator's subjective involvement in events was used to fracture the relationship between reader and fictive reality. There is a crucial difference in *Cat and Mouse*, however: whereas Oskar's story was related by Oskar himself, Mahlke's is narrated by someone else – and not just anyone else, but the very person who was his principal persecutor. Grass thus provides himself with a narrator who has every reason to be ignorant of the true nature of the protagonist, and to misrepresent the truth even when he does know it, since his own sordid role would otherwise be too nakedly displayed. For good measure, Grass also adds a third source of uncertainty, in that he endows his narrator with a defective memory of what 'really' happened all those years ago.

Whilst there is no really critical lapse of memory on Pilenz's part, Grass incorporates so many little lapses that a powerful compound effect is achieved – 'I don't remember which summer it was', 'I'm not sure whether', 'I don't know whether', 'It is perfectly possible that', 'sometimes I am certain and sometimes I have my doubts whether', 'I almost seem to remember': such

90

phrases are typical. Did Pilenz really talk to Tulla's cousin, or only imagine that he did? – 'Either in my thoughts or in reality I tried to strike up a conversation with him about Tulla' (110; *121*). Did a tram really come with Tulla in it? – '... and then a tram came – or could have done' (157; *170*). And what about Pilenz's hands after he used Mahlke's concoction on his hair? – 'my hands were sticky ... – but maybe the stickiness of my hands is only an idea that came to me later, maybe they were not sticky at all.' (27; *30*).

There is a particularly interesting lapse of memory in connection with the sudden encounter between Pilenz and Mahlke in the Oliva Castle Park in Chapter Ten. At first, the ominous avenue through the trees where the two boys meet is described as 'womöglich dornig' (126; *'perhaps thorny'*, *137*), but in the very next sentence Grass has Pilenz shift from a possibility to a certainty – to the extent even that 'thorniness' is substantivised in the word 'Dornentunnel' (127; *'tunnel of thorns'*, *138*); and a few lines later the image is reinforced even more in what is in fact one of the book's most symbolic vignettes: 'und wir standen uns zwischen wie unter Dornen dünnhäutig gegenüber' (127; *'thin-skinned and vulnerable, we stood facing one another amidst the thorns'*, *138-9*). This does serve to display yet again the unreliability of Pilenz's memory, it is true; but we are also carried beyond it to the fundamental issue of the book's mimetic process: in this shift from the casual 'womöglich dornig' to the intense tableau of the thorn-wreathed confrontation between Mahlke and Pilenz, Abel and Cain, the Redeemer and his dismal betrayer, we have a paradigm of the way that Grass contrives to impart a grand archetypal dimension to his tale of an eccentric teenager in the suburbs of Danzig. And later, in the crucial context of Mahlke's ultimate failure and his futile but noble gesture rejecting Klohse and the social order he stands for (see below, pp. 152, 167), this symbolic dimension of the Oliva encounter is highlighted beyond doubt: 'Aber der Grosse Mahlke befand sich in einer Allee, ähnlich jener tunnelartig zugewachsenen, dornenreichen und vogellosen Allee im Schlosspark Oliva, die keine Nebenwege hatte und dennoch ein Labyrinth war' (154; *'But the Great Mahlke had started down a path resembling that tunnellike, overgrown, thorny and birdless path in Oliva Castle Park, which had no forks or byways but was nonetheless a labyrinth'*, *167*).

Undoubtedly the most notable of Pilenz's lapses of memory are those concerning Mahlke himself – such as the apparent lapse concerning Mahlke's last moments before his (putative) death, when Pilenz professes to have forgotten whether his companion said anything before disappearing: '... Did he say something more over his shoulder? ... I don't think I heard you say "Well, see you tonight!"' (173; 187); as we shall see, Pilenz's role in this final episode is such that the reader must have strong suspicions that this is not genuine forgetfulness but just a cover-up. What is also particularly striking is Pilenz's inability to remember what Mahlke actually looked like; one minute he says he believes he had light blue eyes (14; 17), then he says he believes he had light grey eyes (19; 21), and a little later: 'he had grey or grey-blue eyes, bright but not shining, anyway certainly not brown' (44; 49). The uncertainty is neatly expressed in the gravitation from positive to negative, from 'he had grey eyes' to 'he didn't have brown eyes';[3] and the uncertainty is all the more emphatic on this occasion in that two other people are involved who likewise 'knew' Mahlke for years – and who can remember his looks no more clearly than Pilenz: the three can agree only on a makeshift picture of him ('Behelfsmässig wurden wir uns einig'), and when it comes to Mahlke's mouth, they get completely confused as between Mahlke and Tulla Pokriefke. Altogether, this nebulous description of at any rate some parts of Mahlke's physical appearance has a vital implication: if the narrative can offer only a tentative picture of Mahlke's visible, outward nature, how much more tentative must its picture of his inward nature be. And we touch here on one of the book's most remarkable features: whereas the narrative mode of *The Tin Drum* was such that the reader all too easily assumes that he knows the 'truth' about Oskar, the reader of *Cat and Mouse* is never allowed to jump to any pat conclusions about Joachim Mahlke. I would even go so far as to say that Grass created in *Cat and Mouse* one of the most deliberately arcane works of German literature.

At the beginning of Chapter Two, Pilenz comes out with the firm assertion: 'Your house was in Westerzeile' (23; 26). In the next sentence but one, however, this statement is just as firmly cancelled: 'No, your house was in Osterzeile.' Another lapse of memory, perhaps? But when in the following pages Pilenz launches into a precise description of the whole street layout, of Mahlke's house, of Mahlke's own room, the reader can no longer credit him with mere forgetfulness, and is driven instead, as he persistently is in the book, to doubt his honesty (the play on 'Westerzeile' – 'Osterzeile' also has another function at a different level of the narrative; see below p. 122). We are faced with something similar in the book's second paragraph: Grass has Pilenz initially 'conjecture' that the sunken wreck was a Czaika-class boat – and then has him show that he in fact knows its history in precise detail (6; *9-10*).

This kind of device for highlighting Pilenz's untrustworthiness (already well known to us from *The Tin Drum*) is used to particular effect concerning his relationship to Mahlke. Thus he claims at one point that he made a special effort to serve as a friend to the other boy ('Gab mir jedenfalls Mühe.', 101; *110*); but this impression of the relationship is immediately exploded again: Pilenz did *not* force himself to be friendly, but was in reality compulsively in thrall to the other boy ('Keine Mühe! Lief von ganz alleine neben ihm'), and there follows a long and graphic evocation both of this total thraldom and of Mahlke's equally complete uninterest (*q.v.*, and see also below, p. 106 f.). The episode in the Oliva Castle Park is brought to a close with just the same kind of contradiction: Pilenz at first flatly denies that he turned round to see Mahlke after their parting – but then goes on to confess that he did look back, not once but several times (whereas Mahlke, it is implied, did not bother; 128; *139*). As I shall argue, it is precisely Pilenz's total but unrequited involvement in Mahlke that Grass creates as the background to his role as 'Cain'.

The attack on Mahlke in the first paragraph, and the episode of Mahlke's final disappearance, not only constitute the brilliant start and finish of the novella, they also mark the precise beginning and end of the 'cat and mouse' relationship of the two boys. And it is at these two critical points that Pilenz's misrepresentations are at their most blatant. At the beginning, it is the cat's attack on Mahlke's Adam's apple that is misrepresented – the event which at once activates the meaning implied in the title and dust-jacket symbol, and at the same time prefigures the whole essential action of the book. At first Pilenz claims that the cat pounced spontaneously at Mahlke's throat; then a new version immediately follows: it was perhaps 'one of us' that set

93

the cat on Mahlke; but this version in its turn is superseded by another: it was perhaps the narrator himself who was responsible. The very next sentence then confirms this final version as the fictive truth: 'I, who called your mouse to the attention of this cat and all cats'; and each time this crucial act is referred to later on, Pilenz is always shown to have been its perpetrator – except in those cases where it is Mahlke who recalls the incident, when it appears that he is the only person who does not know who was responsible (Grass has him ascribe it to Schilling (116; 127) and to Kupka (122; 133), never to Pilenz).

As for the closing stages of the book, Pilenz's account of things prickles with contradictions. When collecting food from Mahlke's home for the other boy's escape, did he really enquire whether the army were already after Mahlke for desertion? His first statement on the subject is a flat contradiction: he asked no such question, he claims, but if he did, then the answer was 'no' (166; 179). In front of Mahlke, however, he alleges that the authorities have already twice come in search of him, and that his mother has already been taken away (167; 180). The reader is allowed no certainty here – but what he is given to infer is that Pilenz deliberately lies to Mahlke in order to be quite sure of getting rid of him, in that Mahlke is much less likely to abandon his escape plan once he believes that he is already being hunted as a deserter (cf. 162; 175: 'Don't be stupid. I can't show my face in Osterzeile. If they're not there already, it certainly won't be long.') As for the dinghy that Pilenz hires to row Mahlke out to the wreck: Pilenz tells the reader that he hired it for two hours (168; 181) – but he later hurries Mahlke on with the excuse that he had been able to get the boat only for an hour and a half (171; 184). And there is similar uncertainty over the tin-opener: Pilenz claims that he twice reminded Mahlke to take it down into the boat with him – but then Pilenz also says that he had in fact hidden the thing beneath his foot (173-4; 187). In both these cases, again, the likely implication is that Pilenz's equivocation masks a Cain-like treatment of Mahlke; but at the surface level of the narrative, at least, this is no more than 'likely'.

Pilenz's lapses of memory and his misrepresentations certainly play their part, but they are greatly exceeded in importance by the factor of Pilenz's ignorance. This is often only of token significance, as in the very first paragraph: 'Mahlke was asleep. . . . Mahlke was asleep or seemed to be.' But what really counts is that Pilenz is profoundly ignorant concerning the novella's most decisive area of meaning: the inner world of Joachim Mahlke. In Grass's lapidary phrase: 'Und seine Seele wurde mir nie vorgestellt. Nie hörte ich, was er dachte.' (37; *And as for his soul, it was never introduced to me. I never heard what he thought.*', 42). And this incomprehension concerning Mahlke is repeatedly pointed up throughout the narrative, as at the beginning of a sub-division of Chapter Two, when a volley of questions and interpretations about Mahlke is summed up in the remark: 'We racked our brains and we couldn't understand you!' (32; 35); or again at the close of Chapter Six: 'We were always talking about you. We would lay bets: "What's he going to do now? . . ."' (77; 86).

In accordance with this, Pilenz can never firmly state what was in Mahlke's mind in any particular situation. Hence, although the lectures by the two ex-pupil holders of the Knight's Cross, and Mahlke's reaction to them, constitute critical points in the story, Pilenz on the one occasion makes no attempt to interpret Mahlke's inner response (85 f.; 95 f.), and on the other can offer only conjecture: 'I suppose the Lieutenant's talk didn't agree with you.' (64; 73). A few lines after this conjecture, Chapter Five ends with one of the novella's most poignant depictions of Mahlke as he strides clown-like through the winter evening with his oversize shawl and his rows of luminous shapes, trying to disguise his suffering ('Lied'; see below, p. 121 – but again, Pilenz can only guess at the other boy's motives: 'But you said to yourself no doubt' etc. (65; 74). Even the depiction of Mahlke praying at mass emphasises the enigmatic, with his hands forming a roof 'directly in front of his forehead and its thoughts' (118; 129); and the sub-division then closes with Pilenz saying that he will pay Mahlke a visit and take a really close look at him, since 'there must be something behind it all' (118, 'Da muss doch was dahinter'; 129. When Pilenz does visit him in the next pages, Mahlke typically has his back to the light, with his face therefore hidden in shadow – a position that Grass carefully re-creates when 'cat' and 'mouse' encounter one another in the school corridor at the beginning of the end: 146; 159).

As with Pilenz's defective memory and lack of candour, the motif of his ignorance about Mahlke comes to a head at the close of the book, so further increasing its sense of openness. The first open question is whether Mahlke really did find Tulla in the tram and go off with her on the evening before his disappearance: Mahlke claims that he did, Pilenz flatly denies it (161; *174*). Even in general, the narrator knows little (or, alternatively, admits little) about what kind of relationship there was between Mahlke and Tulla, if any, and volunteers only such indefinite observations as this: 'No, he didn't much fancy Tulla, though they say there was something between them later.' (42; *48*). But the question of whether Mahlke spends the evening (or night) with Tulla is linked with a far more fundamental one: the question of his motives. Why does he fail to report back for duty? Why does he, a hero distinguished with the Knight's Cross, wish to flee his country and its war? At the narrative level of what Mahlke actually says, and what Pilenz understands, no adequate explanation is forthcoming – any more than it is anywhere in the narrative. There are only Mahlke's claims that it is because of Tulla and because he feels he has done his bit, and his denial that fear has anything to do with it – a denial that Pilenz again flatly contradicts (161; *174*. As we shall see, fear is in fact a considerable issue in the book.) Again, with Mahlke on the run a little later, there is complete uncertainty on the surface of the narrative as to whether Mahlke genuinely had crippling stomachache: Mahlke claims that he did ('I can't swim ... I've got a belly-ache.'; 167; *180-1*) – but Pilenz rejects this: 'even today I can't make myself believe in that belly-ache' (168; *181*); and the reader is even more in two minds when he remembers the much earlier statement that, no matter what kind of food Mahlke stuffed inside himself, he never spoiled his stomach (30; *33*).

Why does Mahlke devour the unripe gooseberries at all? And is his stomach-ache perhaps just a pretence because he is afraid to dive down into the boat? – a refuge that is anyway not his suggestion but Pilenz's (162; *175*). Or is he telling the truth when he says that he is too ill to swim, and does he drown in consequence? It is in this respect of Mahlke's ultimate fate that Grass disguises the truth most thoroughly, for the concluding pages centre unremittingly on the uncertainty – or professed uncertainty – of the 'cat' about the fate of the 'mouse', with Pilenz's virtual hysteria when he hears no signal from inside the boat, his time spent staring out at the wreck through field-glasses, his post-war searchings for some trace of the missing Mahlke.

There is nothing but circumstantial evidence: Mahlke's failure to give a signal, his boots still standing on deck the following morning, the same ships still lying in the roads. This all points to his death – but as with Joseph Koljaiczek in *The Tin Drum*, there is no body; and Mahlke's failure to give a signal means little when we remember Pilenz's much earlier remark: 'often he was gone for as much as an hour; we would begin to pound frantically, but he never answered.' (72; 81). As I shall argue: at the level of the inner story, of the fable of Cat and Mouse, the hero's destruction is implicit in the whole conception of the book; but at the level of the ostensible narrative the issue is left emphatically obscure, and the book thus ends as it began in a flurry of enigma.

CHAPTER II

Bleak Images

After the powerful figurations of *The Tin Drum*, the reader of *Cat and Mouse* might reasonably anticipate more of the same kind – and he is not disappointed. Metaphoric motifs and imagery indeed acquire a special function in Grass's oblique novella: it is they above all that serve to point the meaning beneath the manifold ambiguities of a forgetful, dishonest and uncomprehending narrator. Thus the book as a whole is projected in terms of just such an image: the ominous image in word and picture that confronts the reader even before he picks up the volume. I shall follow up the forms of this paramount image of cat-and-mouse in a while; but let us look first at some of the secondary images in the book.

A fleeting but typically expressive example is the labyrinth image that Grass introduces with double reference both to Mahlke's symbolic confrontation with Pilenz in the Oliva Castle Park, and to his equally symbolic final confrontation with Headmaster and Party functionary Klohse, when he waylays him in the street and slaps him: the description of the tree-lined avenue where this gesture is enacted explicitly draws a comparison with the avenue in the Park where the two boys met, and in so doing it not only reinforces the earlier emphasis on the surround of thorns, but also picks up an apparently neutral detail of the earlier passage – the fact that the avenue in the Park was 'ohne Nebenwege' (127; *'without forks or byways', 138*) – and invests it with a rich significance: 'der Grosse Mahlke befand sich in einer Allee, ähnlich jener ... Allee im Schlosspark Oliva, die keine Nebenwege hatte *und dennoch ein Labyrinth war*' (154; *'the Great Mahlke had started down a path resembling that ... path in Oliva Castle Park, which had no forks or byways but was nonetheless a labyrinth', 167*).[4] The image is no sooner come than gone. But it epitomises all the same the whole spirit of the fable, in which the fugitive Mahlke repeatedly imagines that he has discovered a way out, only to end up each time more lost and more exposed than ever.

After *The Tin Drum*, no reader is likely to miss the short sentence that comes almost exactly halfway through the opening paragraph of *Cat and Mouse*: 'The wind was from the east, and the crematorium between the United Cemeteries and the Engineering School was doing its work'; with this inclusion of death in the book's tense figuration of the Cat's first assault on the Mouse, the essential tenor of the story is quietly indicated.[5] Not that *Cat and Mouse* has anything of the welter of deaths that marked *The Tin Drum* – but this is a function of its economy as a novella, and does not mean that death is any the less central to the book, which indeed remains the only one of Grass's works to date in which the protagonist dies, or, as we must say, probably, possibly, presumably dies. Furthermore, *Cat and Mouse* is not randomly placed in time but is set precisely in the years of the Second World War, the worst period of death and destruction yet known in history. This context of mass dying is explicitly and powerfully evoked in part of a remarkable subdivision of Chapter Nine (118-19; *129-30*; below, p. 146), a virtual prose-poem in which Grass generates great tension by building up a driving pattern of rhythms and repeats, while at the same time suspending its key element until the last word but one, with the result that reality stands revealed only at the very last moment – the reality of the 'vorherrschenden Leichengeruch', the pervasive stench of corpses which, so Grass describes it, lurked behind the banal and tidy façade of National Socialist Germany, much as in *The Tin Drum* the noxious, dreadful spirit of the National Socialist 'disaster' infiltrated every household in the Reich (and in *Dog Years* later on, Grass will insistently use the image of the stench of death in his mighty sequence on the 'Knochenberg', the mountain of concentration camp bones; see below, pp. 181 ff.).

In the context of *The Tin Drum* we have already cited what is perhaps the grimmest single figuration of existence in the novella: the bleak cycle in which the boys chew the seagull droppings that blanket the boat, spit the slimy residue over the side, a slime which is then snatched up in mid-flight by the swooping gulls, who meanwhile constantly layer the boat with new excrement (7-8; *10-11*); and the metaphorical point is driven home by the closing words of the sub-division: the remark that the gulls no doubt noticed nothing odd ('merkten wohl nichts') as they devoured the doubly excremental gobs of the boys' spit and their own faeces. At this stage (it is almost the beginning of the book), Mahlke is the only one not involved in the grim cycle, in that he never chews the droppings; but it is one mark of his essential unfreedom that, when the imagery is taken up again a little later in the tale, it is he alone that is involved: enticed by Tulla Pokriefke, he masturbates into the sea and the gulls pounce on his sperm and scream for more (40-1; *45-7*). The imagery is not new, of course: in *The Tin Drum* Grass had the seagulls swoop down and devour Agnes's vomit in the episode of the horse's head; but in *Cat and Mouse*, the images of the seagulls, and of various forms of excrement and decay, are used so extensively that they become a kind of dominant presence in the book – a constant token of the threatening order of existence of which Joachim Mahlke is a representative victim.

As for the gulls, their metaphoric function is concisely established in the opening pages, not only through the depiction of the excremental cycle, but by the fact that the narrative almost immediately describes them as swooping about according to some pattern – but a labyrinthine pattern that is beyond understanding: 'In all kinds of weather the gulls flew ..., grazing the remains of the binnacle, then wildly up again, according to some indecipherable plan' (7; *10*). The narrative at one point specifically describes the gulls as having the function of a Greek chorus ('ein als griechischer Chor funktionierender Möwenpulk', *105*; *114*), and in fact there is no single significant event on the sunken boat where the gulls' sombre presence is not explicitly evoked; and it is altogether typical that when the scene of action is created in the second paragraph of the book, the gorged company of gulls ('ein Volk vollgefressene Seemöwen') is the very first element of the setting to be conveyed.

As one might expect, given that Mahlke is the protagonist and the gulls a kind of omnipresent Greek chorus, the relationship between these two elements of the tale is repeatedly pointed up, the depictions of Mahlke's non-participation in the excremental round, and his subsequent emphatic involvement in it, being

100

only two instances among many. But the role of the gulls is especially marked in the closing stages of the narrative when Mahlke goes under for the last time. They are first brought back into the picture – 'the customary gulls' (170; *184*) – as Pilenz rows Mahlke over the last stretch of water towards the wreck. Other references follow, but one is particularly fraught: Mahlke's wave to the gulls on boarding the boat is presented as being like some long-lost uncle's greeting on his first visit in years: ' "Halloh, Kinder, Ihr habt Euch überhaupt nicht verändert!" ' (171; ' *"Hello, boys and girls, you haven't changed a bit!"* ', *184*). The levity here is ironic, for what the words really do is to emphasise yet again that, despite Mahlke's frenetic efforts, the reality represented by the gulls, the chaotic 'indecipherable plan', remains immutable; as Pilenz, the human representative of that reality, is given to remark earlier on: 'nothing changes around here' (133; *144*). Finally, the whole motif of the seagulls reaches its climax in the matter of Mahlke's putative death. The pattern of things was prefigured much earlier, when it seemed to the others that Mahlke must certainly have drowned (in fact he had found his way into the radio-cabin): the gulls are described as circling the boat ever more tightly – 'they must have noticed something' (69; *79*). And now, with Mahlke once more vanished within the wreck and giving no sign of life, the gulls again show a response, but a far more telling one than before: for the first time in the story, the gulls are described as suddenly all quitting the boat, as though they had no further business there. Pilenz alleges that their abrupt departure is 'for no apparent reason' ('ohne lesbaren Grund', 174; *187-8*) – but for the reader the implication is clear: the departure of the 'chorus' means that Mahlke is dead. When Pilenz returns next day to stare out at the boat through binoculars, the gulls are back around their old haunt, and again the implication is clear: the Mahlke phase in the bleak cycle of existence is done and finished, and everything is back to 'normal' – a point that is also beautifully made in the description of the water after Mahlke's last dive into the boat: 'Das Wasser über der Luke fand ins gewohnte kurzwellige Spiel.' (174; *The water over the hatch resumed its usual rippling play*', *187*).

As with the associated motif of the gulls, the motif of excrement and decay is established in the story's first stages, for the fourth paragraph begins with the remark that seagull droppings had collected and dried on the minesweeper from the moment it was sunk, and the whole of the rest of the paragraph, which concludes the introductory sub-division of the novella, is given over to excremental imagery, and above all to that bleak image of faeces-food-spit-faeces that we have already discussed. The rust of the boat, and the seagulls' excrement: these are the twin images that echo time and again throughout the book, indeed the phrase 'Rost und Möwenmist' (*'rust and gull-droppings'*) itself becomes almost a refrain. And not only is the boat covered with rust and faeces, it is also a decaying wreck in itself, becoming ever more ruinous throughout the time-span of the story – while the layer of faeces becomes ever thicker ('Only the encrusted gull-droppings had come through the winter in good shape and, if anything, had multiplied.'; 69; 78). As with the gulls, the rust and excrement imagery culminates pointedly in the paragraph depicting the lack of any sign of life from Mahlke after his final disappearance; and what is more, the rust and droppings, like the gulls, are described as breaking away from the boat at this juncture: at Pilenz's frenzy of blows against the deck, 'Flakes of rust went flying, crumbs of gull-droppings danced at every blow.' (175; 188); and although far less compelling than the image of the gulls' departure, this too may perhaps be taken as another sign that it is all over, and that the fugitive Mouse has gone to its symbolic and almost ritual death.

Grass not only makes excrement and gathering decay the symbolic central setting of Mahlke's activity, but he occasionally also uses the same kind of imagery elsewhere in his figuration of the hero. It is thus no empty aside when Pilenz, transfixed by the sight of Mahlke's National Socialist Labour Service hat when they come upon one another in the Oliva Castle Park, not only describes the hat as uniquely ugly and ill-proportioned, and gives its nickname of 'Arsch mit Griff' (127; *'arse with a handle'*, 138), but also defines it as being 'saturated with the colour of dried excrement'. A little later, it is typically a military latrine heaped with the worm-ridden faeces of Pilenz's generation ('der madendurchwachsene Auswurf meines Jahrgangs', 137; 150) that Grass makes the setting of one of the book's most strident evocations of Mahlke's suffering, of his Passion that echoes the crucified Christ's: the epitaph-like inscription 'MAHLKE STA-BAT MATER DOLOROSA ...' that the hero had carved deep in a beam, and which his oppressor savagely hacks to pieces. As *Dog Years* will show with expressive insistence later on, excrement is for Grass one of the truest images for the vile and sordid reality beneath the surface of the National Socialist era.

There is one other arresting use of the image in the novella that has a very different significance: the cryptic case of Mahlke and the unripe gooseberries in the closing stages of the book. He writhes in the sand in apparent agony, and is sent hobbling off into the sand-dunes by Pilenz to vomit and excrete (*168; 181*). We have seen how open the question is left at the surface level of Pilenz's narration; but a coherent meaning presents itself in terms of the inner story: Mahlke's systematic devouring of the unripe gooseberries is directly analogous to Agnes Matzerath's behaviour in gorging herself to death after her experiences with the horse's head; is it not with him, as much as with Agnes, an outward, physical mark of a profound collapse within?

CHAPTER III

Persecution and Suffering

'*Cat and Mouse*'

If there is one theme above all others that characterises the
'Danzig Trilogy', then the theme of persecution and suffering
undoubtedly has a strong claim. As we have seen, it was central
to *The Tin Drum*. Joseph Koljaiczek, Stephan Bronski, Agnes,
Jan, Matzerath, Herbert Truczinski, Sigismund Markus, the
'Dusters', Fajngold, Schwester Dorothea: all become victims at
some time, and commonly lose their lives in consequence.
Most of the great images of the book reflect the theme too: the
horse's head sequence, 'Faith Hope Love', the 'merry-go-round',
Kurt's beating up of Oskar. Above all, the conception of Oskar
himself expresses the theme: Oskar as 'Judas' and 'Jesus', Oskar
as the murderer of his mother and his two presumptive fathers,
and Oskar as the victim, mortally afraid of being driven from the
minimal asylum of his bed. As for *Dog Years*, we shall find the
book even more profoundly informed by the theme, in that its
whole dialectic arrangement is in terms of the Cain and Abel pair
of Walter Matern and Eddi Amsel. But, as its title suggests and
its opening paragraph demonstrates, it is in *Cat and Mouse* that
Grass's preoccupation with persecution and suffering is most
purely and powerfully expressed.

After Grass's use of the 'Schwarze Köchin' song, and his many
other borrowings in *The Tin Drum* from the world of children
– whose ritualistic behaviour clearly seems to him to demonstrate the fundamental but normally well-disguised patterns of
existence – it is no surprise to find him drawing on children's
lore to formulate the theme of his novella, the title of which
echoes the German game-cum-song of the same name (a game
which, though apparently little known by German children

today, was popular before the Second World War, and was, I am told, a hot favourite among the children of Danzig): the children stand in a circle, with one of them inside the circle as the mouse, another outside as the cat; they sing the traditional song, and the 'cat' then goes for the 'mouse' – whose capture is a necessary part of the game, which otherwise cannot carry on.[6]

It is with just such an attack, in symbolic terms, that Grass's novella begins, thus bearing out the implication of its title; and from this opening paragraph onwards, the cat and mouse imagery is repeatedly evoked, so that the reader is continually led to conceive the story in terms of the symbolic event on the playing-field. Even the distribution of the imagery throughout the narrative is pointed: in the first two expositional pages, the cat is mentioned no less than fourteen times; then in the following ninety-five pages – that is, in all the pages which, as we shall see, convey Joachim Mahlke's seeming achievement of freedom – the image is used only five times (and even then is not used at all in the fifty pages from page 45); but from the novella's crisis onwards – that is, from Mahlke's theft of the Knight's Cross, the event which confirms his situation beyond the pale, and thereby initiates the phase leading ultimately to his (presumable) death – from this point, the imagery of the cat is brought to the fore again and recurs every few pages right through to the end. Within this general distribution, there is another significant grouping, too, namely a division into two quite distinct cycles of imagery: the first cycle, from the second paragraph to the close of Chapter Eleven, always refers back either explicitly or implicitly to the symbolic act of the first paragraph, while the second cycle, coinciding precisely with the two chapters of the book's catastrophe, recreates the image afresh in the shape of the ominous, slinking cat in the school show-case (146; 159),[7] and goes on to bring the fable beautifully full-circle by pointing up the final re-enactment of the sports-ground aggression – and by thus delineating the truth that lurks beneath the blanket of ambiguity in Pilenz's, the persecutor's, narration.

Pilenz (and the Others) and Mahlke

However effective the cat and mouse image is in giving point and shape to the story, it *is* just an image, and therefore inadequate of itself to make up the body of the narrative, which in Grass's prose world is always derived from banal, ordinary reality. Thus the book's essential image of persecution, and the (futile) struggle to reach freedom, is given substance in the shape of two Danzig schoolboys and their relationship – two figures that are timeless and archetypal in their meaning, and yet thoroughly local and everyday in their outward existence and social context. Before we get on to the central matter of Joachim Mahlke himself, this question of the relationship between him and Pilenz (and their other class-mates) calls for consideration.

One key element in the relationship has already been mentioned earlier on: the fact that Pilenz is virtually in thrall to Mahlke (much as Matern in *Dog Years* will be in thrall to Eduard Amsel). Pilenz, it will be remembered, claims that he had to force himself to associate with Mahlke – but then has to admit that in truth there was no question of forcing himself (101; 110); and the passage in which this admission occurs amounts in fact to the book's most extensive picture of Pilenz's thraldom, with its details of how Pilenz would have done anything for Mahlke, how he went right out of his way so as to be able to accompany Mahlke to school, how he was the first to copy Mahlke's pompom invention, how he took to wearing a screwdriver round his neck, how he served at mass only in order to stare at Mahlke and his vulnerable throat (a motive that betrays not only his compulsive involvement but also his latent aggression).

Pilenz's abject subordination goes together with another important element in the relationship, and that is its imbalance and lack of any mutuality. For it is fundamental to Mahlke's existence that he is a being apart, a being quite beyond the 'normal' sphere to which Pilenz and the others belong – a separateness that both enables him to become a grand hero, the 'Great Mahlke', and also isolates him as a classic victim, as the vulnerable 'mouse' and fugitive in an inescapable labyrinth. All Mahlke's energies are directed towards one particular end, and

106

he is entirely unconcerned about Pilenz and the others (thus ironically remaining blind to the fact that Pilenz is a kind of Trojan horse that helps to render futile all his heroic achievements on other fronts). Thus, for instance, Mahlke is very rarely given to express himself to the other boys in the story, and over a third of the book passes before he utters anything of significance at all; he is even defined in terms of his reticence at one point, when he is referred to as 'der Einsilbige' (literally 'the monosyllabic one'; *115; 126*). The boys are full of admiration at Mahlke's doggedness in refurbishing the radio cabin – 'But Mahlke ignored our admiration and grew more and more monosyllabic' (*72; 81*); he lets them help him to hack a hole in the ice covering the boat's hatchway – 'But even without our help Mahlke would have finished his hole.' (*56; 63*); Pilenz would have done anything that Mahlke had told him to do – 'But Mahlke said nothing and just accepted it without a word or gesture when I ran after him' (*101; 110*); Pilenz would even have stolen the naval officer's medal if asked – 'But Mahlke attended to his own affairs' (*102; 111*).

Mahlke's insistent separateness also has to do with another crucial form of imbalance in the boys' relationship, and that is the ambivalence in attitude towards him. The passage describing Schilling's and Pilenz's visit to the ice-bound boat with the two girls conveys this ambivalence very clearly: the two boys are furious at Mahlke ('wütend') for having captured all the girls' attention, but cannot help singing his praises all the same (*51; 58*); once they have left him behind on the boat again, however, they promptly change their tune, and viciously ape his appearance to make him seem as ridiculous as possible – and whereas before it was Mahlke's magnificent feats that they had extolled, it is now characteristically his Adam's apple, the mark of his essential weakness, that they chiefly ridicule (*54-5; 61*). Nowhere is this ambivalence more pointedly, even schematically expressed than at the close of Chapter Six, following the story of Mahlke and the radio cabin:

Zwar bewunderten wir Mahlke; doch mitten im verquollenen Getöse schlug die Bewunderung um: wir fanden ihn widerlich und zum Weggucken. Dann tat er uns ... mässig leid. Auch fürchteten wir Mahlke, er gängelte uns. Und ich schämte mich, auf der Strasse mit Mahlke gesehen zu werden. Und ich

war stolz, wenn Hotten Sonntags Schwester oder die kleine
Pokriefke mich an Deiner Seite ... traf. (77)

*Of course, we admired Mahlke; but in the middle of the soggy
din our admiration shifted into its opposite, and we thought
him so repulsive we couldn't look at him. Then ... we felt
moderately sorry for him. We were also afraid of Mahlke:
he had us on a string. And I was ashamed to be seen in the
street with him. And I was proud when Hotten Sonntag's
sister or the little Pokriefke girl met the two of us together.
(86)*

Needless to say, it is in Pilenz that this ambivalence is most
significant. As well as the evidence already mentioned, there is
for instance his reaction to Mahlke's absence during one summer
holiday: he finds the summer empty without Mahlke, but he is
also glad that he is 'rid' of him, and that he doesn't have to go
tagging along behind him ('Besonders ich war froh, ihn los zu
sein, ihm nicht hinterdrein zu müssen', 111; *122*). But his ambivalence shows itself most crucially in the way that his compulsive attachment to the other boy is matched by a recurrent urge
to break his thraldom and get Mahlke out of his system. This
may just show itself in the mind, as in the context of his swim
out to the boat to rejoin Mahlke and his 'borrowed' Knight's
Cross: 'As I swam and as I write, I tried and I try to think of
Tulla Pokriefke, for I didn't and don't want to think incessantly
of Mahlke.' (99; *108*; a remark, incidentally, which obliquely
demonstrates the irony that Pilenz's own unfreedom was and
still is at least as great as that of his victim!) There is a much
more telling case of ambivalence in Pilenz's mind immediately
after the boys' portentous encounter in the Castle Park at Oliva,
when Grass has him remark, apropos of Mahlke's year-long
absence: 'sah ich eine Katze ..., lief mir sogleich die Maus
durchs Blickfeld; doch weiterhin übte ich mich im Zögern und
blieb unschlüssig, ob das Mäuschen geschützt, ob die Katze zum
Fangen gestachelt werden sollte.' (128; *'if I saw a cat ..., the
mouse ran into my field of vision forthwith; but still I hesitated,
undecided whether the mouse should be protected or the cat
goaded into catching it.', 140*). So much for Pilenz's ambivalent
thoughts – but when it comes to his actions, the pattern turns
out to be exactly the same: Pilenz does spend most of his time

108

tagging along willy-nilly behind Mahlke, but he also makes sporadic attempts to break free (just as Matern will do in *Dog Years*). Hence his violent hacking away of Mahlke's inscription on the military latrine (138; *151*); hence, above all, his treatment of Mahlke in the closing stages of the book, when he not only revels in being 'on top' for a change, but jumps at the chance of getting rid for ever of the cause of his servitude. He fails abysmally on both occasions, of course: the raw, smashed patch of wood where Mahlke's name had stood proves even more eloquent than the inscription itself had been (138; *151*), and similarly, the consequence of Mahlke's disappearance is that Pilenz finds himself more deeply enmeshed than ever, especially because he incurs something entirely new: a remorseless sense of guilt (again, Pilenz foreshadows Walter Matern in this, as we shall see).

But however significant all this emotional ambivalence and private psychology undoubtedly are within the story, they are equally certainly not of central importance. Much as Pilenz's guilt in the 'present' is first and foremost a contrivance to account for the fact that he narrates the story at all,[8] so his psychological contortions in the narrated past are chiefly meant, not for their own sake, but as a way of convincingly motivating the essence of the character, which is his role as persecutor, as the 'cat' of the title. The inner chronology of the novella makes this perfectly clear: it is emphatically conveyed that, prior to Mahlke's first successes in swimming, Pilenz had scarcely even been aware of his existence, let alone been deeply involved:

Bevor Du schwimmen konntest, warst Du ein Nichts ... Dennoch glaube ich, wir sassen in der Sexta oder später, jedenfalls vor Deinen ersten Schwimmversuchen, eine Zeitlang in einer Bank ... Später hiess es, Du hättest bis in die Quinta hinein eine Brille tragen müssen; fiel mir nicht auf. Auch Deine ewigen Schnürschuhe bemerkte ich erst, als Du Dich freigeschwommen hattest ... (32)

Before you could swim, you were a nobody ... And yet I believe that in the First form or maybe it was later, certainly before your first attempts at swimming, we shared a desk ... Later someone recollected that you had worn glasses up to the Second form; I never noticed them. I didn't even notice

109

those eternal laced boots of yours until you had made the
grade with your swimming ... (35-6)

Earlier on, the second sub-division of Chapter One had established
precisely this point in its trenchant opening sentence, saying that
at the start of the war Joachim Mahlke could neither swim nor
ride a bicycle and went completely unnoticed ('fiel überhaupt
nicht auf', 8; *11*; the sentence is then echoed on page 33; 36).
It is thus made plain that Pilenz's symbolic aggression in the
opening paragraph is *not* to be understood as a private act
generated by the frustrations and emotions of a particular
relationship, but as something much larger: as the response of
the eternal cat to the eternal mouse – to use Grass's own specific
image (25; 28). Quite apart from the book's inner chronology,
the sheer disposition of things powerfully conveys the same impression: first come the title, the ominous beast of the dust jacket,
and the opening paragraph, which all go to create an archetypal,
fable perspective; and only subsequently is the 'local' apparatus
of Pilenz's private relationship to his classmate gradually
developed – though the cat-and-mouse imagery throughout the
narrative ensures that the fable perspective remains in force.

CHAPTER IV

Joachim Mahlke - the Static Aspect

Although Grass's *Cat and Mouse* may often nudge the reader into looking at the story rather as Tom Stoppard's *Rosencrantz and Guildenstern Are Dead* looked at *Hamlet*, it is nonetheless certain that it is Mahlke that truly dominates the stage. As Grass has Pilenz explicitly declare: 'but I'm not going to speak of myself, my story is about Mahlke, or Mahlke and me, but always with the emphasis on Mahlke' (25; 28); or again, much later: 'but this is not the place to tell my story ... – here I am speaking only of you' (125-6; 137). Beyond this fact of his predominant place in the book, however, there is precious little else about Joachim Mahlke that is unambiguously clear, for as we have already seen, Grass makes him as enigmatic as possible by his choice of narrative mode. The reader must scan for the truth behind the dubious façade of Pilenz's tale, and a truth may indeed be discerned, but indirectly, as though by a series of mirrors, and very tentatively, for Grass consistently baulks the reader in his desire to feel in firm and confident possession of reality. But the meaning behind Mahlke and the book as a whole is not only put at several removes from the reader, it is also extremely complex within itself (in this respect of combined arcaneness and complexity, *Cat and Mouse* is a clear forerunner of *Local Anaesthetic*). The approach adopted here is to make an analysis firstly in terms of the static aspects of Mahlke – his outward, physical appearance, and his corresponding inward attitudes; and secondly in terms of the book's dynamics – the mechanism of events leading ultimately to Mahlke's presumable death, and involving both what he himself does, and what is done to him.

Joachim Mahlke's outward appearance is always expressive throughout the book in that it cries out his paramount characteristic: his irredeemable separateness. Above all there is his Adam's apple, his vulnerable 'mouse' – but since Grass uses this to generate the movement of the story, I shall discuss it later on. For the rest, his whole physique marks his natural 'abnormality': the sharply protruding back of his head, his blotchy back and washboard-like spine, his reddish, almost lashless eyelids, his yellowish lips and huge, bleached hands, his enormous genitals, and, above all, his bright red, protruding ears, which are picked out over and over again in the narrative. But Mahlke is distinct from the normal mass of people not only in a congenital way, but chiefly by reason of his conscious attitude and relationship to existence; and this is reflected in the kind of appearance that he affects: the 'old-fashioned boots' that he chooses to wear at all times of the year, and which are repeatedly evoked (they have to do with the important motif of his dead father), the plethora of bits and bobs with which in turn he covers his vulnerable throat, and then, most telling of all, the centre parting that he gives to his hair, and which ostentatiously crowns his appearance throughout the novella.

In almost all cases, this striking hair-style of Mahlke's is symbolically figured. Sometimes its significance is in terms just of a particular context, as on the occasion of Pilenz's Sunday visit to the home of his 'friend', when a change in Mahlke's hair serves as a quiet image of his frailty in the face of the 'cat': Pilenz relates that, whereas Mahlke's hair had been securely lodged in its customary place at the start of the visit, it was all collapsed and frailly trembling ('brüchig zitternd', 120; *131*) by the end; elsewhere, in the context of the *Luftwaffe* lieutenant's speech, Mahlke's hectic and crucial inner response is signalled in part by the way his hair goes awry and his parting is destroyed ('zerstört', 64; *73*). Much more importantly, though, Mahlke's centre parting also has a constant emblematic value: at once both 'solemn' and 'ridiculous' ('ernst', 'affig'), his parting is a chief mark of his combined role as 'Clown' and 'Christ', as the lone performer in the ring who is a genius at futility, and as the vain saviour – not the triumphant Christ of the Resurrection and the 'living Church', but the stricken and forsaken victim of the Passion, the child of the timeless *Mater dolorosa*.[9] Mahlke's hair is repeatedly figured in this emblematic way – and often within clusters of symbolic motifs that are intense in their effect, and which are amongst the book's distinctive features; but let us cite just the final, typical reference at the start of the 'catas-trophe' phase, which neatly hints at the fact that, despite all heroic appearances, everything is essentially the same, that Mahlke's Knight's Cross does not make him any the less a clown and vain saviour (the context is the boys' cat and mouse con-frontation at the school towards the beginning of Chapter Twelve):

die graue Feldmütze ... erinnerte mit rechtwinkliger Knautsch-falte ... an den Mittelscheitel Deiner Schüler- und Taucher-jahre, als Du vorgabst, Clown werden zu wollen. Dabei trugst Du bevor und nachdem man Deine chronischen Halsschmerzen mit einem Stück Metall geheilt hatte, keine Erlöserhaare mehr. Jene alberne streichholzlange Bürste, die damals den Rekruten zierte, ... hatte man Dir oder hattest Du Dir geschnitten. Dennoch Erlösermiene ... (147)

your grey field hat ... with its rectilinear crease down the middle recalled ... the parting that divided your hair in your schoolboy and diving days, when you planned, or so you said, to become a clown. Nevertheless, the redeemer's hair-do was gone. Even before curing your chronic throat trouble with a piece of metal, they must have given you that ludicrous brush cut which was then characteristic of recruits ... But your countenance was that of a redeemer all the same ... (160)

Evaluating Mahlke's outward appearance is one thing, but trying to discern his inner attitudes and his relationship to the world around him is quite another, given the extreme obliqueness with which they are conveyed. Pilenz, it will be remembered, is confes-sedly uncomprehending, and quite ignorant of Mahlke's soul and mind ('seine Seele wurde mir nie vorgestellt. Nie hörte ich, was er dachte.') The reader must glean the truth *despite* the narrator, as it were, and is entirely dependent on inference and deduction.

It is easy to deduce that Mahlke's chosen appearance reflects an inner state that makes him quite different and separate from his fellows, thus compounding his congenital differentness. But what is this inner state, and what is the motive force within it? This, it seems to me, is the fundamental question about *Cat and Mouse*, the question on which any serious interpretation of the book must necessarily hinge. My own conviction is that what we are to infer as Mahlke's prime and fatal distinction is an *undue awareness*, an electrifying insight into that destructive order of existence betokened, for instance, by the 'Schwarze Köchin' of *The Tin Drum*, the seagulls in *Cat and Mouse*, and – if in a somewhat different sense – the dynasty of dogs and the scarecrow pandemonium of *Dog Years*. Both Eduard Amsel and Oskar Matzerath are also beset by a similar crucial awareness of existence. But their responses to it are critically different from Mahlke's: whereas Amsel shields himself behind his protean disguises and behind his art, and whereas Oskar retreats to the refuge of his asylum bed (threatened though that is in the event), Mahlke's reaction to his awareness is to struggle desperately for freedom and safety in a strenuous 'Flucht nach vorn', an attempt to escape the enemy by outsmarting it at its own game.

Nothing implies this more clearly than the opening paragraph of the second sub-division of the book, a paragraph that serves to give the reader retrospective insight into the development of things *before* the symbolic event of the book's beginning: the three-stage development from zero, as it were, to Mahlke's first apparent pre-eminence. The zero stage consists of the hero's initial anonymity – and safety (the juxtaposing of these two factors in the narrative being of course no stray coincidence):

Als Joachim Mahlke kurz Kriegsbeginn vierzehn Jahre alt wurde, konnte er weder schwimmen noch radfahren, fiel überhaupt nicht auf und liess jenen Adamsapfel vermissen, der später die Katze anlockte. (8)

When shortly after the outbreak of the war Joachim Mahlke turned fourteen, he could neither swim nor ride a bicycle; there was nothing striking about his appearance and one missed the Adam's apple that was later to lure the cat. (11)

The middle section of the paragraph goes on to depict the second stage, consisting above all of Mahlke's dogged attempts to learn to swim; and the closing sentence then describes the third stage: Mahlke's sudden success at swimming. As ever, no reasons or motives for Mahlke's behaviour are explicitly cited. But there is a crucial pointer all the same: the terms in which, in the

114

paragraph's emphatic end-position, the fruition of Mahlke's strenuous efforts is expressed: '– und [Mahlke] schwamm sich frei.' It is admittedly easy to miss the significance of these few words; the English version, for instance, does not reproduce them at all, and there are those who have claimed that they are incidental and have only a mere technical meaning, since 'sich freischwimmen' does have the sense: 'to pass one's fifteen-minute swimming test'. But the whole tenor of the book makes it unquestionable that it is one of the metaphoric senses of the phrase, namely the idea of escaping from some predicament or other, that is uppermost here, so that an English rendering of the words would have to be something like '– and swam his way to freedom'. And in case the book itself is not evidence enough for this, there is Grass's own remark, in a letter following a public dispute on the subject: 'Wenn Mahlke sich freischwimmt – "... und schwamm sich frei" – spielt diese Sentenz natürlich nicht nur auf das Freischwimmen und das damit erschwommene Freischwimmer-Zertifikat an; denn indem Mahlke sich frei-schwamm, begann seine eigentliche Geschichte.' (*When Mahlke sich freischwimmt – "... und Mahlke schwamm sich frei" – the words used don't of course just refer to passing a swimming-test and to the swimming-certificate gained thereby; for Mahlke's real story began when he managed to sich freischwimmen.*)[10]

The phrase at the end of the paragraph thus serves as a key that unlocks the guarded meaning of the paragraph as a whole: we are given to infer that Mahlke in his adolescence suddenly became a conscious, knowing being – but inordinately so, since he was afflicted with an awareness not only of the vicious pattern acutely expressed by the war ('die Schlacht, die schon dage-wesen, die immer wieder kommt'), but also of his own frailty and proneness, his virtual unfreedom, with the result that he was suddenly driven to struggle for some position of strength and freedom – a position which the closing words of the paragraph might seem to suggest he has already reached, in however token a way. But there is a profound irony, an irony that will inform the book at every turn: Mahlke's awareness is disastrously partial. He is driven to action by an irresistible insight into the inimical nature of existence, but he remains blind to the fact that it is precisely his phenomenal 'Flucht nach vorn' that first exposes his 'mouse' to the gaze of 'one cat and all cats' (6; 9), and which makes him ever more exposed and vulnerable in direct proportion as his seeming successes become ever more brilliant. It is thus only through his recognition of the labyrinthine, deadly order of things that he becomes its victim, and makes himself – to use Grass's own phrase, coined to describe Döblin's protagonists – a vain 'hero against absurdity'.[11]

When one turns from the particular paragraph in Chapter One to the book as a whole, one finds the same oblique method of conveying the cardinal fact of Mahlke's awareness: nothing ever spelt out in so many words, but enough individual clues to put the meaning beyond doubt. Just such, for instance, is the description of Mahlke's eyes in one powerful evocation of him in his 'monumental solitude': 'terror-stricken, watery blue eyes that see more than is there.' (49; 56). When Mahlke himself describes the times as 'times like these when everything is getting more or less out of joint' (121; 132), this is certainly sententious and rhetorical (it is of course an echo of *Hamlet*, I, v), but at the same time it is also a real expression of his view. And again, Mahlke's inner orientation is suggested when Grass has him say that he has been reading a lot of Kierkegaard, and that Pilenz should read Dostoievski sometimes – 'It will help you to understand all sorts of things' (156; 169). But Mahlke's letter home from the Russian front is particularly pointed; for one thing, he specifically laments the desolation wrought on people and country by the war, and underlines its questionableness ('You can't imagine how run down everything is here, how wretched the people are and all the many children ... Sometimes I begin to wonder what it is all for – but I suppose it has to be.'; 133; 144); but this is not all, for Grass has this lament lead on immediately to an elaborate, portentous enquiry as to whether the sunken boat is still to be seen. The implication is clear: Mahlke may soon feel in need of a bolt-hole like that of the radio cabin hidden in the boat. This potential function of the cabin was established from the moment of its discovery, above all through the seemingly gratuitous remark of Mahlke's that is yet another pointer to his secret awareness: 'Good place to hide in if things get hot.' (71; 80) – and his subsequent re-equipping of the place included such survival items as candles, a primus stove, and stores of fuel and food. Though when it comes to the point, his would-be refuge will ironically prove to be the death of him.

I shall argue that it is this fundamental awareness of Mahlke's

116

that lies behind the whole sequence of his actions, from his first learning to swim to his attempted final flight. But it is also in the light of this awareness that the various dominant motifs of the novella gain their full significance.

One such motif is that of Mahlke's dead father, which is introduced emphatically within the first few pages:

> Mahlke war einziges Kind zu Hause.
> Mahlke war Halbwaise.
> Mahlkes Vater lebte nicht mehr.
> Mahlke trug im Winter wie im Sommer altmodische hohe Schuhe, die er von seinem Vater geerbt haben mochte. (11)

> *Mahlke was an only child.*
> *Mahlke was half an orphan.*
> *Mahlke's father was dead.*
> *Winter and summer Mahlke wore old-fashioned boots which he had doubtless inherited from his father. (14)*

The motif then recurs periodically in Chapters One to Four, the first of the book's four sections (cf. below, p. 131), the reader gathering that Mahlke's coat and stuffed owl both derive from his father, in addition to his old-fashioned boots, and also that his pompoms are made from the unravelled wool of his dead father's socks; later (in Chapter Seven) it is said that his shirt, too, appears to have been his father's. Taken together, these details have the effect of establishing a clear relationship between Mahlke and his father's memory. And this is emphasised by a further reference in this first section : in the fusillade of questions and comments that preface Pilenz's remark that he and his class-mates racked their brains but still could not understand Mahlke, there is just one attempted explanation : 'Maybe it's got something to do with his father's death.' (32; 35). At this stage of things, the reader is given no clue as to what was so special about the man's death, nor any explanation as to why Mahlke apparently fosters his father's memory. But then in the last two sections of the book, involving Mahlke's winning of the Knight's Cross (Chapters Nine to Eleven) and his flight and disappearance (Chapters Twelve and Thirteen), the motif comes fully into its own.

Its active significance first begins to show through in the

closing lines of Chapter Nine, when Mahlke explains the photograph of a locomotive and two men that Pilenz sees hanging in the other boy's house: 'The Great Mahlke said: "My father and Labuda the fireman, shortly before they were killed in an accident near Dirschau in '34. But my father managed to prevent the worst and got a posthumous medal."' (123; *134*). It is no random coincidence that medal ('Medaille') is the note on which the chapter ends, for the last five chapters, of which this is the first, are centrally concerned with medals, with Mahlke seeming to tread brilliantly in his father's footsteps by himself winning the Knight's Cross. But there is a decisive difference, already intimated in these closing lines of Chapter Nine: whereas the father was given his medal by society for *preventing* destruction, the son is given his for *wreaking* it.

It is in this same context in Chapter Nine, too, that we are first allowed to glean what the nature of Mahlke's attachment to his father's memory might be: not only does he outwardly sport his father's clothes, but his inner awareness is also determined by the same humanity that was his father's. This is suggested above all by his remark when he stops his aunt's innuendoes on the morals of Pilenz's mother: 'If Papa were still alive, he wouldn't like it, he wouldn't let you speak like that.' (121; *132*); and the narrative evokes a sense of equivalence between father and son by adding: 'Both women obeyed him or else they obeyed the departed engine driver whom he quietly conjured up' (the same impression is conveyed a little later, when Grass has Mahlke's aunt say that he was never one to complain – 'jenau wie sain Vater', 130; *just like his father*, *142*).

This humanitarian base to Mahlke's awareness is of critical importance; and it is implicit not only in the father motif, but also in the mention of Kierkegaard and Dostoievski, in his lament on the misery in Russia, in his rescue of the boy trapped inside the sunken boat (68; 77-8), in his prevention of the contraceptive jape (28; *31*), and especially, as we shall see, in the novella's key motifs of Christ, Clown and Suffering. It is implicit, too, in the very first words of any importance that Grass has Mahlke utter in the book, just after the *Luftwaffe* lieutenant's lecture about the exploits that won him his Knight's Cross:

Ruhig und wehleidig, als wollte er von den langwierigen Gebrechen seiner Tante erzählen, kam die Stimme: 'Jetzt müssen sie schon Vierzig runterholen, wenn sie das Ding haben wollen. Ganz zu Anfang und als sie in Frankreich und im Norden fertig waren, bekamen sie es schon, sobald sie Zwanzig – wenn das so weitergeht?' (64)

Calmly and mournfully, as though speaking of his aunt's chronic ailments, his voice said: 'Now they need a bag of forty if they want the medal. At the beginning and after they were through in France and in the North, it only took twenty – what if it keeps on like this?' (73)

Taken superficially and in isolation, this might seem to be no more than a cynical complaint that it will be all the harder for Mahlke to get hold of his own Knight's Cross in due time. But when considered in the context of the persona and the book as a whole, it becomes clear that what Mahlke is truly doing is lamenting in all his awareness at the cruel inflation of the equation 'x units of death and destruction = 1 unit of glory and honour'.

These words do reflect Mahlke's humanity; but they also express the desperate paradox which it entails: what good is a humanitarian spirit in an era in which destruction is at a premium? It is surely in such terms that we must understand the culmination of the father motif towards the book's end, when Mahlke, in outlining the lecture he had so ardently wanted to deliver at the Conradinum, gives a grotesque description of how he achieved his phenomenal tank corps successes: he had a vision each time of the Mother of God clutching to her womb the photograph of his father with fireman and locomotive, and had only to aim at his father's engine, and with it Mary's womb, in order to wipe out yet another Russian tank and its occupants (169-70; *182-3*). This brutal image (which is also a travesty of coitus, a desperate metaphor of human relationships and love – see below, p. 126) crystallises what seems to be the main implication of the chapters on Mahlke's participation in the war: that the era has no room for the generous, constructive humanity that Mary's child and Mahlke's father both stand for in their different ways, and for Mahlke to have any chance of escaping from the 'cat' and the 'labyrinth', he has ultimately to act against his deepest spirit, he has to play the cat's own game and shoot at the images both of his father's humanity and of the womb whence came the incarnation of Love and Brotherhood. In this same context, too, the gross disparity between the circumstances of Mahlke's winning of his medal, and his father's winning of his, is clearly pointed up, for Mahlke says that he would not have talked just about himself in the lecture – 'Wollte über meinen Vater und Labuda. Hätte ganz kurz das Eisenbahn-unglück vor Dirschau. Und wie mein Vater durch persönlichen Einsatz. Und dass ich am Richtaufsatz immer an meinen Vater.' (169; *My father and Labuda, the fireman. A few words about the accident by Dirschau. How my father through his courage and self-sacrifice. The way I always thought of my father as I sat there at the sights.'*, 182). Earlier on, towards the beginning of the final section (Chapters Twelve and Thirteen), just the same point is made, but with pungent irony, when Pilenz is given to remark : 'I talked, in order to give him courage, about his father ... his father's death near Dirschau, and his father's posthumous medal for bravery : "How happy your father would be if he were still alive !" ' (149; *162*) – for in reality nothing would be less likely to give Mahlke's father joy than the grounds for his son's supreme distinction.

The spirit represented in Mahlke's father is thus utterly extinguished in the kind of society effective in the book – and this is finely reflected in the way that the father motif itself ends up by being symbolically cast into oblivion by none other than Pilenz, the 'cat'. Whereas Mahlke had half-asked Pilenz to bring the photograph of his father and Labuda on his return to the sunken boat that evening, Pilenz does no such thing; he does go and fetch the photograph (which he had already eyed on his visit to get food, 166; *179*), and he does bring it with him when he comes to stare out at the boat next day. But it is the final token of his being that after getting rid of Mahlke himself, he also disposes of the one surviving symbol of his spirit by doing away with his father's photograph, burying it in his case beneath his underclothes and assorted odds and ends and ultimately losing it in the fighting at Cottbus (177; *190*)[12] – a deed which re-enacts his eradication of Mahlke's name from the Labour Service camp latrine, just as his final betrayal of Mahlke himself re-enacts the fable's opening paragraph.

Mahlke as a Sufferer, as a Clown and Christ figure : these are key motifs that we have already touched on – motifs which

Grass exploits and combines so intensively that they amount to the book's most powerful figuration of the hero's monumental separateness and failure; but, what is more to the point here, they express more cogently than even the father motif does the central matter of Joachim Mahlke's fatal awareness.

The explicit notion of suffering is not often used in the book, but it is a forceful one all the same in that it is only ever set in particularly charged contexts. The first such context, towards the beginning of Chapter Two, involves a characteristic bunching of motifs: it speaks of Mahlke in terms of clown, Christ, centre parting etc. etc., and in terms of his trying to distract the 'eternal cat' from his 'eternal mouse' – but it also speaks of his 'saviour's' face as expressing 'suffering', as though from some 'raging inward sense of pain' (25; 28). Later the blackboard caricature of Mahlke as Christ, complete with halo, represents his eyebrows as 'raised in pain' ('schmerzlich gehoben'), and his face as a whole appears as a 'countenance of suffering' ('Leidensmiene', 45; 50), while the powerful evocation a few pages later of the Clown Mahlke in his 'monumental solitude' likewise describes his eyebrows in terms of suffering (49; 56). But much the most intensely explicit image of suffering anywhere in the book comes in the next chapter (Chapter Five) when Pilenz once again visualises his 'friend' coming clown-like through the snow, decked out this time with his array of luminous plaques – and solely concerned to distract attention from his 'Leid', his affliction and his profound suffering and sorrow (Leid has a large meaning in German for which there is no single English equivalent):

ein dürftiges Gespenst, das allenfalls Kinder und Grossmütter erschrecken kann und von einem Leid abzulenken versucht, das in schwarzer Nacht ohnehin verdeckt bleibt; aber Du dachtest wohl: keine Schwärze vermag diese ausgewachsene Frucht zu schlucken, jeder sieht ahnt fühlt sie, möchte sie greifen, denn sie ist handlich; wenn dieser Winter doch bald vorbei wäre – ich will wieder tauchen und unter Wasser sein. (65)

a pathetic sort of ghost, capable at most of scaring children and grandmothers – trying to distract attention from an affliction that no one could have seen in this pitch darkness. But you said to yourself no doubt: no blackness can engulf

121

this ripe fruit; everyone sees, suspects, feels it, wants to grab
hold of it, for it is ready to hand; if only this winter were over
so I could dive again and be under water. (74)

Quite apart from anything else, this beautifully conceived passage shows once and for all how Mahlke's awareness of suffering and sorrow lies behind his strenuous actions; and nowhere in the book is the manner of his Passion more poignantly evoked than here.

As for the Christ motif: it parallels the motifs of cat and mouse and Mahlke's father in functioning most strongly in the latter half of the book, where it greatly illuminates the final sequence of events. But although it has no immediate bearing on the action of the first half, it is none the less asserted more or less from the beginning, like all the book's principal motifs. We have already seen how the 'saviour' image is used of Mahlke in the context both of the 'eternal cat' – 'eternal mouse' passage in Chapter Two, and of the blackboard caricature that closes Chapter Three. There is also the subtle but telling detail of the street that Grass chooses for Mahlke to live in: 'Osterzeile' – 'Easter Row', a detail that is carefully established at the beginning of Chapter Two (23; 26). But there is also another and particularly important pointer in this first half of the book: the motif of the Passiontide sequence *Stabat Mater dolorosa*, which Mahlke is twice described as reciting (21, 73; 23-4, 82). Only on the second of these occasions is Mahlke's 'favourite sequence' ('Lieblingssequenz') explicitly identified as the *Stabat Mater*, and furthermore both passages seem at first sight to be nothing more than reflections of Mahlke's cheery mood on the two particular occasions; in truth, though, they both typify the ironic method of the book, for there is a sharp contradiction between Mahlke's cheeriness and the deathly lamentation of the sequence[13] – and it is the sorrow of the Passiontide sequence that is borne out by the fable, not Mahlke's transient gaiety. These passages thus quietly prefigure the closing phase of the story; and given these and the other more direct depictions of Mahlke in Christ-like terms, combined with the various evocations of suffering and sorrow, the reader is soon made aware that Joachim Mahlke's existence is not only to be understood in a specific sense (Germany under National

122

Socialism) and in a universal sense (cat destroys mouse, and always has done), but is also to be understood as if silhouetted against the most memorable Passion of Western culture.

In the second half of the book this perspective is steadily reinforced by various additional uses of the Christ motif, several of which we have already mentioned elsewhere, such as the boys' thorn-wreathed confrontation in the park, and above all the symbolic episode when Pilenz hacks away the lapidary inscription 'MAHLKE   STABAT MATER DOLOROSA ...' As so often, though, it is in the closing phase of the narrative that the motif really comes into its own. The first paragraph of the final chapter, with Mahlke attending mass for the last time, makes the point with delicate, beautiful subtlety, when – after steadily building up its 'soap-bubble' imagery – it concludes:

Gusewski [hob] die Hostie, liess mit vollendeter Lippenstellung die ganz grosse und entsetzt in der Zugluft zitternde Seifenblase wachsen, hob sie mit hellroter Zungenspitze ab: und sie stieg lange, ehe sie fiel und nahe der zweiten Bank vor dem Marienaltar verging: 'Ecce Agnus Dei ...' (159)

Gusewski lifted up the Host and began with full-rounded lips to blow the big bubble, the bubble of bubbles. For a moment it trembled terror-stricken in the draught; then with the bright-red tip of his tongue he sent it aloft; and it rose and rose until at length it fell and passed away, close to the second pew facing the altar of the Virgin: 'Ecce Agnus Dei ...' (172)

For it is Mahlke who always sits in the second pew from the front (18, 113, 114; 21, 124-5, 125), Mahlke, too, who rose and rose only to fall and become as nothing, and Mahlke whose death will re-enact the sacrificing of the *Agnus Dei*, the Lamb of God; and it seems to be the whole hope of Salvation that bursts into nothing along with this 'fearfully trembling bubble of air'.

There is just one other small but insistent detail that points up the motif beyond all doubt: the novella as a whole scarcely ever bothers with mentioning days of the week, and why should it? – but come the closing sequence of events, days of the week are suddenly carefully specified – to clear symbolic effect: Mahlke, the archetypal child of the *Mater dolorosa*, dies on a *Friday* (and there is nothing that implies his death more certainly

123

than the Christ motif in general and its culmination in particular). The first such reference tells us that Mahlke slapped Klohse on a Thursday (155; 168); later, after Mahlke's final disappearance, Grass has the narrator remark: 'Ever since that Friday I've known what silence is' (175; 188); and on the following page, with Pilenz back home in time for lunch, there is the curt detail: 'There was no fish' – it would indeed be grotesque if Mahlke's Judas were to enact the symbol of abstaining from eating meat; then finally, on the same page, the day following Mahlke's disappearance is explicitly named as a Saturday.

Mahlke is thus shown to be 'crucified', to be a victim of that process of persecution so often reflected in the Bible, from Cain's fratricide onwards, the process so sharply evoked in the psalmist's words that serve as the Introit on the same Passiontide Friday as the *Stabat Mater*: '*Miserere mihi, Domini, quoniam tribulor: libera me, et eripe me de manibus inimicorum meorum, et a persequentibus me: Domine, non confundar, quoniam invocavi te. In te, Domine, speravi, non confundar in aeternum: in justitia tua libera me. – Miserere mihi.*' – Except that the gracious God besought in the Introit is absent for Mahlke, and the 'fleeing mouse' (169; 182) remains undelivered '*de manibus inimicorum meorum et a persequentibus me*', and *is* confounded '*in aeternum*'. It is plain that Mahlke's gross and desolate 'Leid' is nothing local or physical, but existential, like the ancient sorrow proclaimed so plangently in the verse from *Lamentations* that is fixed as the Tract for the same Friday: '*O vos omnes, qui transitis per viam, attendite et videte, si est dolor sicut dolor meus*'.

An intriguing question arises here: given that Grass's whole figuration of Mahlke amounts to a dismission of the gracious God of Christianity, what are we to make of Mahlke's own apparent devotion to Catholicism? – witness, for instance, his insistent attendance at mass (so insistent is it that it brings his expulsion from the *Jungvolk*, 31; 34), his need to go to confession when Tulla has goaded him into masturbating (42; 47), the request in his letter home that a mass be said for his dead father (133; 144), etc., etc. One thing is certain: Mahlke's ardour has in truth nothing to do with God, or with Christianity in any normal sense, but instead consists of a solitary, eccentric fixation on the Virgin Mary. This fact, though everywhere implicit, is

124

actually stated through Mahlke himself towards the close: 'Of course I don't believe in God. ... I believe only in the Virgin Mary' (156; *169*; – the remark is then repeated in telescoped form in the following paragraph). And the point is further reinforced a few pages later, when Mahlke's claim that he is no longer as afraid after attending mass as he was before it, is followed by this exchange: '"I thought you didn't believe in God and all that stuff." "He's got nothing to do with it."' (161-2; *175*). But what is the significance of this compulsive irreligious attachment to Mary?

What it amounts to above all is one further token of Mahlke's fatal awareness and separateness: Mary and the 'Marienkapelle' ('*St Mary's Chapel*') are a sanctuary for the frail Mahlke just as Anna Koljaiczek and the uterine warmth of her skirts were for Oskar. Having exposed himself to 'one cat and all cats', Mary (together with the memory of his father) is the one thing he can cling to, and it is no coincidence when the narrative, in seeking to explain the motives for his actions, puts Mary and his urge to disguise his 'mouse' in immediate juxtaposition: 'Whatever he did, from diving to his subsequent military accomplishments, was done for her, or else ... to distract attention from his Adam's apple.' (43; *48*). When inside the sanctuary of the 'Marienkapelle' itself, Mahlke even feels able to let the sign of his weakness show through undisguised: as he kneels at the altar-rail he has 'abandoned all caution' and 'exposes that agitated mouse' (58; *65*); or on another occasion at the altar-rail: Mahlke 'exposed to view a bare, unguarded neck that concealed none of its secrets' (114; *125*).

What a vain refuge this is, however (just as the boat proves to be)! Oskar was safe from all menace once tucked up beneath his grandmother's skirts; but who is in this very sanctuary of the 'Marienkapelle' but Pilenz, constantly spying on the mouse? – 'Whenever Mahlke knelt at the altar rail, ... the altar boy ... would peer into Mahlke's shirt collar', 'And if I continued to gratify Gusewski with my services as an altar boy, it was only in order to gaze at Mahlke's neck during Holy Communion.' (30, 101; *33-4*, *111*).[14] And how do the above-mentioned passages continue that speak of Mahlke abandoning all caution at the altar rail? In the one case his exposed throat is described as 'that agitated mouse, that I might have caught in my hand, it was so defenceless'; in the other case Pilenz goes on to describe it as 'the

125

restless mouse ... which had once attracted a cat and had tempted me into putting the cat on his neck.' It is of course entirely typical of the book's irony that the one place where Mahlke believes himself secure (leaving aside the equally ironic matter of the radio cabin) is in fact the place where he is most thoroughly exposed to the forces that beset him.

One aspect of Mahlke's relationship to the Virgin Mary is undoubtedly drastic: he sees in her not so much the divine being as the woman[15] – so much so that he physically desires her. This is made clear in the important context of Mahlke's last visits to mass before he goes off to military service and the seeming consummation of his struggle: the words 'schon begehrlich' are used to describe his altar-rail posture of yearning towards the Virgin's effigy – calculated words that have an unmistakable ring of sensuality (115; 126); then, two pages later, the point is reinforced beyond any doubt when Mahlke's gaze is described as being aimed straight at the 'belly of the Mother of God'. This desire is satisfied after a fashion once Mahlke gets to the war, for he achieves a kind of union with his beloved each time he destroys yet another Russian tank – but, as we noted earlier, this 'union' is a desperate reflection of human existence and relationships: the hero's phallus is the cannon of a tank, his seed a spray of high velocity shells, the receiving womb the mere imagined vision of the 'Virgin of Virgins', and the bed a battlefield.[16]

Just as in the masturbation scene, therefore, when the seagulls swooped down and devoured Mahlke's semen, the implication of his quasi-sexual act with the Virgin Mary is bleak in the extreme. But in a quieter way the whole relationship of Mahlke to Mary is grim indeed in its implications. It would be bad enough if Mahlke were able to be involved only in one or two *living* people, but nothing signals his alienation more poignantly than the fact that the only two 'people' he appears devoted to – Mary, and his father – are both without real substance, and present only in the form of lifeless mementos: the pendant, medallion, print and statue of the one, the photograph and items of clothing of the other. True, there are allusions suggesting some kind of relationship between Mahlke and the Labour Service camp commandant's wife, and between him and Tulla Pokriefke; but these things are left both obscure and peripheral, and do nothing to

126

detract from the cardinal fact that Mahlke's isolation and alienation are total.

This brings us at last to one of the most richly worked of the novella's motifs: that of Mahlke as a 'clown'. But richly worked though the motif certainly is, the basic situation is dramatically simple: one solitary man in the spotlight, comically masked and garbed, and, all around but infinitely separate from him, the gathered mass of 'normal' people, simultaneously marvelling at his prowess and delighting in his failure.

At the most patent level of the book, there is the laughable abnormality of Mahlke's sheer appearance: his physique and his manner of dress need only the admixture of exaggerated behaviour to mark him out as a comic oddity – and it is typical of the book that he is presented in just such terms from the outset, for the second sub-division of Chapter One describes him as cutting a stock comic figure, 'eine komische Figur', in his dogged, big-eared, knee-pumping efforts on a bicycle (8; *11*). Along the same lines, we hear in due course how the other boys laugh at Mahlke's prayers and recital of the *Stabat Mater* on the boat (20; *23*) – a performance explicitly described a little later as a circus-clown act (23; *26*); how Mahlke only has to eat a bread-roll to send them into stitches (23; *26*); how they guffaw at the blackboard caricature of the hero (45; *51*); and how Schilling ridicules Mahlke behind his back and makes the two girls laugh at the boy they had just been enthralled by (55; *61*). But it is of the essence that Mahlke's 'performances' set him apart as an object of wonder as well as of ridicule (we have already mentioned the other boys' ambivalence towards him, above, p. 107); and it is again typical that the book's second sub-division not only depicts him as cutting a comic figure, but also says apropos of his first great feats on the wreck: 'Mahlke ... stand vom ersten Tag an ganz gross da.' (10; *from the very first day he was an ace*', *13*). Almost from the beginning, he stands as 'der ganz besondere Mahlke, der auf teils erlesene, teils verkrampfte Art Beifall sammelte' (28; *that very special, individual Mahlke, always, in a choice or tortured way, gathering applause*', *31*).

But whether Mahlke appears to the others as a comic buffoon or a wondrous artiste, the implication remains the same: he is not one of them, he is separate and alone beneath the limelight. And the more extravagant his antics become, and the more prodigious the *salto mortale* that he is driven to attempt, so he becomes ever more endangered, ever more exposed – until at last, inevitably, he falls. Failure and profound impotence being thus the secret of all Mahlke's acts, even his most glorious feats are in truth the futile gestures of a clown, of this 'virtuoso of imperfection, of failure, of human and artistic defeat',[17] this 'anti-hero, who is almost more effective, more captivating as a failure than anyone else might be as a success'.[18]

Needless to say, it is not just that the others see Mahlke as a clown and performer – the fiction is decisively that he sees himself in such terms, and acts accordingly. This is established in the opening paragraph of Chapter Two, with the fourteen-year-old hero's reply to a question in class as to his career intentions: 'I'm going to be a clown and make people laugh' (23; 26). What is more, Grass not only specifically describes the occasion of this statement as being *after* Mahlke's learning to swim (' – damals konntest Du schon schwimmen –'), thus obliquely showing that it has to do with Mahlke's awareness (this point being driven home two pages later: 'no sooner had he learned to swim, than he made up his mind that ... he would be a clown in the circus'); not only does Grass do this, he also clearly expresses the un-comic reality behind the clown's mask: Mahlke's face when he speaks his reply is so deadly serious that not a soul in the class-room laughs, while Pilenz is even taken with fright ('ich bekam einen Schreck').

From this early point in the book, the Clown motif is steadily intensified. For one thing, Mahlke's own wish to be a clown is repeatedly referred to (cf. 38, 47, 65, 116, 147; 43, 54, 74, 127, 160). Above all, though, Mahlke's actual behaviour is persistently expressed in 'performance' terms: the sunken boat is described as giving him his first 'Auftrittsmöglichkeiten' (33; *chance to perform*, 36); his general relationship to Tulla, and his antics on the boat with the stolen Knight's Cross, are both described as a 'circus act' (37, 104; 43, 113); his postures are 'stylised' and 'affected' (37, 114; 42, 125; – it is in this latter context that it is said of Mahlke that he could have done a stage routine as Jesus); his huge spotted tie is his 'new trick' (92; 101), while his first wearing of it is 'Mahlke's necktie première' (91; 100); and there are also various descriptions of his activities as 'perfor-mances', 'brilliant tricks', 'exhibitions' (41, 56, 106; 47, 63, 115). And of course the reader is never in doubt as to the reasons for this incessant and flagrant display: Mahlke is desperate to hide his enticing 'mouse' and escape its potential aggressors. In the poignant image that closes Chapter Five, he makes himself into a clown because he feels driven to distract attention from the inviting full fruit of his 'Leid', his affliction and sorrow.

CHAPTER V

Joachim Mahlke and the Book's Dynamics

Mahlke's fatal awareness, his struggle for freedom, his signal
failure: these, I have suggested, are the three constituent stages
of the story. The second of these stages is by far the longest: it
occupies no less than the first eleven of the book's thirteen
chapters, the first stage being virtually hidden away in Chapters
One and Two, while the final stage takes up only the last two
chapters. Indeed it is the *second* stage, not the first, that is
expressed in the splendid opening paragraph of the book. As I
have argued before, it is essential to grasp this, for it is a fundamental error to assume that the opening – anachronic as it
is – represents the true beginning of the story (in one critic's
words: '... Mahlke has a gigantic and very conspicuous Adam's
apple. Being forever painfully conscious of this lump in his
throat since a cat once attacked it, taking it for a mouse, he
tries to divert his own and everyone else's consciousness of his
huge Adam's apple by excelling in various skills and feats.'[19])
What really comes first, despite appearances, is that cardinal
awareness in Mahlke that drove him into the limelight with
his bicycling and his swimming, and which thus attracted the
Cat's attention. The opening paragraph, then, is not the true
beginning of things; but what it does do, and that most powerfully, is to establish the all-important imagery in terms of which
the development of the book is organised: from this point
on, Mahlke's enormous Adam's apple stands as the mark of his
weakness, and his desperate struggle for freedom henceforth
expresses itself almost exclusively in his urge to find some
adequate means of counteracting the blatant symbol of his
throat.

This major importance of the Adam's apple motif is well
reflected in the fact that it is far and away the most frequent
and variegated single element in the narrative. It is thus men-

tioned no less than thirty-one times as 'Hals' (*neck*), fourteen times as 'Adamsapfel' (*Adam's apple*), ten as 'Gurgel' (*throat*), and is variously represented as 'Artikel', 'Knorpel', 'Rücken-flosse', 'Hüpfer', 'Fahrstuhl', 'Ding', 'Ausgeburt', 'Blickfang', 'Kennzeichen' and 'Kropf' (*article*, *piece of cartilage*, *dorsal fin*, *jumping jack*, *lift*, *thing*, *abortion*, *eye-catcher*, *distinguishing mark*, *goitre*). As well as this rich incidence, there is also the fact that Grass includes a number of explicit glosses on the motif's significance. It is thus spelt out that Mahlke's Adam's apple is nothing less than his 'motor and brake' (103; 112), and likewise all his actions were undertaken 'to distract attention from his Adam's apple' (43; 48); or there is the curt paragraph that begins Chapter Three: 'He was not a thing of beauty. He ought to have had his Adam's apple repaired. Possibly that piece of cartilage was the whole trouble.' (37; 42) – then, only a few lines later, Pilenz's classic remark about never having got to know the soul or the thoughts of his 'friend' is immediately followed by the assertive statement: 'What is left in the end are his neck and its numerous counterweights.'

Right at the outset of this Second Part, I argued that *Cat and Mouse* is a deliberate and pure example of the novella genre, above all because it classically depicts one single dynamic and extraordinary development.[20] We can now take this further and see in more detail how astonishingly poised and measured the novella is in the way it unfolds. For we soon find that the book is ordered in four distinct sections: there are two longer sections of four chapters each, with fifty-four and fifty pages respectively, the last two chapters (that is, Seven and Eight) being the critical centre of the book, with seventy-three pages before and seventy pages after; there then follow two shorter sections of three and two chapters, involving in turn thirty-five and thirty-four pages. This delicate balance in the book is all the more astonishing in that it reflects the classical balance of the sonnet, even to the point of showing a pause at the end of the 'octet' (one almost feels cheated that the 'sestet' should have been left incomplete). As for the burden of the four sections, this may be summarised as follows:

1. Mahlke's awareness, and his first attempts to secure freedom: the attack on his Adam's apple: Mahlke's diving
   prowess, and the first series of compensatory disguises – the

'bits and pieces' around his neck ('Klamotten am Hals', 32; 35).

2. The first Knight's Cross phase. Mahlke, faced with the inadequacy of everyday disguises, becomes oriented towards the Knight's Cross, the one thing that seems capable of counteracting his vulnerability. The medal theft: Mahlke's provisional, vicarious attainment of the Knight's Cross; Mahlke's expulsion: the fatal, though latent, crisis.

3. The second Knight's Cross phase. Mahlke and the War: his 'proper' winning of the Knight's Cross: his pre-eminence and the apparent imminence of safety.

4. Mahlke's downfall. Klohse and the 'Conradinum': Mahlke's flight and (?) death.

What we now need to look at is the way Grass gives his story momentum through these four distinct groups of chapters.

The Beginnings: Chapters One to Four

It has long since become clear that Grass's novella is centred in manifold irony — above all, the ironic discrepancy between the appearance of Mahlke's steadily mounting success, and the irrefutable, destructive reality of the labyrinth from which he is ever trying to escape. This key irony is expressed through the overall structure of the book: no matter how great are the interim triumphs of the Great Mahlke, it is the Cat that has the first word and the last, and which even squats malevolent and lowering on the dust-jacket, belying in advance the hero's grand successes. As for the first group of chapters, we find just the same telling pattern: not only does it begin with the attack on Mahlke's throat, but in its closing paragraph this same weak spot is dwelt on, with Pilenz ominously mentioning how easily he could have pounced on the hero's defenceless, agitated mouse (58; 65).

Once the narrative gets under way in the second sub-division of Chapter One, Mahlke's shift from anonymity to singular pre-eminence is conveyed with almost breathtaking rapidity: within a matter of paragraphs we hear how he at last learns to swim, outstrips the others on his first journey to the wreck, and immediately establishes his supremacy with a quick volley of diving exploits, culminating in his demonstrative display with the fire-extinguisher. This instant and absolute supremacy of Mahlke's is then variously confirmed in the rest of the chapter. As far as swimming and diving are concerned, he is always first to the boat (11; *14*), and he brings up an endless succession of wondrous booty – above all, the extra-special screwdriver, the bronze plaque, and the silver medallion of Mary. But there is also another sphere in which Grass has his hero excel : that of school gymnastics. Whereas previously he had avoided such activity on the grounds of sickliness, he sets about mastering it at the same time as he applies himself to swimming lessons (12; *15*) – and within a few lines of our being told this, we also learn of his outstanding success: he is up with the leaders apparently at once, and is later to surpass even the best with his thirty-seven knee circles on the horizontal bar ... However, the book's incessant ironic procedure ensures that the reader is always aware of the reality confuting the hero's achievements. The first sub-division sets the characteristic pattern, its two scene-setting middle paragraphs being bracketed by grim omens: there is not only the vicious attack on Mahlke's 'mouse' at the start, but also the paragraph at the close that so forcefully establishes the motifs of rust and excrement and, above all, the motif of the choric sea-gulls, with the black cycle that they represent, and their swooping and soaring according to an 'indecipherable plan'. Then in the second sub-division, Mahlke's 'swimming his way to freedom' and his phenomenal success on the boat are sharply relativised by the remark that, although the hero's screwdriver does to some extent distract attention from his throat, it is still incapable of entirely hiding 'that fatal piece of cartilage'. And at the end of the chapter, it is the destructive order of things that again prevails: within the last dozen or so lines the *Stabat Mater* lamentation is first introduced, there is the symbolic detail whereby the medallion of Mary and her child is placed between two 'heroes' of war, that is, between two representatives of death and devastation – and there is the recurrence of the book's crucial motif in the sudden reference to 'jenem Adamsapfel, der einer Katze als Maus gegolten hatte.' (21; *'the Adam's apple that a cat had taken for a mouse.'*, 24).

As for the other three chapters making up the first section, the pattern remains very much the same. On the one hand, Mahlke appears to consolidate his position beyond question. His general prowess in the water makes him, in the book's explicit formula, 'the great swimmer and diver Joachim Mahlke' (39; *44*), and earns him a 'legendary reputation' within the school (31; *35*). There is also a whole series of events that exhibit and enhance his singular pre-eminence : his recovery and repair of the gramophone, his prevention of the contraceptive joke, his demonstrative devouring of the tinned frogs' legs, his superlative performance in the masturbation episode. And similarly it is Mahlke who is always first to the boat, Mahlke alone who can reach the submerged wardroom, Mahlke who is best at reciting details of the world's warships, Mahlke who first introduces or even invents the pompom craze. The episode in Chapter Four is particularly expressive, when Pilenz's two girl-cousins are taken out to see Mahlke on the ice-covered wreck : Pilenz and Schilling – despite themselves – extol their classmate's exploits and fame as a diver ('Tauchertaten' and 'Taucherruhm', 51-2; *58-9*), the two girls address him as 'Herr Mahlke' and call him 'Sie' instead of 'du', and their two escorts are made to look small indeed : 'He turned us into shivering little boys with running noses, standing there definitely on the edge of things' (52; *59*). But betwixt and between these various assertions of the hero's pre-eminence, the bleak underlying reality is repeatedly apparent. Chapter Two opens with Mahlke's desperately serious desire to become a professional clown; there is a tell-tale cluster of the clown, suffering, and saviour motifs (– among others; 25; *28*), and the caricature incident makes the same kind of point; Chapter Three begins by observing that Mahlke should have 'repaired' his Adam's apple; the attack on his throat is twice recalled (32, 43-4; *35, 49*). The masturbation episode is doubly trenchant : it does enable Mahlke to out-perform his class-mates yet again, but it also represents a clear symbolic lapse on his part, and points to the essential impotence of his will : whereas communal masturbation is just a harmless pastime for the other boys (a 'Sport' and 'Spielchen', 38, 39; *44*), Mahlke has always abstained from it, just as he has always abstained from joining in the grim excremental cycle involving the seagulls and the boys' excrement-filled spittle; but Tulla drives him into betraying his standards – to the voracious delight of the gulls (41; *47*).[21] The sharp significance of all this is characteristically emphasised through Mahlke's own manifest reaction : his Adam's apple suddenly goes wild ('geriet ausser Rand und Band', 39; *45*), and he hits Tulla in the face – just as he hits

134

the caricaturist at the close of the chapter, and Klohse towards the end of the book (acts of violence which, like his actions in the war, also demonstrate the unviableness of his inherited humanity).

In Chapter Four, which prepares the way for the new developments of the second section of the narrative, Mahlke's fundamentally hopeless situation is made more patent than ever, in that he is virtually bereft of his disguise of excellence: the winter ice has deprived him of his boat, of his main sphere of distinction, and when he treks out to cut a hole in the ice above the hatchway, his relationship to the boat shows itself to be reduced to the same remote, insubstantial form that marks his relationship to his father and to the Virgin Mary. It is in this chapter, too, that he is so expressively figured as a clown striding resolutely but pathetically through the snow in his suffering and his 'monumental solitude' (49; 56-7). And as we have seen: the whole first section closes as it began with an evocation not of Mahlke's excellence, but of his infinite vulnerability in the form of his agitated, exposed and all too easily graspable mouse.

We know that it is Mahlke's awareness, and his consequent powerful will to attain freedom, that are the driving force behind his actions – but it is striking how many pointers there are in this first section to the intensity of his will. A dynamic and urgent intent is implicit, for instance, simply in the remarkable difference between Mahlke's rapidly achieved preeminence, and his previous sickly state, a general sickliness that had not only meant his being excused from school gymnastics and swimming (8, 11), but had even caused him to be sent to school a year later than normal (28; 31). But the descriptions of his actions convey his determination most clearly of all: he is 'grimly determined' (8; 11) in his efforts to learn to ride a bicycle, 'earnest and dedicated' (9; 12) in his swiming practice, and 'fanatical' (36; 39) in his diving off the wreck, while his face is described in the intense 'cluster' passage towards the beginning of Chapter Two as 'gently resolute' (25; 28). As for his general activity on the boat, this is no idle boyish pastime, but a deliberate and arduous task: 'Mahlke didn't make things easy for himself: while we dozed on the boat, he worked under water' (14; 17).

The boat itself has a key role in these first four chapters: like the Knight's Cross later on, it serves as the focus for Mahlke's will and energy ('It provided you, Joachim Mahlke, with a goal'; 35; 38), and it is only when Mahlke, as yet unable to master swimming, hears the other boys' fabulous tales of the wreck that he gets a 'mighty stimulus', and 'swims his way to freedom' within a fortnight. As we know, the other and much more intensive 'focussing' device here (and elsewhere) is the Adam's apple motif. The most evident mark of this is the succession of disguises with which Mahlke attempts to distract attention from his 'mouse': screwdriver, Mary medallion, ironmongery, 'various amulets' ('Klimbim'), tin-opener, 'bits and pieces around his neck' ('Klamotten am Hals'), 'pendants on strings, bootlaces and chains', 'pompoms', the scarf with its clownishly enormous safety-pin. In the classic formulation towards the beginning of Chapter Two: 'he always had something or other dangling from his neck to distract the eternal cat from the eternal mouse.' (25; 28). But as well as this adoption of sheer physical disguises, it is also the case – as I have already argued – that Mahlke's whole struggle for freedom, and with it his every action, is expressed in terms of his urge to defeat the implications of his throat.

The Second Section: Chapters Five to Eight

In this second section of the book the narrative pattern changes considerably, in the sense that there is very much less dynamism than before. The first four chapters covered a period of more than two years, and concerned Mahlke's drastic change from being 'nothing' to being seemingly 'everything'. But Chapters Five to Eight cover a period of only some six months, and involve a phase of reaction and reorientation rather than of action.

Chapter Four, we noted, marked a low point for Mahlke; for one thing, the boat was denied him by the weather; for another, he began to run out of adequate decoys for his throat ('the winter must have been hard for him because diving was out and the pompoms had lost their efficacy'; 49; 56). It is this state of things that is echoed in the opening paragraph of Chapter Five, with its emphasis on Mahlke's dissatisfaction with the pompoms but lack of anything better (59; 68) – but this is just by way of a contrastive introduction to the critical new departure which immediately ensues: within a dozen or so lines, we are confronted first with the speech-making ex-pupil bearing around his neck the Knight's Cross, the 'begehrten Bonbon' ('*coveted lozenge*'), and then with Mahlke's hectic response – expressed, as always, through purely tacit, outward means: Mahlke's ears turn bright red as he sits watching and listening with the rest of the school, he sits stiffly back, and he rips off his pompoms and throws them on the floor (59-60; 68-9). This reaction in itself, and the forceful rhythm with which it is described, make the point very clearly: from now on, all Mahlke's will and energies will be focussed on one thing: the Knight's Cross – and we see at the beginning of the next chapter that even the sunken boat has been supplanted as his goal, for he proves to be no more interested in going out to the boat than he is in continuing to make use of the pompoms (67; 76).

But this is not all there is of Mahlke's response to the ex-pupil and his medal. A three-line paragraph tells how the end of the speech is followed by tumultuous applause from the assembled school – but not from Mahlke (63; 72). Mahlke's awareness and separateness are vividly apparent here, for this refusal to applaud plainly reflects his conscious, egregious re-jection of that glorification of war and destruction that the young officer and his medal symbolise – and this is strongly reinforced at the close of the sub-division, when Grass has Mahlke utter substantially his first words of the book (64; 73); for as I have already argued, these lines make sense only when read as a lament by the humanitarian Mahlke at the gross inflation of the 'glory/destruction' equation.

However, Grass also has Mahlke show a further marked reaction to the situation:

Er schwitzte ... Noch nie, selbst in der Turnhalle nicht, hatte ich Mahlke schwitzen sehen ... Mahlkes Angströhren, diese zwei, vom siebten Halswirbel gegen den ausladenden Hinter-kopf stossenden Muskelstränge, glühten und perlten. (64)

He was sweating ... Never, not even in the gym, had I seen

Mahlke sweat. It stood out in beads on Mahlke's fear cords, those two bundles of sinew running from the seventh verte-bra of his neck to the base of his jutting occiput. (73)

That this description is loaded with meaning is clear from the sheer insistence on the fact of Mahlke's sweating, and from the explicit emphasis on its uniqueness ('Mahlke didn't sweat even at the parallel bars'; 12; *15*). As for the nature of this meaning, it is the odd word 'Angströhre' that gives the reader the necessary signal. If it were not for the explanatory phrase that follows it, the German reader would be puzzled indeed, for the word is an archaic colloquialism for 'top hat', and normally has nothing to do with human anatomy;[22] but the reader is saved from puzzlement by the accompanying defin-ition – and can thus freely take the symbolic point of the word, which is that *fear* is the true cause of Mahlke's profuse and extraordinary sweating, a kind of existential fear that we shall find again at another critical juncture: Mahlke's ultimate dislocation and flight (below, pp. 153 f.). The grounds for this secret fear are easy to see: in this decisive phase of the nar-rative, Mahlke, in opting for the Knight's Cross to the virtual exclusion of all lesser things such as the pompoms and the like, and his feats on the wreck, makes one of his most critical choices, second only, perhaps, to his initial decision to seek freedom and his final decision to give up and flee. And it is a choice that enmeshes him absolutely in absurdity; for his essen-tial spirit is the humanitarian one of his father and of the Virgin Mary, and yet the only apparent path to freedom entails the most flagrant violation of that spirit. And it is appropriately in this context that we find the novella's sharpest image of Mahlke in his plight as a futile 'hero against absurdity': the depiction of him as a pathetic, ineffectual clown, striding through the winter twilight bedecked with the 'miserable makeshifts' ('billigem Ersatz') of his luminous shapes, and trying desperately to distract attention from his 'Leid', from 'this full fruit' which he imagines all are out to grasp and yet which would have remained unnoticed had he himself not drawn attention to it (65; 74). What is also apt is that this depiction, with its emphatic end-of-chapter evocation of the bleak reality from which Mahlke will in fact never be able to free himself, constitutes a return of the ironic pattern so characteristic of the earlier section (Chapters One to Four); and it is a fresh irony that this evocation of reality, and Mahlke's turn towards his ultimately greatest distinction, should be juxtaposed in this chapter.

Chapter Six, the second chapter of the second section, is in one sense a kind of interlude, in that its substance – the discovery and refurbishing of the wireless cabin – does not form part of the central action : Mahlke's search for an adequate 'counterweight', for something that will counterbalance the implications of his throat. But the chapter has an integral function nonetheless: it helps to illuminate Mahlke's current state; it prepares the way for the catastrophe; and it creates an effective lull before the two chapters that constitute both the centrepiece and the disguised crisis of the book.

Mahlke's reorientation away from his previous activities is made plainer still in the short sub-division that opens the chapter. Originally it was Mahlke who pleaded to be allowed to join the other boys in their swim out to the wreck, and when he did join them, he wore a screwdriver round his neck as a (vain) decoy, and drove himself on, 'hideously contorted' (25; 28), ahead of everyone else. Now, however, the situation is pointedly different. It is the others who pester Mahlke to join them, and he does so only against his will ('widerwillig'); as for his manner of swimming: 'He swam without his screw-driver, stayed between us, two arms' length behind Hotten Sonntag, and for the first time I saw him swim calmly without contortions or splashing.' (67; 76). Once on board the wreck, he shows complete indifference, especially as regards his erst-while prime activity of diving ('no one could persuade him to dive'). There are two other pointers in this finely detailed little sub-division, both concerning his reaction to submarines sur-facing in the bay: they alone arouse him from his indifference; but he takes no part in the others' enthusiastic waving to the crewmen coming out on deck (68; 77). We are clearly to infer that Mahlke is aroused because submarining is one means of winning a Knight's Cross (as will shortly be evidenced by the lieutenant commander), but that he no more endorses its cruel implications than he did those of air warfare when he refused to join in applauding the *Luftwaffe* lieutenant.

As already suggested, the episode of Mahlke's discovery and

dedicated refurbishing of the wireless cabin, which takes up virtually all the remaining pages of this chapter, is not intended to have a dynamic function, and we have discussed its implications in earlier contexts, in particular the role of the wireless cabin as a potential refuge. One other aspect of these pages, however, is decidedly relevant: once again, there are repeated evocations of the destructive background reality. Mahlke may surpass the others with his lone access to the wireless cabin (though it is later suggested that Störtebeker may have invaded his hideaway! – 110, 116; *121, 127*), he may have his secret 'plans' and refurbish the cabin 'according to plan' (71; *80-1*), and he may be in an 'aggressive good humour' (73; *82*) – but the real order of things prevailing behind these appearances shows through incontrovertibly in the motifs of the seagulls and their excrement, in the attendant signs of the war, and in the other boys' extreme ambivalence towards the hero, so powerfully expressed at the close of the chapter. And it is Mahlke himself, of course, who recognises that he may well need a bolt-hole, and who recites the novella's ominous theme song, the *Stabat Mater dolorosa*. Then finally, almost as the last lines of the chapter, the key motif of Mahlke's throat is again introduced: 'What's he going to do now? I bet you he's got a sore throat again. I'm taking all bets: some day he's going to hang himself, or he'll get to be something really big, or invent something terrific.' (77; *86*). And the last sentence of this is at once both ironic and prefigurative: in positing two apparently contrary alternatives, it in fact anticipates both sides of Mahlke's dual destiny: his acquisition of highest honours, and his ultimate abandoning of everything.

The crucial developments that make Chapters Seven and Eight the major turning point of the book are signalled without delay: the short first paragraph of Chapter Seven (incidentally the only chapter with no sub-divisional breaks) tells us not only of the bemedalled naval officer's appearance in the school hall, but also of his decisive effect: he causes the abrupt end of Mahlke's renewed activity on the wreck, and he 'gave all conversations about Mahlke a new, though not fundamentally new, turn' (79; *88*). The sentence is phrased with nicety: Mahlke's interest in the Knight's Cross is 'new' only so far as other people and their 'conversations' are concerned – the reader knows that in truth it goes back some six months to the air-force lieutenant and his speech; and this interest is not 'fundamentally new' because of course it relates to the driving motif of Mahlke's Adam's apple.

Grass has Mahlke's reactions to the second ex-pupil and his medal follow just the same ambivalent pattern as his reaction to the first, and thus considerably strengthens the impact of these chapters and puts their cardinal importance beyond doubt. Just as he abstained from applauding the fighter-pilot (and waving to the submarine crews), so he avoids joining in the admiring laughter around the lieutenant commander (86; 96); there is an extra detail, too: Mahlke is described as not wanting to go to the speech of honour at all, and as having to be virtually dragged along by Pilenz (80; 89). A major part of Mahlke's response on the earlier occasion was his crisis of fear (or so at least we inferred) – and there is just the same element here except that the physical token of it is trembling in place of sweating (80, 81; 89, 90). As with the earlier passage in Chapter Five, the inference of fear seems all the more founded when considered in the light of the narrative's final stages: the fugitive Mahlke is described not only as sweating, but as trembling too (164, 168; *177, 181*), and in the later context fear is explicitly mentioned (161; *174-5*; one thinks inevitably of Kierkegaard's *Fear and Trembling* – all the more so since Kierkegaard is specifically invoked in the book through Mahlke himself).

As for the other side of Mahlke's response – his powerful attraction to the Knight's Cross – this is only fleetingly expressed in the first half of Chapter Seven: the bemedalled officer is said to look in Mahlke's direction in the school hall, and 'Mahlke zuckte, fühlte sich wohl erkannt' (81; '*Mahlke jumped, feeling no doubt that he had been recognised*', 90); the reader himself infers the missing explanation: Mahlke imagines himself recognised as an aspirant to that same supreme distinction which the ex-pupil on the stage already possesses. The scene changes to the school gymnasium, and the intense degree to which Mahlke's energies and will are now aroused is conveyed by well-tried means: he is described as being contorted and horribly ugly in his strenuous exertions to equal the ex-pupil's exhibitionist prowess on the horizontal bar (87; 96) – for it was just such an ugly contortedness that signalled

141

his original will to be pre-eminent in both gymnastics and swimming (12, 25; *15*, 28. See also below, page 143). But there is a physical indicator of another kind, too: after his horrible contortions on the horizontal bar, Mahlke's Adam's apple dances about like some mad and persecuted thing ('tanzte ... toll und wie gestochen', 87; *96*), and thus the reader is reminded once more of the real object of all Mahlke's endeavours. This is reinforced in the last phase of the chapter, concerning the missing Knight's Cross: once the narrative has fixed on Mahlke as the person responsible (89, 90; *98, 99*), there is a whole page that concentrates on him and his Adam's apple: first his vain attempts to button up his collar over his 'distinguishing mark', and then, as the very last of his 'everyday' decoys, his donning of the tie with its enormous knot.

Chapter Eight, although of cardinal importance, is somewhat similar to Chapter Six in functioning for most of its extent in static rather than dynamic terms: in its first, ten-page sub-division, no significant change or development intervenes at all, and it is only in the two short sub-divisions at the close that we are presented with succinct – and critical – developments.

In the long first sub-division (the longest unit in the book except for Chapter Seven), there is a splendid suspension effect, as if the story were being held still a while at the top of its arc before being allowed to start on its downward sweep. For the first few pages the narrative marks time with more or less peripheral details, and it is only from page 99 (*108*) that it begins to turn to central issues, above all the evocation of Pilenz's ambivalent and ambiguous relationship to his 'friend' (100 f.; *109 f.*) which we have already variously discussed. Then towards the end of the sub-division, there is the depiction of Mahlke almost deliriously enjoying his first, if only token, taste of what a Knight's Cross might do for him; in the book's precise formulation: 'For the first time the Adam's apple which as I still believe ... was Mahlke's motor and brake, had found its exact counterweight.' (103; *112*).

In the two-and-a-half-page sub-division that follows, the story begins to gather momentum once again, and it is characteristically Mahlke's forceful will that is the motive power: regardless of Pilenz's attempts to dissuade him, Mahlke is resolutely bent on carrying out his own intentions, and goes to Klohse to admit having taken the medal – with the result that he is promptly expelled. The short sub-division that closes the chapter (and so also the whole second section) is devoted exclusively to this one event of Mahlke's expulsion, and this helps to establish its critical importance; for although it seems harmless enough at first, and is indeed played down by Pilenz in the final paragraph, it is none the less this event which will ultimately lead to Mahlke's undoing.

But this episode does leave the reader with an even bigger conundrum than usual: *why* does Mahlke make his fatal confession at all? The hero's actions are never explained in as many words, but they are all readily comprehensible in terms of his general awareness combined with his specific drive to counteract the implications of his vulnerable spot – all, that is to say, except this critical confession, which certainly has nothing to do with distracting attention from his 'mouse'.[23] It seems to me that there is only one explanation that we may reasonably cobble together from the narrative as a whole – namely that Mahlke's confession bears out the ethical base to his awareness, and that it is all of a piece with such acts as his prevention of the contraceptive prank, his abstention from the masturbation sessions, his rescue of the half-drowned youngster from within the wreck. Once again here, Grass's speech 'Über meinen Lehrer Döblin' supplies us with a fitting concept, for in the same passage in which he spoke of Döblin's 'heroes against absurdity', he also described them as having 'Kierkegaard's honesty': is it not just such a radical and deliberate honesty that we are to infer in Mahlke when he admits to removing the medal?[24]

Returning to Chapter Eight as a whole, it has one other striking feature: Grass again makes the narrative taut with irony. It would appear on the one hand that Mahlke is close to freedom at last: he has found a full 'counterweight' in the Knight's Cross, his Adam's apple quietly sleeps beneath the skin of his neck (103; *112*), he himself prances about with gay abandon for the first time ever, and whereas he had swum out to the boat 'frantically and with much splashing and foaming ('wild und mit viel Schaum', 97; *107*), he goes back to the shore at a steady, well-balanced pace ('in ausgeglichenem Tempo', 105; *114*). It is here, too, that he is first aggrandised

143

as 'the Great Mahlke', a designation that is repeated as much as four times in ten lines (97; *106*).[25] And Pilenz describes him in the middle of his joyous cavortings as having lost his normal saviour-sufferer countenance (104; *113*). Such is the emphatic appearance – but an appearance that is belied by a different reality. At the close of the very first paragraph of the chapter, Joachim Mahlke's true position is laconically shown: 'Dir war nicht zu helfen' (95; *'You were beyond help'*, *104*) – an expression that is used on no fewer than three other occasions in the book (37, 133, 151; *43*, *145*, *163*). Other intimations of reality are the prominent motifs of the boat's rust, and the seagulls and their excrement. But the clearest signs of the truth are in the lines dwelling on Pilenz's relationship to the hero. For one thing, the prime symbolic event of the novella is cited again for the first time in almost sixty pages, when Pilenz tells how he is still in thrall to the memory of his 'friend', and how he continually talks about him to Father Alban – and about 'cat and mouse and mea culpa' (101; *110*). This not only firmly re-asserts the cat-and-mouse pattern, it also implies its eventual outcome in the words 'mea culpa', and this is taken up again in the telling passage that opens the second sub-division of the chapter, when Pilenz laments that if Mahlke had hidden the medal, or if he had never become involved in Mahlke ' – then I should not have to write now and say to Father Alban: "Was it my fault if Mahlke later ..."' (104; *114*). From these things, as from the whole pattern of the book so far, it is plain that the confident poise and grandeur of the Great Mahlke are just as sharp an irony as the initial one when he appeared to swim his way to freedom. And it is apt indeed that this characteristic pattern of irony should add its force to the critical centre of the book.

The Third Section: Chapters Nine to Eleven

In the first chapter of this third section there is just one major development: Mahlke joins the war. Already in the second paragraph we gather that he, alone amongst all his class-mates, has volunteered for pre-military training, and later in the chapter, when Pilenz sees him for the first time since his expulsion, Mahlke himself admits to having volunteered for war-service in the tank corps; and when Grass has him say: 'That's the only branch that still has a chance' (116; 127), we recognise at once what this bears on: his single goal of the Knight's Cross.

Once more in this chapter, the reader is carefully kept in suspense: the five-page opening sub-division, the longest in Chapter Nine, tells of many things – of Pilenz's interest in Tulla, of Störtebeker's possible invasion of the wireless cabin, of Pilenz's ambivalence towards his 'friend', etc., etc. – but tells us conspicuously little of Joachim Mahlke (the fiction being that he is away at his pre-military training). Suddenly though, in the opening lines of the next sub-division, he is there in close-up again, and a powerful sequence ensues – powerful, because it adds yet more to the ironic tension between bleak reality and the aspirations and attitude of the hero.

As the closing paragraph of this second sub-division, there is the longest piece of direct speech from Mahlke so far, and its mood is beautifully created in the lines that introduce it:

Er ... lachte auf neue Art ungezwungen, plauderte, plauderte. Er, der Einsilbige, sprach übers Wetter – Altweibersommer, goldene Fäden in der Luft – und begann unvermittelt ... im gleichen Plauderton zu berichten: (115)

He ... laughed in a free and easy way that was completely new, and talked and talked. He who was always so monosyllabic talked of the weather – Indian summer, threads of gold in the air – then suddenly, in the same conversational tone ... : (126-7)

With his cheerful, easy manner, Mahlke would seem to have become a new person, to have found liberty after all, and this appearance takes clearer shape in what he chattily says to Pilenz (116; 127). He mentions having volunteered for active service, but immediately side-tracks by alleging that he little likes the war and little understands his own volunteering. And he carries on in just the same dismissive way: he professes to believe that his choice of the tank corps is a bit silly and pointless, and that his erstwhile wish to be a clown was a childish

145

whim, implies that he could not care less about his enforced change of school, and claims to be unconcerned about Störtebeker's reputed invasion of the wireless cabin. Most important of all, though, the 'Great Mahlke' speaks of the cat's attack on his 'mouse' – but speaks of it as if it were some remote bit of history, and describes his consequent fixation on his Adam's apple as a nonsensical aberration from which he has long since recovered. But this appearance is manifestly spurious. For one thing, the reader knows full well that Mahlke in reality does have a driving purpose in joining the war; and if Mahlke's professed attitude towards school and boat seems unconvincing enough even here, it will be completely belied by his subsequent actions in the final chapters of the book. But the most clamorous lines in this passage are those on the Adam's apple/cat-and-mouse motif, for they are a strident irony: whereas Mahlke claims to have put the whole business behind him, these very lines – addressed to Pilenz of all people – are the first since the novella's opening to re-tell the original symbolic act in any detail, and to make it a present reality again. This irony is heightened, too, by what has gone before it in the sub-division; for it is there that Mahlke rashly lets his throat be 'bare and defenceless', allowing Pilenz to fix his gaze on that 'restless mouse ... which had once attracted a cat and tempted me into putting the cat on his neck'.

The third and fourth sub-divisions of the chapter are unremarkable for any particular development of the action; but whereas the third has a kind of local, consolidating function, it is not too much to say that with the fourth (118-19; 129-30) Grass contrives with brilliant, poignant effect to confirm what is perhaps the novella's most significant dimension. For what we are offered here is a kind of prose poem, a sombre and beautifully rhythmed elegy that goes far beyond the immediate action of the story and gives new shape to one of the early Grass's fundamental themes: the grim relationship between sameness and sterility in social living, and the brutal spirit that animated National Socialism; a relationship expressed in the passage's arc from the deadly sameness of the Osterzeile houses with their ornamental frogs and sentimental bird houses, to a driving evocation of what is termed the 'prevailing stench of corpses', the 'vorherrschenden Leichengeruch'. Without going into all the poetry of these fifty lines, we can but note such prominent

146

devices as the verbal echoings of sameness, the persistent use of pairs to evoke sameness (especially in the second sentence), the incessant rhythmic flow. The opening sentence is particularly expressive on account of its triadic stress pattern, its suspensions and rhythmic repeats, its extensive use of long vowels. The triadic structure of this first sentence is then also used for the piece as a whole, with its three distinct sections of *circa* seventy, sixty-four and seventy stressed syllables (the second section beginning at 'Schritte', '*steps*', the third at 'man sollte glauben', '*It might be supposed*'). And of course the crucial words – 'vorherrschenden Leichengeruch' – are suspended to the very end of the piece, and to the end of a sentence of twenty-six lines.

Quite apart from anything else, this sub-division is the only passage of intense writing in the book that does not bear directly on the specific characters and events of the story. But that is precisely what gives it its particular force, for it helps to demonstrate that the fable of Joachim Mahlke relates inherently to its setting of time and place: as I shall shortly try to show, there is a necessary link in *Cat and Mouse* between the (presumable) death of its protagonist, and the 'prevailing stench of corpses' that it ascribes to National Socialist Germany.

In the final sub-division of Chapter Nine – Pilenz's Sunday tea with the Mahlkes – the sombre spirit of the 'Leichengeruch' passage is carried on in a sense, but with direct reference to the hero and his frail situation, as is at once conveyed by the opening paragraph with its image of Mahlke's hair collapsing from careful orderedness into trembling ruin. This is a tableau part of the narrative, however, not a dynamic one, and we have already considered its various effects, above all the symbolic confrontation of 'cat' and 'mouse', and the crucial story in the chapter's last lines of the constructive heroism of Mahlke's father – in contradistinction to the son's aspirations. Again here, the book's irony is sharply apparent:

Fast möchte ich mich erinnern, Mahlke erwähnte lachend ... seine, wie er es nannte, weit zurückliegenden Halsgeschichten, brachte auch – und Mutter wie Tante lachten mit – das Katzenmärchen zum Vortrag: diesmal setzte ihm Jürgen Kupka das Biest an die Gurgel ... (122)

I almost seem to remember that ... Mahlke laughingly men-

tioned the old nonsense about his neck, as he put it, and
even went so far – his mother and aunt joined in the laughter
– as to tell the story about the cat: this time it was Jürgen
Kupka who put the cat on his throat ... (133)

Mahlke may laugh and dismiss his 'Halsgeschichten' as mere by-
gones. But the narrative logic is such that the reader is well
aware that the hero is still secretly driven by the same old compulsion – and that he is bound to fail in the end. It is indeed the
stench of corpses, like the rust and excrement layering the
wreck, that is the dominant reality.

We have already dwelt on the poignant tableau in the first
sub-division of Chapter Ten: the portentous, thorn-wreathed
confrontation of the two chief characters. Not that this passage
functions exclusively at the symbolic level of the book's cat/
mouse, Cain/Abel, Judas/Jesus pattern: it is also finely expressive in terms of the quotidian, surface level of the story, in that
it creates the precise mood of a failed relationship, of a lack of
any positive bond between the two boys – 'and the distance
between us increased' (128; *139*). In this, the passage helps to
back up Pilenz's persecutor role with a strong psychological
motivation: here, as elsewhere, he is figured as one who is
incapable of achieving warm, balanced, fulfilling relationships,
and in whom the vindictiveness born of frustration would be
thoroughly in character. We know this kind of situation well
from *The Tin Drum*, where Oskar's vicious attempts to kill
Maria's foetus were actions of just this order; and we shall find
the same thing on a systematic scale in *Dog Years* in the person
of Walter Matern.

Mahlke's hectic activity and brilliant successes on the Russian
front: this is what is chiefly recounted in the following sub-
division (128 f.; *139* f.) – and the description of him as being
'at it again' ('Mahlke [war] wieder am Zug', 131; *142*) further
emphasises that his present activity is indeed a continuation of
all he has undertaken before. The Great Mahlke is clearly
advancing towards his most grandiose triumph – but in Pilenz's
dark words at the close of the sub-division: 'Nothing changes
around here' (133; *144*): reality is ever-present, not least in the
person of Pilenz himself. And it is on just such a note that the
sub-division begins, with Pilenz remarking that during Mahlke's

148

year-long absence at the Front, the sight of a cat automatically reminded him of the 'mouse' – whereupon he professes to be undecided whether to protect the mouse or encourage the cat (128; *140*). Then at the end, Mahlke's hopeless predicament is stressed with great force in a trenchant single-paragraph sub-division that brings the whole chapter to a close. And the same expression is used that we have noted elsewhere: Mahlke is 'beyond help'; for no matter what happens, he cannot escape the logic of his situation – above all the logic of 'die Katze und die Maus' (133; *145*).

The ironic pattern continues in Chapter Eleven, the climactic chapter of the section – with the effect that what seems to be Mahlke's most glorious triumph is in fact the promise of his end. There is a strong build-up to Mahlke's supreme distinction: the flashback to his time at the Labour Service camp that magnifies his separateness and his pre-eminence (138 f.; *152* f.). Once again, the enormity of his hair, his ears, his genitals, his Adam's apple is evoked, and we are told of two typical feats: his calm recalcitrance towards the C.O. and relationship with his wife, and his discovery of the arms cache (which earned him a preliminary medal). The flashback is soon followed by the first intimation that Mahlke has made it at last, that he has won the Knight's Cross and so battled his way through to the only 'exact counterweight' for his vulnerable throat (141; *155*); and this is confirmed in the two echoing paragraphs of the chapter's final sub-division: 'A former labour service man from Tuchel-North battalion, serving first as a simple gunlayer, then as a sergeant and tank-commander, always in the thick of battle ... and so on and so on', and 'A son of our city, always in the thick of battle, first as a simple gunlayer, then as a tank-commander, and so on and so on.' (142-3; *156*). But this story of success – abrupt and oblique and begrudging enough in itself – is punctuated by paragraphs of a contrary indication: between the flashback and the first intimations of Mahlke's Knight's Cross is a paragraph that not only describes the hero's erstwhile class-mates as quasi-conspirators in their attitude towards him, but also includes the image of a cat crouching in wait for its prey (141; *154*); then between the first suggestion of the Knight's Cross and its final confirmation is an emphatic paragraph of tumbling dialogue that recapitulates Mahlke's frantic struggles, reaching further and further back in time until it fixes on the crucial event of the opening paragraph – and drives home Pilenz's part in it (142; 155-6). This most extensive recapitulation so far of the opening event has a double function: it dramatically highlights the persecution theme once more, and it prepares the way for the new cycle of cat and mouse imagery that ensues at the start of Chapter Twelve and goes on to epitomise the catastrophe. Apart from all this, however, there is another decisive pointer in Chapter Eleven that belies the hero's achievements: it is here that Pilenz symbolically tries to obliterate his 'friend' when he hacks away the poignant inscription: 'MAHLKE STABAT MATER DOLOROSA ...'

The Fourth Section:
Chapters Twelve and Thirteen

In its movement, this final phase of the narrative is sharply different from all that has gone before it: whereas the first eleven chapters covered some four and a half years and described Mahlke's slow ascent to supreme distinction, the last two chapters amount to a rapid catastrophe that is all over in a matter of days.

The rout is prefaced in characteristic fashion, however, in that Grass first of all steadily inflates the balloon of irony to bursting point: Mahlke, with his Knight's Cross dangling around his neck, is shown as being full of the illusion that he is free at last, and that his 'chronic throat troubles' (147; 160) are finally cured. All his words to Pilenz as they wait for Klohse in the school corridor connote the blind assumption that he is already safely back within the pale, and that his speech-of-honour, like those of the air force and naval ex-pupils, will follow as a matter of course: 'My speech is ready, every word of it.', 'I'll look in later with Klohse, we'll have to discuss the seating arrangement on the platform.', 'Have a little patience, my dear Pilenz: all the problems associated with the bestowing of the medal will be discussed in my lecture.' (148; 161). The whole dialogue is tense with irony, what with Mahlke's extravagant confidence and stilted language, and Pilenz's rhythmic refrain concerning headmaster Klohse's supposed response: 'He'll be very pleased.' But the balloon promptly bursts: all Mahlke's expectations, both immediate and profound, are confuted when Klohse arrives and first ignores him, then makes it clear that, Knight's Cross or no Knight's Cross, he still remains *persona non grata* for the Conradinum (149-50; 162-3). With this, Mahlke's undoing is certain, and indeed the whole first sub-division of the chapter, as well as re-asserting all the cardinal motifs of Mahlke's father and the Virgin Mary, of Adam's apple, centre parting, saviour and clown, fairly bristles with evocations of threatening reality: the tableau of Pilenz and Mahlke, Cain and Abel, once more in confrontation with one another (146 f.; 159 f.),[26] but above all the persistent image of the cat creeping up on its prey, and steadily acquiring 'more and more significance' (149; 162) throughout the passage, while the 'mouse' at Mahlke's throat, at first asleep and at peace, slowly wakes up to the danger besetting it.

The sub-division that follows is one of the novella's most critical, in the sense that it is here that the story finally tips over to its conclusion. In narrative terms: after more than four and a half years, the hero demonstratively and irrevocably abandons his struggle for freedom. The beginning of the sub-division tells of Pilenz's various attempts at making alternative arrangements for Mahlke's speech. But Mahlke is interested only in appearing within the community of his own old school ('from the start he had but one aim in mind: the auditorium of our school'; 152; 165) – and this is soon ruled out completely: Klohse's refusal is confirmed by higher authority, and Klohse even puts it to Mahlke that it would perhaps be proper for him not to impose himself on the Horst Wessel school either (the school he had gone to after his expulsion) – 'he might prefer, like a true hero, to choose the better part of speech and remain silent.' (154; 167). Mahlke's response to this situation is clear-cut and irreversible: 'And taking the advice Klohse had given him in his letter, Mahlke chose the better part of speech, heroic silence; without a word he struck the headmaster's smoothshaven face left right with the back and palm of his hand.' (155; 168). This is a decisive act of Mahlke's, and it is essential for the reader to see it in its proper light. Emil Ottinger, in his criminological study of the book, makes the fundamental mistake of seeing Klohse and his society as proper and legitimate, and Mahlke as a 'schizoid', a 'delinquent', a 'schizophrenic hypochondriac' who is venting a mere 'vengeful defiance' ('Vergeltungstrotz') in his wanton 'aggressiveness' against his headmaster.[27] This is clearly wrong. In Grass's own words in an interview, Mahlke's calculated treatment of Klohse is 'eine erwachsene Tat' ('*a mature act*').[28] It is a symbolic action that betokens his final turning away from the society which Klohse – National Socialist *Amtsleiter* (party official) as well as head of a supposedly humanistic grammar school – stands for. And similarly: Mahlke turns resolutely away because Klohse's own action in rejecting him was equally symbolic, being the final sign that Mahlke, for all his frenzied struggles and distinction, has no entry to the 'ordered' and 'moral' society of Amtsleiter Klohse, the same society that expels Meyn and Matern from the SA on account of cruelty to animals and petty theft, just as it expels Mahlke from the Conradinum for his fateful peccadillo involving the naval officer's medal. Mahlke's partial awareness and the urgency of his purpose had misled him into striving for an unattainable goal; once disabused, he responds with characteristic determination and energy – but it is too late to extricate himself from the labyrinth, and too late to escape the crouching cat.

From the opening words of the last sub-division in Chapter Twelve, Mahlke is already a fugitive: 'From that point and that moment on, we ran through lifeless suburban streets' (*155*; *168*), and the whole physical setting in the first half of the sub-division is an expressive image of Mahlke's isolation and his irrevocable position outside the community: far from being shown within any firm communal context such as home, school, fraternity of class-mates, Mahlke is seen wandering erratically around the streets accompanied only by his ultimate betrayer. One image in particular concentrates this poignant meaning: the picture of Mahlke pausing in his errancy to stand on bridges, neither Here nor There but suspended in a kind of Nowhere, with the Striessbach beneath him, a filthy, stinking little river rank with leeches, rats and rubbish (*156*; *169*). Another fleeting detail underlines the central theme of isolation: 'Wir ... starrten dann – *und jeder für sich* – in den Bach' (*156*, emphasis added; '*we gazed ... – each for himself – into the stream*', *169*); and this gains extra cogency when we recall the final paragraph of *Dog Years*, where Amsel and Matern are pictured together but infinitely separate – and which ends with words 'Jeder badet für sich.' ('*Each of us baths by himself.*')[29]

The second part of the sub-division – echoing the novella's

beginning with its '. . . and once' (157; *170*) – brings about a fresh development: Mahlke's departure in what the two boys think might be Tulla Pokriefke's tram. This is no casual spicing of the plot: Grass had Pilenz claim at one point that he was keen on Tulla (110, *121*), and later that he tried, in vain, to seduce her (130; *141*) – Mahlke's subsequent claim to have slept with Tulla (161; *174-5*) therefore supplies extra motivation for the other boy's treachery which ensues the same day. Finally, the closing paragraph of the chapter is important too, where Grass has Mahlke imply that he has deserted the army – for this adds to the depiction of Mahlke's settling of accounts with Klohse in showing how the hero has cut himself off completely from society, and thus, after years of delusion, made the outward appearance correspond to the essential reality.

Mahlke as a sacrificial lamb like the crucified Christ: we have already seen how well this is conveyed in the opening paragraph of the final chapter. But the paragraph has another element of the same order: it begins with a resonant piece of liturgy: 'Misereatur vestri omnipotens Deus, et, dimissis peccatis vestris . . .' (159; *172*); then again: 'Indulgentiam, absolutionem et remissionem peccatorum vestrorum . . .' The 'sin' that Grass doubly evokes here is no metaphysical, religious thing, but something existential, that constant drive in men to afflict one another, the drive that this novella exemplifies in the relationship of Pilenz and Mahlke, Cat and Mouse – ' "Misereatur vestri omnipotens Deus, et, dimissis peccatis vestris . . ." hob es sich seifenblasenleicht von Hochwürden Gusewskis gespitztem Mund . . . und . . . spiegelte Dich mich alles alles – ' (' *"Misereatur vestri omnipotens Deus, et, dimissis peccatis vestris . . ." The words issued light as a soap bubble from Father Gusewski's pursed lips . . . mirroring you me everything everything – '*). It goes without saying that in this conception of existence the notion of an 'omnipotens Deus' can be nothing but an irony, and the 'peccati mundi' remain an undiminished, unredeemed reality. It is the very absence of Grace that is conveyed by the quoting of the Blessing here, just as the absence of Salvation is connoted by Gusewski's 'Ecce Agnus Dei . . .' rising like a fearfully trembling bubble and falling then to disappear into nothing.

In the ensuing paragraphs figuring Mahlke at the altar-rail the crucial element is the emphasis on his profuse sweating (159-60;

153

173): what we have here, as before, is an oblique but powerful indicator of fear; indeed it is in this context that Grass creates the one passage of the novella that dwells explicitly on the subject of fear (161; *174-5*). Not that Mahlke is physically afraid – there is nothing in the book that remotely suggests such a thing. His is that same kind of existential fear that increasingly possessed Oskar Matzerath, an over-powering sense that the seagulls, the excrement, the cat's attack, the 'Schwarze Köchin' are the true tokens of reality, and that Mahlke's previous basis for action was about as firm and stable as Jan Bronski's house of cards.

The passage of direct speech from Mahlke in which the idea of fear is explicitly introduced is a characteristic one: far from having Mahlke directly express the truth, Grass has him peddle an entirely false impression. As when he casually spoke earlier on of volunteering for the army, etc., he affects great gaiety here; he claims to have had a grand old time with Tulla, declares that it is because of her that he wants to quit – and because he has simply 'done his bit'; he denies being afraid at first, but then admits to it; and maintains that he is going to apply to the authorities for transfer – whereas in reality he has already turned his back on the authorities and their society. The material effect of this blatantly false information is that the reader, as ever, is prevented from taking the narrative façade for granted, and must glean the truth from behind it.

Immediately after this come the first signs of Pilenz's incipient treachery: he refuses to put Mahlke in touch with the Störte-beker gang, turns down his plea to hide in the Pilenz family's cellar – but then himself suggests the wreck. And although he twice claims to want to have nothing to do with it now that Mahlke has deserted ('Ich will nichts damit zu tun haben', 'Aber ich wollte abermals nichts damit zu tun haben', 161, 162; *174, 175*), he in fact scarcely lets Mahlke out of his sight from this point on, on the oft-repeated and blatantly specious grounds that 'Regenwetter verbindet' (161 ff.; *rain is a binder*, *175* ff.). For the first time in the two boys' relationship, it is Mahlke who requires something of the other boy, and who is thus the weaker party. Earlier in the book, Pilenz was shown as being sharply alive to the slightest variation in the power relationship, as on the occasion of the naval officer's speech, when he sniffed a chance to 'get on top' ('Ich witterte für mich Oberwasser', 80; *89*), or again, after Klohse's rejection of the hero, he rejoiced at the sense of once more being on top ('wieder einmal bekam ich Oberwasser', 150; 163) – but in this present case, Pilenz is not just fleetingly on top, but has the other boy completely at his mercy.[30] And his automatic response is to exploit his power, and try to get rid of the pervasive presence that Mahlke has long been for him, just as he tried symbolically to destroy the presence by obliterating the inscription, and just as he will do again when he carries away the photograph of Mahlke's father.

The sequence with the young boys towards the end of the sub-division is penetrating indeed, for at this key juncture, just prior to the hero's disappearance, it brings a last evocation of the paradox that all the hero's calculated campaign of violence and conscious betrayal of his own true spirit have availed him nothing, have delivered him neither from the labyrinth nor *de manibus inimicorum meorum et a persequentibus me*. The whole of Mahlke's present awareness and attendant fear are concentratedly manifest in these few paragraphs: he tells the war-happy young boys of his part in the war 'in a hoarse voice' (163; 176); trembling and sweating overtake him once more; and finally, when the boys harp on the question of Mahlke's army leave, thus touching the raw nerve of his break with society, he tears free and runs away. But perhaps the most telling effect of the passage arises from the way it contrasts Mahlke and the little boys: on the one hand the secure innocence of the children for whom war and destruction are just a game, on the other, the driving, fatal insight of the Great Mahlke, who fell victim to reality through becoming too aware of it.

As for the four other sub-divisions that follow and bring the book to its close, we have already looked at them on various occasions, and seen how effective they are: all the motifs of the book are brought to a head, Pilenz is at his most treacherous and the narrative at its most oblique, Mahlke fulfils his essential victim role, the fable is brought full circle by a re-enactment of the original symbolic persecution. But there is one forceful aspect of this closing phase that does call for extra comment, and that is the typical matter of Joachim Mahlke's outward appearance and behaviour – for there is a most dramatic change in these last pages. Mahlke trembles and sweats and speaks hoarsely while with the boys; he breaks free and runs away pell-mell; he stuffs himself with unripe gooseberries (on the analogy, I suggested, of Agnes Matzerath and her expressive and suicidal diet of fish); he rolls in agony in the sand, and has to be kicked into getting up by his 'friend'; a renewed bout of trembling and sweating again points to fear (168, 169; *181*, *182*). But then, suddenly, the tables are turned once more: as the boat crosses the water, Mahlke begins to sketch his intended speech – and in so doing transforms himself into the Great Mahlke again, and pushes Pilenz back into his wonted inferior status: it is Pilenz who is pouring with sweat by the time they reach the wreck, while Mahlke is calm, relaxed, entirely free of sweat and trembling, and plainly dominant (170; *183-4*). He had removed his grandiose Knight's Cross after the encounter with the boys (165; *178*), but once on the wreck he hangs it round his neck again and strides cheerfully, confidently, about, chatting and joking, as though on top of the world. In its whole tone, this passage strongly echoes the earlier one in Chapter Eight depicting Mahlke's antics on the boat with the naval officer's medal – and it is just as clear here as it was on the other occasion that what is involved is *irony*: by borrowing the officer's Knight's Cross, Mahlke for the first time achieved an 'exact counterweight' for his throat, and falsely concluded that he was within reach of freedom; now, back on the wreck with his own Knight's Cross, he is shown as imagining that, whatever other avenues have been closed to him by Klohse and the rest, at least he is certain to gain freedom of a kind by fleeing the country ('Look at that bucket, the one next to the tanker, she's lying pretty low. I'll bet she's a Swede. Just for your information, we're going to row out there as soon as it gets dark.'; 171; *184*). But only minutes after these words, only minutes after he has seemingly re-asserted himself as the Great Mahlke – he is dead (or rather: presumably dead). And so the novella's ironic counterpoint of imagination and reality is brought to its powerful conclusion, with Grass arranging the fiction so that even Joachim Mahlke's very last act is begotten, like all his significant acts, of a fatal concourse of insight and blindness.

I say 'brought to its conclusion', but this is not strictly correct. For in the one-page tail-piece which so neatly bridges the gap between the past and the narrator's present, Grass adds a final touch to the novella's splendid irony: it is seemingly Pilenz, the Cat, who triumphs when Mahlke's greatest victory has brought him his downfall; but in fact it is the Mouse that has the last laugh, albeit from beyond the grave. Pilenz tried to obliterate the latrine inscription, but the macerated wood inflicted the memory of Mahlke on him even more intolerably than the inscription had done – and so it is here: his attempt to get rid of Mahlke once and for all only makes him a far greater, far more haunting presence than ever before: 'Denn, was mit Katze und Maus begann, quält mich heute' ... (177; *For what began with cat and mouse torments me today*, 190).

CHAPTER VI

Settings of Time and Place: The Unmasking of a Society

Grass could have located his Cat and Mouse fable in any other historical time and place, or he could have given it the indeterminate setting of his early plays – but he chose to bestow on his story the exact time-scale of the Second World War, and to give it the setting not just of National Socialist Danzig and Germany generally, but of precise locales that have a strong symbolic function within the book. The full purpose behind all this will become apparent in due course, but Grass's own comment on the implications of Joachim Mahlke's downfall powerfully reflects the trend: 'Sein Fall decouvriert Kirche, Schule, Heldenwesen – die ganze Gesellschaft. Alles schlägt mit ihm fehl.' ('*His downfall exposes church, school, the hero-business – all of society. In his failure is the failure of everything.*')[31] Whatever else it may be, *Cat and Mouse* is certainly an attempt to highlight a gravely flawed society.

The War

The opening words of the book, with their slight fairy-tale resonance, might seem to invoke a purely fictional time-scale. But of course the true inception of the story, Mahlke's sudden awareness and hectic activity, is not described until the second subdivision – and this real beginning is expressly associated at the very start of the paragraph with the beginnings of the Second World War: 'When shortly after the outbreak of war Joachim Mahlke turned fourteen, he could neither swim nor ride a

158

bicycle, there was nothing striking about his appearance'. Within a few months of the start of hostilities, Mahlke's fateful odyssey is under way, as this same paragraph makes clear – and in the light of the book as a whole, the reader may readily infer a causal connection : the hero's awareness is triggered off by the reality of the War, by this most gross and violent manifestation of the 'Schlacht, die schon dagewesen, die immer wieder kommt' (*'battle that was and will always recur'*). On turning to the other end of the story's time-span, we likewise find that Grass links the close of the tale with the close of the War : Mahlke goes to his presumable death only in June 1944, it is true, but the final paragraph before the tail-piece describes how Pilenz consummates his treachery by burying the photograph of Mahlke's father beneath his underwear and finally losing it in the fighting at Cottbus – fighting that occurred in the closing weeks of the war (and in which Grass himself was taken prisoner by the Americans). Thus both the beginning and the end of the fiction, the inception of Mahlke's spirit and its final symbolic liquidation, are precisely linked to the beginning and end of the historical War (and one also finds that this link is reinforced throughout the narrative in that the time-scale of the War is repeatedly used to express the time-scale of the story).

The relevance of the War is even more marked when it comes to the general physical setting of the story : a continual succession of incidental references ensures that the War is at the very least the unfailing backdrop to the action – references to war-vessels of all kinds, barrage balloons and ack-ack emplacements, Hitler Youth and the BDM, military hospitals and convalescent troops, Stutthof concentration camp and the Todt Organisation, Hitler and Göring, the fighting in Greece, France, Russia, the North – etc., etc. And it will be remembered that the smell that is described as the predominant one throughout all the nation is the stench of death.

As for the characters – and institutions – that Grass places in this belligerent environment, it is a principal feature of the book that their reality of being and doing relates profoundly to the reality of the War. One characteristic detail here is the way that the minds of the various characters, especially the boys, are shown as being imbued with the spirit of the war. Thus for instance there is nothing new that the naval officer can tell Pilenz and his fellows about submarine warfare and its history, for they already know everything off pat (82, 84; *91, 93*), just as they know by heart the vital statistics of most of the world's warships (see especially 33, 156, 172; *36, 169, 185*) – it is worth noting that Mahlke is not only the most proficient at this, but also has his bedroom decked out with two model gun-boats, a photograph of a naval hero, and assorted photographs of 'highly decorated fighter-pilots and Panzer generals' (25, 27; *28, 30*). Even when Pilenz goes to the Mahlkes' for Sunday tea, there is a whole page of conversation centred on the War (121-2; *132-3*); and the young boys who crowd round the fleeing hero towards the end know exactly the geography of the Russian Front, and are hungry for bellicose detail. Undoubtedly the most trenchant instance of war-talk, however, is included in Chapter Four, just before the allusion to the kneeling Mahlke's 'agitated mouse that I might have caught in my hand': the fact that the inimical order of things, in the shape of Heini Pilenz, threatens Mahlke even in the would-be haven of the 'Marienkapelle', is echoed to marvellous effect in the way that the Proper of the mass, the salvationary re-enactment of Christ's sacrifice, is confuted by a dialogue of destruction carried on by the two servers in counter-point to their liturgical responses:

'Introibo ad altare Dei – In welchem Jahre lief der Kreuzer "Eritrea" vom Stapel? – Sechsunddreissig. Besonderheiten? – Ad Deum, qui laetificat juventutem meam. – Einziger italienischer Kreuzer für Ostafrika. Wasserverdrängung? Deus fortitudo mea – Zweitausendeinhundertzweiundsiebzig. Wie-viel Knoten läuft er? – Et introibo ad altare Dei – Weiss nicht. Bestückung? – Sicut erat in principio – Sechs Fünfzehnzenti-meter, vier Siebenkommasechs... Falsch! – et nunc et semper – Richtig. Wie heissen die deutschen Artillerieschulschiffe? – et in saecula saeculorum, Amen – Sie heissen Brummer und Bremse.' (57)

'Introibo ad altare Dei – say, when was the cruiser Eritrea launched? – '36. Special features? – Ad Deum, qui laetificat juventutem meam. – Only Italian cruiser in East African waters. Displacement? – Deus fortitudo mea – 2172 tons. Speed? – Et introibo ad altare Dei – Search me. Armament? – Sicut erat in principio – six 155 millimetre guns, four seventy fives... Wrong! – et nunc et semper – no, it's right.

Names of the German artillery training ships? – et in saecula
saeculorum, Amen. – Brummer and Bremse.' (64)

– and how sharply, ironically relevant the liturgy is: 'as it was in the beginning, is now and ever shall be'; for it applies exactly to the War, 'die Schlacht, die schon dagewesen, die immer wieder kommt'.

One of the most fascinating aspects of the book's treatment of the War is the way that Grass's own humanist feeling at times breaks through the complex narrative apparatus of mirrors, façades etc. – just as it did in *The Tin Drum*, and does again later in *Dog Years*. The most intense and poetic instance of this in the novella is the 'stench of corpses' passage. But we find the same forcefulness, though very differently conveyed, in the key sub-divisions concerning the two ex-pupils' speeches of honour. For what Grass does here, quietly but most tellingly, is to expose the false postures associated with the cult of war and war heroism, postures that conspire to disguise the brute reality of death and devastation. The *Luftwaffe* fighter-pilot describes his deadly activities like some harmless game ('it was pretty much the same as in the old days when we played handball in our good old school playground'; 61; 70), and he makes the whole school laugh with funny stories about parachuting dogs and pyjama-ed pilots – but Grass follows this immediately with the cold douche of reality: 'The lieutenant ... had finished at our school in '36 and was shot down over the Ruhr in '43.' (62; 71). The unmasking effect is much sharper at the end of the pilot's speech, where the narrator is set aside for a moment and Grass's own involvement and concern show clearly through: the pilot, we read (63; 72), jumps directly from a schoolboy joke to a mention of three dead class-mates – justifying their death automatically on the grounds that they have 'doubtless not fallen in vain' – and then jumps just as quickly away from this area of grim reality to round off his speech in a blithe, unthinking way ('leichthin'). A powerful sense of what one can only describe as indignation at such glossing-over of reality comes across from the particular formulations Grass uses in this passage – and this is even more the case when it comes to the submarine commander's speech. The second ex-pupil's killer missions have caused more than 250,000 tons of shipping and their crews to go down to the bottom of the sea (83; 92), but instead of confining himself to this reality, he indulges in grandiose, false evocations of nature, dripping with outrageous similes and metaphors. Grass creates brilliant pastiches which he puts in the man's own mouth (83, 84; *92, 93*); but he also has Pilenz highlight their self-evident absurdity with remarks like: 'When he started brushing in sunsets, it was really embarrassing' (84; *93*), and: ' "So it must be", these were his actual words, "when birds and angels bleed to death" ' (84; *94*); and there is finally a devastating breakdown of the glut of falsehoods with which the officer ends his speech (85; *94*). It scarcely needs to be said, perhaps, that what Grass is so vehemently out to expose in both the episodes in question is just a different form of that same conscious or unconscious posturing, that same fundamental want of integrity in society, that we found so powerfully demonstrated in *The Tin Drum* – and which we shall find again in *Dog Years* in the person of Walter Matern.

It might be noted here that Grass's specific ironisation of the two 'heroic' holders of the Knight's Cross in Chapters Five and Seven has a constant and striking counterpart throughout the novella in general, in the ironic treatment of the Knight's Cross itself. The medal is mentioned on almost innumerable occasions from Chapter Five onwards – but just as Brecht in his *Conversations of a Refugee* persistently and disparagingly speaks of 'Der wie heisst er doch gleich' ('*whatsisname*') instead of 'Hitler', so Grass in *Cat and Mouse* evokes the Knight's Cross only by means of irreverent paraphrases, giving it its proper name only once, and that in the final paragraph, and calling it, among many other things, 'unaussprechlich' (89; *'unutterable'*, *98*), an 'Ausgeburt' (103, 146; *'brainchild'*, but also *'abortion'*, *112, 159*), 'das Ichsprechesnichtaus' (146; *'the Iwillnotutterit'*, *159*). The word 'Ritterkreuz' ('*Knight's Cross*') is of course no ordinary neutral noun, but a highly charged symbol implying a whole received set of values; and Grass's blatant, consistent avoidance of the term is just one more means – like his contrasting of the medals awarded to Mahlke's father and then to Mahlke – of throwing in question the values themselves, and thus of uncovering the 'Heldenwesen', the whole phenomenon of 'heroism' in a war society.

As will be clear, it is in relation to Joachim Mahlke himself that the war motif is most pervasively expressed: war is no mere external context, it is an integral part of the story of Mahlke's struggle.

On the face of it, the early part of Mahlke's struggle – his bicycling, gymnastics and swimming – might appear to have nothing to do with the War. In fact, there is a profound connection even here: as I have suggested, it is the War that triggers off Mahlke's awareness, and which sets him going on his hectic way, a way that will involve him eventually in the most furious battle-front of all. Meanwhile, although his interim activities do not directly concern the War, Grass carefully intimates the essential connection by the location he chooses as the centre of these activities: a warship, a sunken Polish minesweeper that is emphatically established as such by the end of the book's second paragraph – and whose belligerent history is precisely dove-tailed with the story of Mahlke: it played its short, futile role and sank within the opening weeks of the War, just as Mahlke was moving towards his (equally futile) activity (33 f.; 37 f.). Even later on, when it is no longer the persistent centre of action that it was in the first four chapters, the wrecked minesweeper remains an important and symbolic location: it is the setting throughout Chapter Six (concerning the wireless cabin); it is the setting of the crucial episode at the mid-point of the book when Pilenz swims out and joins Mahlke and his borrowed Knight's Cross; and it is the scene of Pilenz's final treachery. It is thus always a token of 'die Schlacht, die schon dagewesen, die immer wieder kommt' – and with its grim seagull denizens, its covering of rust and excrement, its steady decay throughout the time-span of the story, it is also a token of that more embracing order of destructiveness of which eternally recurrent war is just a part. This being so, it is one of the book's more penetrating ironies that Mahlke both at the beginning of this struggle, and then again at the end, fondly imagines that the warship can be his way to freedom.

As I have already tried to show in its various implications, the war motif is a factor of central importance in the second and third sections of the book, the sections on Mahlke and the Knight's Cross. In a sense, though, it is not until the final section that the war motif comes fully into its own. For it is only here, in the context of Mahlke's sudden, abject downfall, that the motif acquires its full ironic and symbolic force. The beginning of the section sets the pattern; for when we see Mahlke again for

163

the first time since the Oliva Castle Park encounter, there is not only an emphatic description of his Knight's Cross, 'das Ding Ding Ding, das Ichsprechesnichtaus' (146; *'the thingamajig, the Iwillnotutterit'*, *159*), but also a page-long description of his Tank Corps uniform, complete with jackboots and pistol (146-7; *159-60*). There he stands, a personification of military glory, the Great Mahlke – but Pilenz and the cat are poised in wait for him, and within minutes all the expectations of the hero are confounded by Amtsleiter Klohse. From this point onwards Mahlke, the fleeing 'mouse' ('die Maus flüchtig', 169; *182*), is insistently, ironically shown in the now manifestly absurd garb of fierce aggressor (cf. 154, 157, 160, 161, etc., etc.; *167, 169, 173, 174*) – while Klohse and Pilenz, the true representatives of the spirit behind the War, are specifically described as wearing civilian clothes! (155, 145; *167, 158*).

Finally, as with almost everything else in the book, so the war motif, too, is brought to a head in the last few pages: Mahlke wears his uniform on his last journey out to the wreck – and it is his jackboots (together with the symbolic tin-opener) that Pilenz uses to pound the deck with when he shows no signs of life (174; *188*). Next day, when Pilenz stares out at the wreck from the significant vantage point of the local war memorial, Grass has him see nothing but two empty jackboots in a shifting cloud of seagulls. And this seagull-shrouded piece of military kit on the rotting, excrement-covered hulk of a warship is the final ironic vestige of the Great Mahlke.

Home, Church and School

Although it is the school, the supposedly humanistic Conradinum with a Party Official for a headmaster, that Grass chiefly uses to convey his image of society, he also makes expressive use of the quasi-institutional settings of home and church. In the case of Mahlke's home circumstances, what comes across most strongly is an increased sense of his isolation: he is of the stuff of his father – but his father is dead, and there are whole worlds between Mahlke and the simple country folk that his mother and aunt are, a separation that is well expressed in such details as the fact that he has his own self-contained world at the top of the house while the two women live below (24-5, 28; 27, 30), or the fact that they both treat him, not tenderly, as a child, but deferentially, as though he were his father (120 f.; *131* f.). Pilenz's is the only other family depicted in the novella – and we find the same degree of separateness as in the Mahlke family, though for quite different reasons. Pilenz's father is not dead, but he might as well be, for he and his elder son are away at the War, leaving Pilenz exposed to his mother's tawdry succession of men-friends (cf. 135; *148*). And Pilenz's failed relationships in society generally are matched by an equally failed relationship to his family, as is expressively demonstrated in his jealous urge to smash to pieces the 'altar' that his mother erects to the memory of his fallen brother (a brother whom he 'scarcely knew', 135, 136; *148*, *149*), or in the acid description that Grass has him give of his mother's mourning: 'Sie aber trug, inmitten illustriertenseliger Gemütlichkeit, geschäftige Trauer von einem Zimmer ins nächste' (135; *'In an atmosphere of cosy comfort that might have been cut out of a woman's magazine, my mother bustled from one room to the next, in mourning', 148*) – this being just the kind of rankling family set-up that we know so well from *The Tin Drum*.

Grass particularly emphasises one general aspect of the milieu to which both Pilenz and Mahlke belong: a deadly sameness and conventionality that offer little scope for the organic, proper development of those within it. The initial description of Mahlke's street hints at the point: the houses are scarcely to be distinguished one from another ('And each garden had its little bird house on a pole and its glazed garden ornaments: frogs, mushrooms, or dwarfs. In front of Mahlke's house sat a ceramic frog. But in front of the next house and the next, there were also green ceramic frogs.'; 24; 27). But it is of course the 'stench of corpses' passage that most forcibly makes the point, with its positing of a correlation between sterile banality in social living, and the soured, poisonous spirit vented through National Socialism. One of the profound (and traditional) humanist premises behind all Grass's writing is more than usually clear to the eye here: the idea that individuals, groups, nations go haywire because the given forms of society frustrate their natural fulfilment and growth – hence, for instance, the murderous hunch-backed dwarf and asylum-patient Oskar Matzerath.

Although the 'Marienkapelle', the actual church itself, is both more frequent and more highly charged as a setting than either Mahlke's or Pilenz's home, the Church as an institution is not really very much more dwelt on in the book than is the institution of family life. What Grass does demonstrate with some force is the abysmal failure of the Church as a whole to remain uncorrupted by its relationship to a society centred on war and on the spirit of National Socialism. Throughout, Gusewski carries on his ministrations regardless, compromising even to the point of Germanising his name (113; *124*); and when Mahlke's supreme destructive skill has been rewarded by National Socialism's highest distinction, Gusewski is quite willing to have him speak to a gathering of parishioners – and the unbridgeable gulf between Mahlke's battle deeds and the true spirit of the Christian Church is indirectly suggested when Grass has the priest remark: 'Perhaps, to bring his talk into line with the concerns of the Church, your friend could say something about St. George to begin with and conclude with a word or two about the powers of prayer at times of great difficulty and danger' (151; *164*) – essentially the same gross absurdity being implied here as in the graphic metaphor of Mahlke aiming his tank cannon at the womb of the Mother of God. The Church's dereliction is conveyed, too, in the way that Gusewski is incapable of pastorally ministering to Mahlke in his fatal plight: having adapted to National Socialism, how could it possibly be in meaningful communion with a Victim like Mahlke in all his awareness and suffering? Gusewski recognises the boy's distress ('innere Not', 115; *126*) – but only complains about his Marianism; and at the very last, on the occasion of Mahlke's last Communion, Grass has Gusewski again perceive Mahlke's plight, and again do nothing: 'In the dry sacristy Gusewski said: "He must be waiting outside. Maybe we should call him in, but ..."' (160; *173*).

Unlike home and church, the Conradinum is of central importance throughout, from the opening event with its school context, to Mahlke's final disappearance clad in Conradinum gym shorts – an importance that is established with great emphasis and explicitness: a sub-division of Chapter Two ends with a prefigurative paragraph to the effect that Mahlke expected too much from the school (32; *35*); Chapter Ten finishes

166

by implying that Mahlke's preoccupation with the school is one of the reasons why he is 'beyond help' (133; *145*); and above all there are the crucial lines at the close of a sub-division of Chapter Two that first speak of Mary and Mahlke's Adam's apple as motives of his actions, and then add: 'And then, in addition to Virgin and mouse, there was yet a third motive: Our school ..., and particularly the auditorium, meant a great deal to Joachim Mahlke; it was the school that drove you, later on, to your final efforts.' (43; *48-9*).

The decisive fact about the Conradinum, as Grass describes it, is the fact that it fully represents and encourages the aims of the society of which it is part, as is sharply symbolised at an early stage when the point is made that Klohse is an official of the NSDAP as well as headmaster. This mutuality of school and society is most clearly evinced in the two sequences involving the fighter pilot and the submarine commander: they are deemed to have reflected honour on the school by winning society's greatest honour, and are in turn accorded the honour of addressing their *alma mater*. There is seemingly no discrepancy whatsoever between the nature of their medal-winning activities and the spirit of the school; as Klohse says of the naval officer, he is 'Einer von uns, aus unserer Mitte, aus dem Geist unseres Gymnasiums hervorgegangen' (80; *'one of us, from our midst, a product of our school and its spirit'*, *90*). And Klohse himself is described in similar terms when Mahlke gives him his due towards the end: 'Der Geschlagene ... verkörperte ... die Anstalt, die Schule, die Conradische Stiftung, den Conradischen Geist, das Conradinum' (155; *'The slapped man ... embodied the school, its founder, the Conradinian spirit, the Conradinum'*, *168*).

But this description of Klohse is severely ironic: he does embody the spirit of the school as currently constituted – but what he stands for is totally alien to the *essential* Conradinian spirit. For the Conradinum is a humanistic foundation (*Dog Years* will explicitly describe it so[32]), complete with 'Lessing in his niche' (146; *159*), not to mention 'Schopenhauer and Copernicus';[33] and by being entirely at one with the prevailing society, it is by definition entirely at odds with itself – a situation that is well conveyed in the way that Grass has Hitler and Conradi, the school's founder, confront one another across the school hall (81; *90*), just as Hitler and Beethoven confronted one

167

another across the Matzerath's living-room; or there is the equally effective touch when Grass has the submarine commander claim to have celebrated his first destruction of a merchant ship by reciting 'qui quae quod, cuius, cuius cuius ...' (83; 92).

The conviction shared by Klohse, the school, society in general, that they still represent the good old spirit and ethos, is thus a complete illusion, a complete contradiction of reality, just as we saw in the case of Musiker Meyn's expulsion from the SA for 'unworthy' maltreatment of animals, for conduct so 'infamous' that not even his 'worthy' behaviour in the *Kristallnacht* pogrom could extenuate it. The importance of all this for Grass could be no better reflected than by the fact that he makes the entire action of *Cat and Mouse* hinge on it – not just once but twice: the critical events of Mahlke's expulsion, and his final rejection in Chapter Twelve, both arise from a grotesquely false ethic.

The notion of 'worthy' behaviour is first introduced in the novella in connection with the pompoms, which Klohse bans on the grounds that they are 'effeminate and unworthy of a German boy' (48; 55); it then comes properly into its own concerning Mahlke's expulsion: what counts against the boy is not that he has broken some substantive rule about stealing or whatever, but that he has made himself guilty of 'unworthy behaviour' ('würdeloses Verhalten', 107; 117; essentially the same phrase – 'unwürdiges Verhalten' – is used of Meyn in *The Tin Drum*, 241; 201).[34] But it is in the context of Mahlke's final rejection that the whole false ethic is most emphatically exposed: the Labour Service camp and the local Danzig newspaper may acclaim him as a former member and a 'son of our city', but the Conradinum will have nothing to do with him: no matter how greatly – and lethally – he has distinguished himself, it is inadequate to wipe out the 'dishonour' he did to the school by seeming to profane the very same symbol that he himself has since won. And it is the 'good order' of the school and the 'old Conradinian spirit' that are insistently invoked by Party official Klohse to justify the continued exclusion of Mahlke ('Die Ordnung der Anstalt', 151, 153; 164, 166; 'den alten Conradischen Geist', 154; 166) – an attitude that Grass carefully depicts as general by having both Klohse's colleagues and higher authority endorse it fully (153; 166). All this would

168

be fine – except that these ardent, systematic proponents of honour and good order are also exponents, not only of a war society in which killing and destruction are anyway at a premium, but also of the most systematically brutal political regime in history, a regime whose prevailing characteristic is the 'stench of corpses'. And typically enough, this essential identity between the spirit of Klohse's Conradinum and the deathly reality of National Socialism is symbolically suggested a last time in the closing sequence of the book: Mahlke dives down to his presumable death wearing red Conradinum gym shorts – shorts that are not only described as representing 'a piece of school tradition',[35] but whose redness is also depicted as 'Fahntuchrot' ('*flag red*'): the redness of the swastika flag.

At one important level of the book, then, Joachim Mahlke's downfall is figured as a direct result of the inadequacies and flaws of a specific society, above all of a schizophrenic duality of standards – and at the same time his downfall serves to expose these very flaws and inadequacies ('Sein Fall decouvriert Kirche, Schule, Heldenwesen – die ganze Gesellschaft'; see above, p. 158). But however crucial this social element is within the book, we must not lose sight of the fact that it is contained within a larger perspective: that non-specific, fable-like perspective signalled by the very title of the book, in terms of which Joachim Mahlke is first and last an archetypal victim, like Abel or the crucified Christ; a 'mouse' that falls prey to the eternal 'cat' only because he becomes too aware of its existence and futilely attempts to beat it at its own game; a prisoner in a labyrinth which reveals only to those that seek to escape it that it has no exits. In *Dog Years*, too, we shall again find both things, the universal and the specifically social/cultural – but with the striking difference that in the later book it is the specific that becomes the dominant perspective, as the very title once again suggests.

PART THREE

Dog Years

Everybody knew it, and those who have
forgotten – may they remember.

GRASS, *Hundejahre*

CHAPTER I

Introduction

The publishing history of *Dog Years* is a remarkable one. Within three months of the book's first appearance in September 1963 after a welter of press publicity, no fewer than twenty-one impressions had been published, amounting altogether to 103,000 copies – two and a half times the number of copies of *The Tin Drum* published in the entire first two years of its life (41,820), and nearly five times the first two years' production of *Cat and Mouse* (22,000). Subsequent publishing figures, on the other hand, show a quite different picture: Luchterhand have done no printings of the novel at all since that first dramatic run of impressions, and paperback and book-club editions in German amounted by March 1972 to only 400,500 copies – less than a third of the total German-language printings of *The Tin Drum* since its first two years (1,266,300), and less than two-thirds of the German-language printings of *Cat and Mouse* in the corresponding period (650,000).[1]

This striking pattern of market success and (relative) failure was matched by the critical response the novel provoked: whereas its publication was attended by a riot of articles and reviews in countless newspapers and periodicals, there rapidly ensued a kind of oblivion that has remained more or less unrelieved ever since. One result of all this has been that no conventional image of the book has yet gained dominance (as happened with *The Tin Drum*), for no consensus has ever developed concerning either its meaning or its merit. The only fairly common response has been to criticise the novel as 'undisciplined' or 'disordered', a view most aggressively argued by Grass's inveterate detracter, Walter Jens, who described the author as being uncontrollably prolix and devoid of all sense of economy, and the novel itself as being 'like a chaotic Kashubian notebook, a bundle of assorted drafts'.[2] Or there have been those critics who have seen the seeming confusion of the book as the source of its greatness, arguing that it is its sheer creative flow that is Grass's particular distinction; thus Ivan Nagel's review in *Die Zeit* (a follow-up to Jens's in the same paper) spoke of a 'broad stream of remembrance' coursing through the book, autonomously bringing into being 'language, time and reality', and bestowing on them a mighty logic of their own regardless of conventional forms and limitations.[3] For my own part, I do not believe that confusion or formlessness enters into it at all – indeed I believe that what faults there are in the novel derive from an excess of form. And while it is beguiling to see the book, as Nagel does, chiefly in terms of a dynamic, all-powerful 'verbal music', etc., the book is undoubtedly open to a more straightforward interpretation, just as were its predecessors in the 'trilogy'.

CHAPTER II

Persecution and Suffering

The General Perspective

After Mahlke and Pilenz in *Cat and Mouse*, it scarcely comes
as a surprise to find Grass centring *Dog Years* on the relationship between two 'friends' : Eduard Amsel and Walter Matern
are present, if only disguisedly, in the opening paragraph of
the book, and remain its chief protagonists right through to
the last forlorn sentence : 'Jeder badet für sich' (*'Each of us
baths by himself'*). But Amsel and Matern are a follow-up to
Mahlke and Pilenz only in the most superficial sense that *Dog
Years* was published two years later than *Cat and Mouse* :
genetically speaking they are almost certainly very much
earlier, and even pre-date the publication of *The Tin Drum*, as
shown by the wall-plans mentioned in the General Introduction
(Matern, incidentally, was originally conceived not by that
name but as 'The Grinder'; on one wall-plan he is even given
a quite different family name : 'Damaschke'). The two relationships are differently presented in all kinds of ways, but in
essence they are the same in that violence and persecution are
crucial to both of them – a violence that goes hand in hand
with a severe imbalance in the relationship : Matern, like Pilenz,
is permanently in thrall to his 'friend', instead of being on an
equal footing. Strikingly enough, Walter Matern is even fleetingly figured at one point in the same 'cat' role as was Heini
Pilenz, with Amsel implicitly as the 'mouse' whose destruction
is wished for (576; 476); and there is a specific linking up of
the two books in terms of persecution : a tableau-like passage
in *Dog Years* set on the same sportsground as the opening of
Cat and Mouse describes how stones were thrown at Eddi Amsel
and how a hole was deliberately burnt in Jenny Brunies's new

dress – and then goes over into a three-line re-narration of the novella's opening act of aggression (208-9; *174-5*). Or there is the fact that one of the final symbolic gestures in *Cat and Mouse* is also incorporated, in modified but powerful form, at the beginning of *Dog Years*: just as Grass had Pilenz consummate his treachery by throwing Mahlke's tin-opener into the sea, so he has Matern commence the action of *Dog Years* by flinging into the Vistula the pocket-knife that symbolises his relationship with Amsel. It is as if Grass wanted to provide us with demonstrative pointers to the essential identity of the two books – an identity that is even genetic, since *Cat and Mouse*, as we have noted, was originally an integral part of what was later to become *Dog Years* (not the least intriguing feature of the wall-plans concerning *Dog Years*, however, is that none of those I have seen includes anything that has a clear bearing on the novella, despite the fact that some of them date from the period immediately before Grass apparently began writing *Cat and Mouse*).

The event with the knife recalls *Cat and Mouse* in another decisive sense as well: as a dramatic, symbolic, intensely prefigurative opening to the book, it corresponds precisely to Pilenz's and the cat's attack on Mahlke at the start of the novella. It is true that the cat episode was all over after little more than a page, whereas the knife episode is spread over four chapters of altogether twelve and a half pages, in accordance with the novel's epic expansiveness. Nevertheless, the device for achieving dramatic effect is essentially the same in both cases: instead of the action being conveyed in one continuous sweep, it is repeatedly put in suspense by the insertion of tracts of other matter, tracts that are progressively shortened as the action builds up towards its climax. In the 'First Morning Shift' of *Dog Years* there is just the one initial element of the episode: at the precise mid-point of the chapter, Walter Matern is suddenly, laconically created, and there, in emphatic end-of-paragraph position, is his crucial attribute, the mark of his ungentle being: 'er knirscht mit den Zähnen' (9; '*he is grinding his teeth*', *4*). The 'Second Morning Shift' shows him looking for a stone because of his compulsive – and, as we slowly realise, characteristically physical – need to throw something; and it shows him lighting instead on his knife. But this is not all we learn. For one thing, Amsel is introduced into the story,

176

casually and as though he were of little importance; for another, we are given the decisive information that Matern's knife is not just any old knife but a present from Amsel ('Dieses hat ihm Amsel geschenkt', 13; 8). The action comes to a head in the 'Shift' that follows: Matern makes to throw, and there is then a magnificent slow-motion evocation of the throw itself that freezes just at the moment where Matern's arm and empty hand are still outflung; while the point is made not just once but twice more that the knife was a present from Amsel (15; 9-10), and at the close of the 'Shift' its symbolic significance within the boys' own relationship is emphasised beyond doubt: not only was the knife a present from Amsel, but the two 'friends' had also used it to mingle their blood in an act of blood brotherhood (16; 10; but see also 605; 500). The episode is still only half-finished at this stage, and it remains for the 'Fourth Morning Shift' to demonstrate the essential counterpart to Matern's physical, inimical gesture: the other boy's complete but unphysical supremacy over him. But so far as Matern himself is concerned, the cardinal truth is already clear: with his grinding teeth, his scar-covered head, his clenched fist, and, above all, his flinging away of the knife, Walter Matern is a being of inarticulate, treacherous, violent responses. And the symbolic force of the whole episode becomes all the plainer to the reader as soon as he realises that – like the opening events of *Cat and Mouse* – it is anachronically narrated: the first four 'Shifts' show Matern at the age of nine, but the first paragraph of the 'Fifth Morning Shift' goes back in time to the point of his birth, and from this moment on, the story of the two boys' childhood follows a strict chronology.

No sooner has Grass established a sense of violence and aggression through the token behaviour of Walter Matern in the first four 'Shifts' than he intensifies it with a second episode in which the role of antagonist passes from Matern to his grandmother, and in which violence is no longer symbolic but actual – developments that are prefigured in Amsel's closing words to his 'friend' in the 'Fourth Morning Shift': 'Du best jenau wie Daine Oma inne Miehle. Die knirscht och immer midde paar Zähne, wo se noch hädd. Bloos schmeissen tut se nech. Dafier schlächt se middem Leffel.' (18; *You're exactly like your grandma in the mill. All she does is grind the coupla teeth she's still got the whole time. Except she don't throw*

177

things. Only hits people with her spoon.', *12*). At first the two participants in the ritual of aggression are simply sketched in: Grandmother Matern in the opening paragraph of the 'Fifth Morning Shift', and her daughter, poor mad Lorchen, in its last. The first part of the next 'Shift' then sets the scene – Grandmother Matern imprisoned in her chair by total paralysis – and at the same time fills in the background as to how the situation originated (24; *17*): the first physical clash between grandmother and daughter-in-law eleven years earlier, and then, two years later, their battle with wooden spoons that ended with Grandmother Matern suffering a stroke. After this, the main action begins: mad Lorchen wandering in search of her dead lover and so not turning the goose that is roasting for Walter Matern's christening feast; Grandmother Matern's gathering rage as the smell of burning slowly fills her room; and finally, her furious resurrection from her nine-year paralysis and 'hellish', 'dragon-like', teeth-grinding chase after Lorchen with its climax in a hail of blows and cursing (26 f.; *19* f.).

This is not the last of this bursting ritual of aggression, however, for it is most importantly this which Grass describes as the chief inspiration behind the child Amsel's first truly effective scarecrow, a creation that is modelled on the 'spoon-swinging and teeth-grinding Grandmother' (59; *48*), and which is such a horrific spectacle that poor Lorchen is driven even further out of her mind, and the scarecrow has to be destroyed. But even that is not the end of this episode, for Grass turns it into a kind of symbolic refrain by repeating it on no less than two further occasions, as the climax to two verbally almost identical flights of remembrance that are apportioned one to Amsel-Brauchsel and one – ironically – to the archetypal aggressor Walter Matern:

... Und die Zähne knirschen, wenn Walter Matern von links nach rechts mit den Zähnen. Desgleichen die Grossmutter: quer durch den Garten hetzt sie das arme Lorchen. ... Denn sie naht schrecklich, hebt winklig den Arm: und in der Hand am Arm steckt der hölzerne Kochlöffel, wirft seinen Schatten auf das krause Lorchen und wird grösser, immer fetter, mehr und mehr ... (68, 604)

And teeth grind when Walter Matern grinds his teeth from

178

*left to right. Same with his grandmother: all around the
garden she chases poor Lorchen. . . . For terrible she
approaches, raising an angular arm: and in the hand on the
arm the wooden spoon casts its shadow on mad Lorchen and
grows bigger and bigger, fatter and fatter, more and more ...*
(55, 499)

These repetitions are poignant in themselves – but their poign-
ancy is considerably increased by their contexts: in the first
case the passage in question follows immediately on the novel's
first prefiguration of its most critical event, namely the savage
'snowman' attacks on Amsel and Jenny Brunies (67; 54); while
in the second case the renewed evocation of Grandmother
Matern's assault on Lorchen leads directly to a fresh rehearsal
of Walter Matern's violence and treachery towards his 'friend',
ranging from the episode with the knife to his brutal attack
in the snow.

The Violence of National Socialism

The period of National Socialism – the most 'doggish' of the
novel's dog years – is the period covered by the second of the
Books, the 'Love Letters', and it is thoroughly characteristic
that the Second Book's very first reference to Hitler's Reich
subsumes it under a single word, standing emphatically at the
close of the sentence: 'violence' (149; 125). The rest of the
'letter' in question sketches details of the Polish invasion, but
again the brutal essence of it all is concentrated into a single
word: the image of 'the fist' with which Grass ends the letter.
This then serves as the cue for the next letter: the image of
the fist forces itself so strongly on Liebenau's awareness, we
hear, that it interferes with his narration – and this leads
over into the Second Book's most intense and symbolic passage
so far, as Liebenau is driven back to the past beyond the past
he is supposed to be narrating:

Vergangenheit: Es war einmal: Als im Sommer des Jahres
zweiunddreissig: Damals damals damals, als ich ein fünf-

179

jähriger Junge war, zur Zeit der Olympiade in Los Angeles gab es schon Fäuste, die schnell trocken und irdisch bewegt wurden; und dennoch, als merkten sie nichts von dem Luftzug, wurden gleichzeitig Millionen Kinderwagen auf hohen und niedrigen Rädern in die Sonne, in den Schatten geschoben. (150)

Past: Once upon a time: When in the summer of '32: in the days in the days when I was a boy of five, when the Olympic Games were being held in Los Angeles, fists were already being moved swift, dry, down to earth; and yet, as though unaware of the draft that was blowing, millions of baby carriages on wheels high and low were being propelled into the sunshine, into the shade. (126)

(Another crucial theme is included in this passage: the theme of wilful obliviousness concerning Nazi brutality – but we shall come on to this in a moment.)

The Hitlerite principle of violence and brutality found its most monstrous expression in the systematic extermination of the Jews and others, as was already reflected in the earlier books – the 'heavenly gasman' image and the Fajngold-Treblinka episode in *The Tin Drum*, the 'stench of corpses' passage in *Cat and Mouse*; in *Dog Years*, however, the savage reality is mirrored with a new and startling intensity. Although there is prefatory mention of Stutthof concentration camp in the last of the 'Morning Shifts', the theme does not begin to be developed until some two-thirds of the way through the 'Love Letters'. After a remark that two Ukrainian forced labourers were said to have been sent to Stutthof after a row between August Pokriefke and the narrator's father, two short 'letters' follow that are exclusively devoted to Stutthof (324-5; 269-70), the first implying that everyone knew what went on at the camp, the second describing its history, and then steadily building up to an emphatic, explicit conclusion: 'and between 1939 and 1945, in Stutthof concentration camp, Danzig-Lowlands County, people died, I don't know how many.' – a formulation that echoes the *Tin Drum* description of Fajngold: 'he had sprinkled the dead, not one corpse but many, why bother with figures; he had sprinkled dead men and women with Lysol.' (513-4; 413). Within a few pages comes the tale of Oswald Brunies, who is denounced, interrogated, arrested, committed to Stutthof, and never heard of again (330-

180

340; 274-82).[4] But then, little more than a dozen pages later, Grass launches into a sequence on the horror of the extermination system that is the longest and most clamorous of its kind in all his work: the twenty-page Knochenberg' ('*mound of bones*') sequence. The importance of the sequence is clear enough from the text itself − but there is striking external evidence as well: not only has Grass himself said that the 'Knochenberg' idea was conceived before *The Tin Drum* was even finished, and that the Second Book was originally to be entitled 'Knochenberg',[5] but there is also a wall-plan of late 1959 (one of the two plans to be seen in the June 1960 edition of *Du*) which shows the word 'Knochenberg' twice in the dominant central area of its plot diagram, and includes as an apparent potential title the bold legend 'Ice-warehouse and Mound of Bones'.

Grass first introduces the motif of the mound of bones in the short 'letter' on page 356 (295) with which the 'Schlussmärchen' ('*closing fairy tale*') of the Second Book is announced − and then unleashes the 'Schlussmärchen' in general and the 'Knochenberg' sequence in particular with an opening section of startling impact (357; 295-6): instead of the normal neutral tone and normal narrative progression, the reader suddenly finds himself faced with a rhythmic barrage of spare, lapidary phrases with a single resonant message; 'all is impurity' − the word 'rein' ('*pure*') appearing in some form no less than thirty-five times in thirty-four lines. Like the 'stench of corpses' passage in *Cat and Mouse*, this is in effect a poetic threnody in which the aggrieved humanism that lies behind the book as a whole suddenly bursts through to the surface. As in the 'stench of corpses' passage, too, the crucial image is suspended through the rhythmic build-up, and is thus all the more climactic when it does come (especially since the poetic rhythm becomes more intense here than perhaps anywhere else in Grass's prose works): the mound of human bones − neat, white and destined to yield nice, cleansing soap − which are the very image of monstrous impurity (and there can be no doubt in the reader's mind that these are human bones: the first of the two Stutthof 'letters' earlier on ended with the 'joke' about making soap at Stutthof, 324; 269).

After this tone-setting opening to the 'Schlussmärchen', the theme is temporarily suspended and the normal narrative thread resumed. But after four pages there is a symbolic double development. For one thing, the tale begins of the myriad rats and their mass extermination, a tale that is sombrely pointed in several different ways: the ancient catastrophe associations of the rat are explicitly and extensively evoked (363-4; *301*); the systematic extermination of the rats echoes the Nazi extermination of people; and the rats themselves bear witness to the vile meaning of the 'Knochenberg', for it is implied that they grow fat on the remnants of flesh still clinging to the bones ('Everywhere they sat and grew fatter; on what?'; 362; *299*; and see 369 (*305*) for a description of the 'remnants of flesh'). The other development is the emphatic introduction – within a few lines of the introduction of the rats – of what soon proves to be a leitmotif: 'the smell that hung over the battery'. This image, which is repeated as many as twelve times in ten pages, and which closely recalls *Cat and Mouse* and the 'stench of corpses', is instantly recognisable as a symbol of the mound of human bones – and it is with the highly charged explicit confirmation of this symbolism on page 368 (*304-5*) that Grass makes the 'Knochenberg' image actual once more, and begins to bring the sequence to a head. First the scene is set with a description of the white mound in its barbed-wire factory-compound with black smoke swirling from the factory chimney, and the original point is reinforced: the 'pure' whiteness and neatness of the mound are a gross deception, and it is its remnants of flesh and its constant, shifting cover of black crows that reflect its vile reality (368-9; *305*). After this comes a picture of secret nocturnal activity in the factory compound, and this is followed in turn by the key episode involving Tulla: Grass first has her flagrantly declare the truth about the mound – 'That's a pile of bones', 'Bet you it's bones. And what's more, human bones. Everybody knows that.', 'And I'm telling you they come straight from Stutthof, want to bet?' (370; *306*) – and then, in a powerfully suspensive passage, Tulla invades the factory compound and brings back absolute proof of her assertion: a human skull (371-3; *307-9*).

It is here that we come to the real point of the whole sequence. On the one hand it is clearly true that Grass is concerned yet again to mirror the same persecution and inhumanity that figured so large in the earlier books. But there is something else quite new: an insistent emphasis on the contributory con-

182

niving role of the populace at large, on that posture of affected ignorance that allowed the inhumanity to go seemingly unnoticed, and so to grow unchecked. This false pretence is repeatedly touched on in the pages leading up to the Tulla episode ('The smell remained unchanged. But no one inquired after its meaning, although Harry and everyone else had it on their tongues.', etc.; 370; 306), – but it is the whole burden of the Tulla scene itself, with Tulla proving the mound's reality after flaunting its true name against the others' denial ('Harry and many others contradicted, but didn't say exactly what was piled up to the south of the battery'; 370; 306), and flaunting it above all against Störtebeker's systematic attempts to bury the truth in a welter of meaningless verbiage, as typified by his first response to Tulla: 'Though freshly uttered, Störtebeker's answer had been ready for weeks: "We must conceive piledupness in the openness of Being, the divulgation of care, and endurance to death as the consummate essence of existence.' (370; 306).

Just as it opened with vile mounds of human bones, so the 'Schlussmärchen', and with it the whole Second Book, ends on the same image, coupling to it other metonymies for the National Socialist era – but again here, in this most emphatic position in the text, what Grass chiefly focuses on is not so much the monstrousness of the thing in itself, but the guilty connivance and especially the falseness of the people in whose midst it was able to happen; for, as Grass projects them, they not only pretended at the time that nothing was going on, but also sought afterwards to suppress all memory of it. They all flee on the collapse of the Reich, the narrative says; and it continues:

Zurück bleiben Knochenberge, Massengräber, Karteikästen, Fahnenhalter, Parteibücher, Liebesbriefe ...
Nicht bezahlt werden: fällige Steuern, ... Schulden und Schuld.
Neu beginnen wollen alle mit dem Leben ...
Vergessen wollen alle die Knochenberge und Massengräber, die Fahnenhalter und Parteibücher, die Schulden und die Schuld. (427)

Left behind: mounds of bones, mass graves, card files, flagpoles, Party books, love letters ...

Unpaid: taxes ... debts and guilt.
All are eager to start out afresh with living ...
All are eager to forget the mounds of bones and the mass
graves, the flagpoles and Party books, the debts and the guilt.
(353)

It becomes clear here how much difference there is between Grass's attitude in *Dog Years* and his earlier attitude in *The Tin Drum*. For while the characters of Oskar's world were also depicted as conniving at the bestiality of the regime, their connivance was shown as an essentially unwitting, unconscious one. The image in 'Faith Hope Love' of Alfred Matzerath cosily warming his fingers and his feelings over the bonfire of Jewish sacred objects was a classic case in point, as was the whole picture of his involvement in National Socialism: he casually, unsuspectingly gave himself over to it – only to literally choke on it in the end. A comparison between seemingly parallel passages in the two novels illustrates the difference precisely: in *Dog Years* Grass writes – in the 'fists' passage – : 'and yet, *as though* unaware of the draft that was blowing, millions of baby carriages ... were being propelled into the sunshine, into the shade.'; or again, in a much later evocation of the 'forgetfulness' of post-war Germans, voiced through Amsel-Brauchsel: 'They cook their pea soup on blue gas flames *and give it not a thought'* (646; 533) – but contrast with this the operative verb in the 'Faith Hope Love' passage: 'And no one who sets his pot of soup on the bluish flame *suspects* ['ahnt'] that disaster is bringing his supper to the boil'.

There is one further passage in the 'Schlussmärchen' that virtually trumpets out this decisively different attitude, and that is the kind of epilogue to the 'Knochenberg' sequence in which Grass has Liebenau, the narrator, reflect on his involvement in National Socialist Germany as a boy and young man. Liebenau relates how his younger self had revered, among others, Hitler and Heidegger, and then adds:

Mit Hilfe dieser Vorbilder gelang es ihm, einen tatsächlichen, aus menschlichen Knochen erstellten Berg mit mittelalterlichen Allegorien zuzuschütten. Er erwähnte den Knochenberg, der in Wirklichkeit zwischen dem Troyl und dem Kaiser-

184

hafen gen Himmel schrie, in seinem Tagebuch als Opferstätte, errichtet, damit das Reine sich im Lichten ereigne, indem es das Reine umlichte und so das Licht stifte. (375-6)

With the help of these models he succeeded in burying a real mound made of human bones under mediaeval allegories. The pile of bones, which in reality cried out to high heaven between Troyl and Kaiserhafen, was mentioned in his diary as a place of sacrifice, erected in order that purity might come-to-be in the luminous, which transluminates purity and so fosters light. (311)

The words 'gen Himmel schrie' (*'cried out to high heaven'*) declare more stridently than perhaps any other phrase in the narrative Grass's normally unspoken humanist view of the Third Reich's bestiality. But also explicit in these lines is what is arguably the most decisive notion of the book: the dual notion of *reality* ('tatsächlich', 'Wirklichkeit') and *mask* ('mit mittelal-terlichen Allegorien zuschütten'). There is nothing more central to the novel than this antithesis – one could argue that the whole perspective of the book is determined by it, and certainly there can be no doubt at all that it governs the main dialectic as represented by the chief protagonists. Grass, as we shall see, creates in Amsel a figure who always 'sees'; in Matern a figure who always fails to 'see'. And the fiction might be noted here that it is Amsel-Brauchsel, the persona who sees, who is the organiser and controller of the book, which is itself a 'Fest-schrift' (32; 24) for the tenth anniversary of Brauchsel's activity in the mine – activity which consists in creating the scarecrow 'Pandämonium' (103; 86) that reflects his clear-eyed vision!

Persecution and the Main Characters

If there is one figure in the novel that embodies as it were the pure spirit of antagonism, it is undoubtedly Tulla Pokriefke. Walter Matern, it is true, appears from the first as an archetypal aggressor and remains so to the end. But for one thing his activity is diffused throughout the book whereas Tulla's is con-

185

centrated within an almost novella-like sub-plot in the 'Love Letters'; for another, he is other things as well as an aggressor (in particular, he is an inveterate posturer), whereas Tulla's role is centred emphatically on antagonism. It was characteristically she who was indirectly responsible for the two Ukrainians being dispatched to Stutthof, and it was she who not only denounced Oswald Brunies in the first place (334-5; 278), but also sealed his fate at the interrogation by offering him the sweet-jar and thus making him betray his mania (336-7; 279). As is said of her at one point in the narrative, she is 'always to blame or partly to blame' (210; 176).

The grim spirit represented in Tulla is strongly projected from the moment the narrative first concentrates on her at the beginning of the Second Book. She is an inhuman 'thing' rather than a girl ('mehr ein Etwas als ein Mädchen'); she has all the makings of some primitive cutter-off of heads ('Kopfschneider', 146; 123); she has several bouts each day of a kind of contorted spasm of anger – and there is a powerful resonance of 'evil' in the word 'böse' that is used three times in the space of five lines (147; 123); she is always dreaming up schemes against the other children (147; 123-4); and she exploits Harry Liebenau to satisfy her sexuality (147; 124).

Part of the remarkable strength of Tulla's evil 'presence' in *Dog Years*, however, derives from the fact that there was a similar presence in both the earlier books. In *Cat and Mouse* there was the figure of Tulla Pokriefke herself, the very image of rampant sexuality and the cause, in the masturbation episode, of one of Joachim Mahlke's most signal successes-cum-failures. But whereas Tulla was strictly peripheral to the plot of the novella, the same is not true of the corresponding figures in *The Tin Drum* : Susi Kater and especially Luzie Rennwand played a major part in the life of Oskar Matzerath – and there are two particularly penetrating echoes of *The Tin Drum* in Grass's *Dog Years* presentation of Tulla : Tulla inflicts her 'soup' of leeches (310, 315; 257-8, 262) on Jenny Brunies and Harry Liebenau much as Susi Kater inflicted her foul brew of frogs, urine and crushed brick on Oskar; and much as Luzie Rennwand was imagined by Oskar as a corpse by the sea's edge (cf. above, page 35), so Tulla is similarly imagined by Brauchsel-Amsel as a dried-up corpse unearthed from a dike (67, 603; 55, 499) – and the context here is that same flight of remembrance which also

186

relates to Grandmother Matern's persecution of poor Lorchen, and to the critical attacks on Amsel and Jenny Brunies. Like Susi Kater and especially Luzie Rennwand, then, Tulla Pokriefke is yet another 'Schwarze Köchin' figure, an incarnation of the viler, more savage processes of existence. And just as with Luzie Rennwand, Tulla is a presence not only as a real person in the narrative, but also as a powerful memory active in the mind of the novel's main character (and chief sufferer). Thus it is that we hear from Brauchsel-Amsel of a Tulla figure, steeped in violence and sexuality, long before such a figure appears separately in the real action of the book (see 54, 67 and especially 78 f.; *43, 55, 64 f.*).

As for Tulla's actual aggressions in the course of the Second Book, nothing is more typical than the three occasions when she unleashes the black and German hound Harras on Felsner-Imbs, teacher of Jenny, and friend to her other subsequent victim, Oswald Brunies. At first the attack is a relatively harmless one, for Harras prances playfully about and does no more than rip his fleeing victim's tail-coat (213; *178-9*). The second attack is more grave: far from making a game of it, Harras goes straight for his mistress's target, and Imbs escapes injury only by countering the dog's savage leap with his umbrella, while Jenny goes tumbling into the rain-filled gutter (227-8; *190-1*). In the third attack Tulla does not even have to say or do anything, for by this time she has so conditioned the hound that its wolfish instincts are aroused by the mere presence of its victim, and it spontaneously breaks loose and savages Imbs, sending him to hospital for three weeks with a badly damaged thigh (241; *201-2*).

But the person who chiefly attracts Tulla Pokriefke's venom and antagonism is, of couse, Jenny Brunies, Jenny who in all her gross fatness is a born sufferer ('Pummelig unnatürlich sah Jenny aus und musste viel erleiden', 397-8; *329*) – and Tulla's antagonistic relationship to her is soon prefigured in the opening pages of the Second Book, typically enough at the end of a 'letter': 'Your incisors protruded slightly: they were soon to become a source of dread to Jenny Brunies, the foundling from across the street.' (144; *121*).

The Second Book has not gone very far before Grass begins to give shape to this relationship through the tense episode of the pram – an episode that is significantly introduced by the 'fists' evocation of National Socialist violence that we have already mentioned. It all begins with fat Jenny's characteristic refusal to be taken in charge by the other girl, which in turn induces an equally characteristic response of rage in Tulla (153-4; 128-9). The narrative moves to other things in the rest of the 'letter' in question, but the following letter rivets attention back on Tulla with its opening phrase: 'Where is Tulla?', which then becomes a leitmotif that steadily builds up tension through nearly two pages until finally the question is answered when the malefic child reappears once more. There follows a passage that is exemplary for the way it gradually generates more tension with its slow-motion pattern of rhythmic 'Tulla ...' sentences that strike home from among a sequence of other images (157-8; 131-2), until at last the climax bursts on the reader as Tulla spits methodically, symbolically, repeatedly into Jenny's empty pram (watched, incidentally, by Oskar Matzerath! 158; 132-3). Like the symbolic episode that opened the novel, this aggressive act of Tulla's towards the beginning of the Second Book has a prefigurative, tone-setting function. Matern's action with the knife and Tulla's with the pram are even specifically linked through a verbal motif: the phrase 'Vor vielen vielen Sonnenun-tergängen' (7, 8; *Many many sunsets ago*, 3, 4), which began the narrative and then rang through the knife episode itself, is echoed at the very start of the pram sequence in the words 'Vor vielen vielen Jahren rollte ein Kinderwagen' (150; *'Many many years ago there rolled a baby carriage'*, 126).[6]

There are other sporadic episodes in the Second Book that demonstrate Tulla's inimical being and help to confirm her specific role as the hounder of Jenny Brunies ('Tulla hetzte Jenny', 358; 297). No sooner is the pram sequence over than Tulla persecutes her victim beneath the pier, trying to force her to eat jellyfish and threatening to set the dog on her, until Harry Liebenau comes to the rescue (159-60; 134). There is the incident of the leech 'soup', when Tulla not only presses Jenny (and Harry Liebenau) into drinking her vile concoction, but also frightens her with threats of pregnancy (310; 257-8). It is soon after this that Tulla and her gang come upon Jenny and try to inveigle her into the cavernous black ice-warehouse, a plot that backfires only because Jenny is most at home anyway in the building's frozen depths (318 f.; 264 f.).[7] Tulla's most intense act of persecution, though, is her ritual victimisation of Jenny amidst the snow – but since this is part of a larger sequence that also includes the critical attack on Eduard Amsel, let us leave it for a moment while we take a closer look at the Amsel-Matern relationship.

In a certain sense Eduard Amsel, the true protagonist of the novel, is even more of an archetypal victim than Joachim Mahlke was, for while the Great Mahlke brought his downfall upon himself by quitting his safe obscurity and exposing himself to the 'cat', Amsel for his part is desperately at risk from the outset because of his inherent otherness, as manifested most obviously by his spatter of freckles and by his extraordinary fatness (a feature he shares with his co-victim, Jenny Brunies); in Grass's crisp formulation:

> Lächerlich rund und mit Sommersprossen besprenkelt, wie er nun einmal zwei Dörfern täglich unter die Augen geriet, fiel ihm die Rolle des Prügelknaben zu. Wie die Spiele der Jugend auch hiessen, er musste mitspielen, vielmehr, es wurde ihm mitgespielt. (42)

> *Displayed each day ludicrously round and freckle-faced to the eyes of two villages, he became a whipping-boy. Whatever games the children happened to be playing, he had to join in, or rather, he was joined in. (32-3)*

Even in the earliest years of his life, we read in the same context, Amsel was subjected to ritual torture by his constant tormentors ('Peiniger'), and this way of things is emphasised when the narrative comes to describing the eleven-year-old's part in the Conradinum *Schlagball* games:

> Dicklich und kurzbeinig bot er das ideale Ziel beim Einkesseln und Abwerfen. Er war die verletzliche Stelle seiner Mannschaft. Auf ihn wurde Jagd gemacht. Sie zingelten ihn ein und umtanzten ihn zu viert mit mittanzendem Lederball. Genüssliche Finten wurden über ihn weg geübt, bis er sich wimmernd im Gras wälzte und das volle Leder schon spürte, bevor der Lederball kam. (114)

> *Stout and short-legged, he was perfect for blocking out and bouncing the ball off. He was the team's weak spot. He was*

189

tracked and hunted down. Hedging him round, four players would execute a dance in which a leather ball figured prominently. Delectable feints would be practised against him until he rolled whimpering in the grass, smarting under the taut leather even before it reached him. (95-6)

With Amsel so persistently 'harried and tormented' ('gehetzt und gemartert'), it comes as no surprise to find Grass reverting here to the 'Passion' concept of the earlier books: 'after Amsel had enjoyed a gentle childhood to the right and the left of the Vistula, Amsel's sufferings began far from the Vistula. They will not be quick to come to an end.' (115; 96).

Throughout these various childhood persecutions, Amsel appears on the face of it to have an effective protector in the person of his seemingly devoted friend Matern, who for instance deliberately hits high balls in *Schlagball* to give Amsel time to get round the pitch unscathed (114-15; 96), and who, on their first arrival in the boarding section of the Conradinum, forestalls the other boys' attempts to blacken Amsel's backside with shoe-polish (106-7; 89). But it was not at all like this at the beginning, for Matern's first compulsive urge as a young child by the Vistula was to use his brute force in the common affliction of the fat and physically helpless Amsel, not in his defence; it was only subsequently that he did what turns out to be a characteristic *volte face* and switched roles – 'in mid-fight' (42; 33) – from Persecutor to Protector.

We are touching here on what is in fact chronologically the first decisive event of the story: the inception of a strange relationship between the two protagonists in which Matern, though physically supreme, is none the less subordinated by the physically impotent Amsel. I shall shortly argue that this theme of power, physical and unphysical, has a crucial importance of its own, but in the meantime let us consider its significance within the general theme of persecution. And the patent truth here is that the real constant in Walter Matern is *not* his 'loyalty' or his 'protectiveness' towards the scapegoat Amsel, but his inherited (and, in the book's perspective, specifically German) compulsion to physical violence of one kind or another, quite regardless of whether his role at any given moment happens to be that of persecutor or protector (and 'role-playing', of course, is the other decisive constant in the make-up of Walter Matern).[8] It was

190

precisely this pattern that was indicated with anachronic forcefulness in the opening episode with the knife, and the description of Matern's switch from persecutor to protector makes the point even more emphatically: his fists go battering away after the switch just as frenziedly as before – the only difference is that Amsel is no longer their target. But even then, Amsel is far from being permanently safe. Already during the phase of their seemingly deepest friendship as class-mates in Danzig, Matern's original antagonism towards the other boy asserts itself again in the brilliantly created episode involving the underground skeleton, when Matern in his tragical posturings is offended by Amsel's response to the skeleton – a response of curiosity for precise, real detail, of quiet, all-seeing detachment – and smashes him to the ground with his club (93; 77).

But it is only later, when the two 'friends' are virtually adult and when National Socialism is well on its brutal way, that Matern's violence and aggression – and hence the novel's whole theme of persecution – come to a savage climax.

The process begins with Matern at first aggressively acting the part of Communist and general rebel against the regime: he threatens a *Jungvolk* leader with a beating (208; *174*), and later starts a fight with him (224; *188*). But on the very next page after this mêlée we find him switching sides once more, ostensibly to please Amsel, by becoming first an ordinary member and very soon an N.C.O. in an SA troop whose speciality, appropriately enough, consists of picking fights with a Polish student organisation and smashing up its headquarters (226; *189*. Matern is later promoted a second time – and it is clearly implied that the 'devotion to duty' that earns him this fresh promotion is nothing other than his brutal savaging of his 'friend' in the snow; 281; *234*). Then, just after Tulla's second attack on Felsner-Imbs, a whole five-page 'letter' is given over to describing the 'Saalschlacht' ('*beer-hall brawl*'; 229 f.; *192* f.), an event that Matern helps to trigger off, and which is a new symbol of that generalised National Socialist violence in which Matern is now fully involved.

All this, however, together with other incidents such as Matern's near attack on Amsel for ironically sporting a Nazi uniform (238; *199*), and Tulla's third and most savage attack on Felsner-Imbs, amount in effect to a prelude, building steadily up to the plangent, fugue-like evocation of brutality that is the novel's crisis. This main sequence begins with several quiet 'letters' (241 f.; 202 f.) that establish the intensely wintry mood and begin to set the scene : Jenny going sledging with the others on the Erbsberg at the ominous suggestion of Tulla, while Amsel works on his SA robots in his villa at the Erbsberg's foot. But the action soon gets under way : with the Gutenberg monument and its towering bogeyman as her black and frightening 'temple', Tulla makes her first prancing, succubine attempt to force Jenny into the role of a kind of sacrificial victim (248; 207-8). Jenny is able on this occasion to escape – but the dynamism of aggression is now fully established, and in the 'letters' that follow, alternating regularly between the two victims, their dual Passion is slowly unfolded.

In the four 'letters' of pages 249-51 (208-10), everything is brought finally into position : Jenny enters upon her ordeal by rejoining Tulla and her minions after all, and they make their silent, ritual way up the Erbsberg and into the grim realm of the 'temple'; while Amsel is shown bringing his robot Germans-cum-SA men into the garden, gaily, unsuspectingly starting them on their mechanical mindless motions, and himself ironically, provocatively acting the part of Hitler. Then, with a poignant contrary motion in the two 'letters' that follow, the crisis duly begins to break : Jenny, 'puppig flauschig verurteilt' (252; 'doll-like fluffy condemned', 210), is shown moving away from her persecutors towards the black 'temple' and isolation, while Amsel's attackers, 'maskiert vermummt verdächtig' (252; 'masked disguised shady', 211), are shown moving in on their victim from outside the garden. And in the next two 'letters' (253-4; 211-12), the first acts in the dual Passion are at last projected : Tulla and her eight accomplices at the 'temple' scream at the grossly fat Jenny to start her dance; she obediently does so but collapses into the snow, tries again but inevitably fails in her trial and twice more goes tumbling in the snow; while down in the garden, Amsel is caught in the ring of *his* nine attackers, tries vainly to escape – and is smashed to the ground with a fist, comes up again, and is smashed with a second fist.

It is only in the two short 'letters' that follow, however (255; 213), that the sequence, and with it the action of the entire novel, is brought to its climax : Tulla goes over to the moaning, defeated Jenny by the 'temple' and throws her repeatedly down in the snow until she can no longer get up; while, in the garden down below, Matern's antagonism towards his 'friend' reaches its savage high-point as he batters him with his fist again and again after all the others have stopped, and even after his victim has become silent and still in the snow. And what with the rhythmic pounding of the 'teeth-grinding fist' ('knirschende Faust'), and Amsel's mouth bubbling with blood and asking the question: 'Bist Du es? Tsib Ud se?' ('*Is it you? Si ti uoy?*'), this darkly splendid 'letter' is an emblematic tableau of just that process of betrayal, persecution and hurt that we have so often found at the heart of Grass's narrative work. After it, the Passion sequence falls rapidly away to its conclusion, the two sets of attackers being whisked from the scene in a single paragraph (256; *214*), and the characteristic pattern of short 'letters' devoted alternately to Jenny and Amsel being superseded by a run of longer 'letters' of more neutral tone. Thematically speaking, a crucial new sequence immediately supervenes: the description of the metamorphoses which the four protagonists variously undergo – a development that shows beyond doubt how the Passion sequence is indeed the novel's crisis, the key turning-point towards which the prior action moves and the subsequent action looks back. But we shall come to this in due course.

One element in the 'attack' pages which calls for comment is the pronounced motif of the crows. Already prefigured long before in the 'Morning Shifts' (cf. below, p. 207), they are first established in the 'letter' that conveys the beginnings of Jenny's ordeal (252, line 8; *210*, line *31*), and are then mentioned no less than seventeen times in the five pages of the sequence, and several times more in the ensuing few pages. Their most obvious function is as a sheer linking device in the way that Grass has them fly to and fro between Amsel's garden and the Gutenberg monument. Much more importantly, though, they also make connections of a symbolic kind: they are first cousins to the grim chorus of seagulls in *Cat and Mouse* (not to mention *The Tin Drum*); they are emphatically black, like Tulla's monument-'temple' and the masks of Amsel's attackers – and like the novel's paramount motif of the dogs; and they are in league with Tulla in her persecution, behaving 'riotously' on Jenny's third and last fall ('randalierten', 254; *212*) and 'enthusiastically' when she is being shoved back into the snow ('begeistert', 255; *213*); they are also presented as Tulla's minions: 'Tulla dismissed the

193

crows' (254; 212). Most importantly of all, Grass uses the motif of the crows to link up this fictive persecution of two individuals with that historical mass persecution commemorated later on in the 'Knochenberg' sequence, and the connection is immediately established: the 'attack'-sequence image of the crows 'creaking unoiled' (252, 260, also 256; 210, 217, 214) is recreated at the very climax of the 'letter' with which the 'Knochenberg' sequence is begun one hundred pages later: 'But the crows, which are not pure, were creaking unoiled, even yesterday' (357; 296). In the subsequent 'letters' depicting the actual mound of bones and Tulla Pokriefke's escapade (367-73; 304-9), the crows are mentioned fourteen times – and whereas their baneful associations were only obliquely apparent in the 'attack' sequence, here they become starkly evident in that the black crows are repeatedly figured as permanent denizens of the vile and stinking mound of human remains. (It comes as no surprise, a little later, to find the crows in attendance on Tulla Pokriefke's abortion, 385-6; 318-20).

One oddity about the crows in the 'attack' sequence is that, instead of speaking about some indefinite number of crows, as one might expect, Grass in fact specifies that there are *nine* crows (252, 253; 210, 211). At first sight this might seem just a fanciful flourish – but it soon turns out that nine is a number that Grass uses astonishingly often in the book: there are nine of Amsel's robot Nazis, nine of his attackers and nine of Jenny's, Tulla forces Jenny to cover herself with nine leeches, there are nine children in Tulla's gang when she tries to inveigle Jenny into the ice-warehouse, there are 'nine-pronged flames' in the strange inferno towards the end, Matern is nine when first presented at the beginning, Grandmother Matern has been nine years paralysed before her mighty resurrection, the scarecrow that changes Matern from oppressor to protector reflects his violent being in ninefold form. I used to think this an irritating mannerism – but that is clearly a wrong view. The more one looks at Grass's wall-plans, the more it becomes certain that *number* is fundamental to Grass's creative imagination. Thus for instance we see that at one time there were to be nine sections in what was later to become the 'Morning Shifts' of *Dog Years*; while other plans work rigorously in fives and sevens – especially sevens (a typical early plan for what was to become the Third Book of *Dog Years* lists seven characters, and depicts

194

seven sections with groups of seven plot elements within each of the sections; a ballet in seven acts is sketched out on the back of one wall-plan; there were to be 'seven heroes' in *Potato Peelings*, etc.). One cannot be sure what this fascination for number means – if indeed it 'means' anything at all (it would seem to correspond to his fascination for certain partly autonomous images – chickens, nuns, etc.). But one can be quite certain that it plays a powerful part in shaping Grass's material, and perhaps even in bringing it into being in the first place.

To come back to the Passion sequence, there is one particularly resonant element in the depiction of Amsel's savage beating, and that is the motif of fists, a motif that Grass uses as many as nine times, explicitly and implicitly, in the relevant score of lines (254, 255; 212, 213). And what he creates is a remarkable kind of combined metonymy and personification whereby the identity of Amsel's attackers, savage and inhuman as they are, is entirely subsumed into the image of the fist, which appears as a being in its own right. The nine attackers themselves are not mentioned once in the critical lines; instead it is fists that answer Amsel's questions, a fist that grinds its teeth, a fist that carries on battering Eddi Amsel – whose identity as a person is by contrast strongly conveyed. And of course the effect of all this is heightened by the fact that Walter Matern is depicted in 'fist' terms over and over again in the novel as a whole : the image is repeatedly used in the knife episode at the start (13 f.; 8 f.), and again in the description of Matern's switch of roles from oppressor to protector – where his fists are characteristically said to have 'made themselves independent' (42; 33), and there are many other instances of the motif thereafter. Another crucial context in which the motif is used is the evocation of National Socialist violence towards the beginning of the Second Book (150; 125-6) – and thus the reader is encouraged to see that this is the reality of which Walter Matern is representative. Eduard Amsel, for his part, is Matern's categorical antithesis; he is profoundly unviolent – and it is one of the book's many nice conceits that Grass chooses to point this antithesis with what is, in fact, the novel's most concentrated elaboration of the fist motif : a description of Amsel's fists as soft and pink and less tough than the air, fists that were just right for laughing into, fists that were never thumped on tables nor raised in violence, fists that were not really fists at all (200-1; 168).

The Victims and their Otherness

We have seen *how* the separate victims of the book are persecuted. The question that remains is *why*: what is it about
Oswald Brunies and Felsner-Imbs, Jenny Brunies and Eduard
Amsel, that makes them victims at all, and draws the attention
of their oppressors?

As we might expect in the light of *The Tin Drum* and *Cat
and Mouse*, it is the victims' 'eccentricity', their 'abnormality',
their otherness that is the single general reason for their suffering; and as we might equally expect on the basis of the earlier
books, Grass makes this essential otherness show itself even in
an outward, physical way, just as he made Oskar manifestly
egregious by means of his pint size and hunched back, and
Joachim Mahlke by means of his huge Adam's apple and oversize ears, etc.

The way that Grass does this in the case of Amsel and Jenny,
the chief victims of the novel, is to make them both extraordinarily fat. The tableau description of Amsel towards the
beginning of the Second Book is a typical one: 'Eddi Amsel is
what is commonly known as a fatty. His clothes are full to
bursting. His knees are marked with little dimples.... The
general impression is one of boneless waddling.' (145; *122*). It
is the same page, too, which first establishes the fatness of 'die
pummelige Jenny' ('*plump little Jenny*'): 'Jenny was a fat child.
Even when Eddi Amsel was roaming around Jenny ... she
seemed no slimmer.' The novel's very first description of Amsel
in the knife episode is in these same terms: 'was komisch
Rundes' (13; '*a funny round something*', 8), and from this point
until his metamorphosis in the snow two hundred and fifty
pages later, Amsel's fatness is mentioned over and over again, as
is Jenny's in her turn. But this first picture of Amsel as not
just fat, but comically so, also hints at the real significance of
his abnormal shape, which is that it makes him not only distinct
from his fellows but also their butt; again, we find the same
pattern being established concerning Jenny at a very early stage
of the 'Love Letters': 'Some laugh, many smile, because Jenny is
so fat and walks over the boards of the pier on two pillars of

fat' (153; 128). At other points in the narrative, as we have seen, this always implicit connection between the fatness of the two main victims and their suffering is expressly and programmatically emphasised; in the case of Amsel: 'ludicrously round and freckle-faced ..., he became a whipping boy.' (42; 32); and in Jenny's case: 'Jenny looked unnaturally roly-poly and had to suffer much.' (397-8; 329). In the attack sequence itself, the victims' fatness is not particularly strongly stressed – but it features very prominently in the page-long recapitulation in the 'Schlussmärchen' (397-8; 329), and Amsel's fatness is again most prominent in Walli Sawatzki's 'vision' in the Third Book (554, 555; 457-8), as it also is in many of Walter Matern's haunted memories of his erstwhile 'friend'.

So much for the egregious physical appearance of the two main victims. But Grass also makes them distinctive and vulnerable in another, though less physical and outward way: they both grow up essentially as aliens within their particular communities. Amsel's parents were newcomers to the region, while he himself is a part-orphan amongst 'normal' children; and Jenny is a foundling in an eccentric bachelor household. Most important of all, though: Grass casts them in the traditional victim and outsider roles of Jew and gypsy – minority scapegoat categories that are clearly identified as such at one point in the novel, when Grass includes as one of the questions put to Matern in the 'radio discussion': 'Was your friend perhaps a Negro, a Gypsy, or a Jew?' (605; 500).

It is true that Jenny Brunies's gypsy background does not contribute in any precise way to her tribulations, and indeed becomes something of an issue only *after* her persecution and metamorphosis, when she begins to identify with her origins in preference to the society that has oppressed her and annihilated her 'father'.[9] Eduard Amsel's Jewishness, on the other hand, plays a very considerable part in his sufferings, as is indicated early on through a pointedly anachronic passage when Amsel-Brauchsel leaps forward fifteen years to relate how his mother 'confessed' on her death-bed that his father had been a Jew, and how she was afraid for her son in view of the (Nazi) laws then being brought into force (38; 29). And although the narrator soon reverts to normal chronology with the remark that the laws were still mild in Amsel's childhood and did not yet penalise him for his origins (39; 30), it is only a few pages later that we are confronted with fat Amsel in his role as 'whipping-boy' – and with the fact that his Jewishness is indeed involved in it; for someone among his attackers begins to taunt him between blows by calling him 'Itzig!' ('*yid*', '*sheeny*') – and that someone is, of course, none other than Walter Matern (42; 33). The same pattern recurs in other decisive contexts, too. Thus Matern not only batters his friend to the ground in the skeleton episode, but punctuates his blows with the same 'Itzig!' imprecation (93; 77; but see also 96, 102; 80, 85); and again, in the penultimate 'Materniad', Matern in his rage of defeat and frustration fires a last Parthian shot at his 'friend' before sinking impotent to the ground: 'Matern releases a word.... Matern flings a single word, which aims and strikes home.... Several times in succession the word.... Matern takes aim and says: "YID!"' (647; 534). Grass has Tulla use just the same weapon much earlier in the book, when her father puts her up to driving Amsel from the joinery yard – and nowhere is his Jewishness more insistently harped on than here, the word 'Itzich' being used explicitly or implicitly some two dozen times in the space of little more than a page (198-9; *166-7*). This whole passage is magnificently created: the natural amphitheatre of the courtyard lined with flats at whose windows more and more spectators appear, the background roar of the joinery saws, and, on stage, Eduard Amsel, severely distressed but still protected by a kind of shield of irony, slowly retreating amidst the barrage of 'Itzich' taunts thrown at him by the prancing, ubiquitous Tulla.

Most importantly of all, perhaps, the theme of Amsel's persecution as a Jew features prominently in the 'radio discussion' towards the close of the book. For one thing, there is the matter of the knife event with which the novel began. When the episode was first narrated, there was no hint of Jewishness at all; but Grass now retrospectively deepens the fiction by implying, through a careful juxtaposition, that Amsel's Jewishness did indeed have something to do with Matern's flurry of antagonism:

Diskussionsleiter: ... Dasselbe Taschenmesser warf Matern als Knabe in die Weichsel. Warum das Taschenmesser? Weil kein Stein zur Hand war. Warum überhaupt? Matern: Weil die Weichsel immerzu geradeaus floss. Weil ..., weil ..., weil – weil ...

Diskutant: War Ihr Freund etwa Neger, Zigeuner oder Jude? (605)

Discussion Leader: ... Still a boy, Matern threw the same pocketknife into the Vistula. Why the pocketknife? Because no stone was available. But in a more general sense, why?
Matern: Because the Vistula flowed straight ahead for ever-more. Because ..., because ..., because – because ...
A Boy: Was your friend a Negro, a Gypsy or a Jew? (500)

But this is not all: Grass goes on to make antisemitism the main theme of more than five pages of the 'discussion'. Matern is forced to admit to having used the 'Itzig' taunt against his 'friend'; the historical background is filled in, concerning both the origin of the word and the outcome of antisemitism in the extermination camps of National Socialism; and Grass then goes over again from this historical reality to his symbolic fiction by recreating the savage attack on Amsel – and we find now that Amsel's Jewishness was deeply involved in his suffering, for the rhythmic re-narration of the attack climaxes in the lines 'Und Itzich Itzich Itzich hiess/des Onkels Litanei' (610; *'And sheeny sheeny sheeny was/My Uncle's litany'*, 504), and Matern himself slips back for a moment into his attacker's frame of mind, uttering his SA warcry and gloating over the way he and the others smashed the 'Itzich's' face ('– Prügel bekam er, der Itzich!', etc., 611; 505).

Turning now to Oswald Brunies and Felsner-Imbs, the other two in the novel's quartet of victims, we find a considerably different situation. It is true that, like Amsel and Jenny, they are so created that their sheer physical appearance marks them out as distinctive and 'abnormal': Brunies with his moustache scorched by cigars and sticky from his mania for sweets, with great curlicues of hair growing out of his ears, with Eichen-dorff nestling in his dishevelled eyebrows and Heine and Raabe apparent about his mouth and enormous nose (110-11; 92), with his large floppy hat and green loden cape (145; 122); and Felsner-Imbs with his great mane of powdered white hair flowing down over his old-fashioned collar, and his public displays of restoring it to shape with his ever handy brush (187; 156-7) – indeed both Brunies and Felsner-Imbs are clearly splendid continuations of that tradition of eccentrics in post-Classical German literature that Herman Meyer has so well described,[10] Brunies even being explicitly defined as a 'Kauz', an 'Original' (144; *eccentric*, 121). But this physical otherness of the two men is plainly quite different in kind from that of Amsel and Jenny: their fatness, and likewise their Jewish and gypsy blood, are inherited factors for which they are in no way responsible – but the physical appearance and whole eccentric bearing of their two mentors is an index of *attitudes*, of a chosen way of life outside the pale of 'normal' social patterns.

Grass makes this a most important factor indeed in the case of Oswald Brunies, for he depicts him as being not merely eccentric to the normal environment, but positively unsympathetic towards it. In him, we have a character unique in all Grass's writing so far: an incorruptible humanist of the old school who recognises that the society around him is increasingly poisoned by a monstrous inhumanity, who can interpret the 'ample omens of disaster' (to quote *The Tin Drum*) – and who quietly refuses to connive at what is happening.

This quiet rejection of the system is beautifully and portentously conveyed towards the beginning of the Second Book in the context of the pram episode, when a crowd of people, (including the Matzeraths and Jan Bronski) begin singing by the Brösen jetty, led by a group of Nazi *Jungvolk* – and the date, it might be noted, is Summer 1932, when the regime of the fist was steadily establishing itself thanks to the general pretence that it was really not such a regime at all (150; *125-6*). The crowd sings and sings, until:

> Mitsingen wird langsam zur Pflicht. Umblicken: 'Warum der noch nicht?' Seitliches Schielen: ... Sogar der alte Sawatzki, durch und durch Sozi, hält mit.... Und der Herr Studienrat? Kann er nicht wenigstens seinen ewigen Malzbonbon verdrängen und so tun als ob? (154).

> *Little by little it becomes imperative to join in: 'Why isn't he singing?' Sidelong glances: ... Even old Sawatzki is with us, and he's an out-and-out Socialist.... And what about Dr Brunies? Couldn't he at least stop sucking that eternal cough-drop and pretend? (129)*

The point is reinforced at the end of the same letter: everyone is singing, Jews, Poles and Socialists included – but 'Brunies lutscht offensichtlich und setzt Spottlichterchen auf.' (155; *'Brunies sucks ostentatiously and an ironic glint comes into his eye.'*, 130). There is the same kind of passive resistance later on: Brunies is conspicuously absent when the neighbours all throng their windows to watch Harry Liebenau and his father drive off in an official Nazi car to be presented to Hitler just after the invasion of Poland (299-300; 249-50); and we hear in the same context that everyone had responded to the invasion by promptly displaying a swastika flag – or almost everyone: 'Ein Fahnenhalter war leer, stellte alle gefüllten Fahnenhalter in Frage und gehörte Studienrat Brunies.' (301; *'One flagpole was empty, cast doubt upon all the occupied flagpoles, and belonged to Dr Brunies.'*, 250). Harry Liebenau hands in a voluntary composition describing his visit to the Führer's headquarters – but Brunies does not let him read it in class, and demonstratively diverts from its real subject by commenting only on what is incidental within the composition, but in his view more valuable than any number of Hitlers: the paintings hanging in the Zoppot Grand Hotel (305-6; 254). Furthermore, Grass for the first time has Brunies express his distaste for the regime in words as well as action, with his sardonic reference to 'the momentarily reigning warrior caste' and its 'clanking sabres and shouts of victory' (306; 254).

Even more striking than all this, however, is Brunies's distinctive response to speeches of honour made to the school by heroic – i.e. masterfully destructive – ex-pupil winners of the Knight's Cross. At question-time, we hear, the school staff either asked plain technical questions, or wallowed in grandiose rhetoric ('gefielen sich in starken Sätzen') – but not Brunies: 'Dr Brunies asked a holder of the Knight's Cross – I think it was the one from the Air Force – what his thoughts had been on first seeing a dead human being, friend or foe' (331; 275). It was of course this very speech by the *Luftwaffe* 'hero' that was decisive in orienting Joachim Mahlke towards the Knight's Cross in *Cat and Mouse*, and which Grass also made the occasion of Mahlke's first major utterance: his lament on the inflation of the destruction/glory equation (see above, p. 119) – a lament that betrayed exactly that same humanism as does Brunies's pointed question in the novel. Having won the Iron Cross, Walter Matern also comes back to the Conradinum to make 'heroic' speeches to the boys – and Grass again has Brunies pose the same question (331; 275); furthermore, Brunies neatly undoes Matern's belligerent influence (and the same ironic formulations are used here as previously: 'in Frage stellen' and 'Spottlichterchen aufsetzen'):

> Beliebt und gefürchtet wurde er allen und mir zum Vorbild; nur Studienrat Brunies stellte den Feldwebel ... in Frage, indem er Spottlichterchen aufsetzte und Matern bat, an Stelle eines Vortrages über die Kämpfe bei Orel, ein Eichendorffgedicht zu lesen ... (331)

> *He was liked and feared by all, and to me he became a shining ideal; only Dr Brunies ... questioned his sergeant's existence by letting an ironic glint come into his eye and asking Matern, instead of delivering a lecture about the fighting at Orel, to read us a poem by Eichendorff ... (275)*

Oswald Brunies's attitude to the 'momentarily reigning warrior caste' is, of course, a subversive one from the regime's point of view – and the significant fiction of the book is that he is liquidated by the State for precisely this reason, and not because of the peccadillo of the misappropriated vitamin tablets, which serves simply as a pretext. This was foreshadowed in *Cat and Mouse*, when it was said that Brunies was arrested 'ostensibly because he had taken vitamin tablets for himself ... but probably for political reasons' (48-9; 55).[11] Now, in *Dog Years*, the fiction is expanded: we are told that Brunies's pupils furnish evidence of his various utterances, which sound 'subversive and negative'; that his freemasonry counts against him; and that the authorities are already well aware of his anti-social behaviour in failing to display a swastika flag when everyone else does (337-8; 280).

Summarily speaking, then, Oswald Brunies has nothing of that rampant *mauvaise foi* so powerfully figured in the 'Knochenberg' sequence towards the end of the Second Book: he refuses to be taken in by the grandiose deceptions that blind the willing mass, he recognises the brutal, poisonous reality for what it is and refuses to connive at it (Brunies thus correlates most intimately to the figure of Eduard Amsel, as we shall see[12]). And

202

this reflects, as clearly as anything does, the crucial shift of attitude in Grass between the writing of *The Tin Drum* and the writing of *Dog Years*. In the earlier novel there was really no theme of a social reality being ironically revealed behind false masks. *The Tin Drum* mirrored life chiefly in terms of a universal, existential, non-social process far beyond the control of mere individual humans – hence such images as the 'Schlacht, die schon dagewesen, die immer wieder kommt', the vile excremental life cycle, the murderous heavenly merry-go-round owner, and, above all else, the baneful 'Schwarze Köchin'. *Dog Years*, on the other hand, depicts life much more in terms of a *social, cultural* process that is determined by specific factors in specific situations. In this particular sense, Oswald Brunies and especially Amsel-Brauxel are personas that plainly reflect a stage in Grass's gradual shift from the bleak universalism of *The Tin Drum* to his present-day position of complete and precisely defined commitment to what he sees as his *polis* – the Federal Republic of Germany, and to what he sees as the most valid set of political alternatives – those represented by the German Social-Democratic Party. The view of existence implicit in *Dog Years* is accordingly a much less unhopeful one than informed Grass's first novel, as is well reflected in the two chief protagonists: although Oskar Matzerath and Eduard Amsel have a great deal in common – for instance they are both equally victims, Amsel-Brauxel and his co-authors are said to have learnt their trade from Oskar (117; 97), Amsel and Oskar are shown together at one point in a strangely poignant secret huddle (238; 199) – they are none the less categorically different in crucial respects, particularly if one takes identity as the parameter. For Oskar is the supreme embodiment of an all-pervasive principle of 'unidentifiability': he is not sure who begot him, or who is truly his spiritual father, he has no clear sense of his own identity, nor can he really identify the inimical forces besetting him, beyond giving them the symbolic, myth-world designation 'Schwarze Köchin' (and as we saw, this sense of unidentifiability is powerfully transferred to the reader himself). Amsel, on the other hand, has an unchallenged sense both of his own identity and of the true reality of the world around him, and as a result is able – thanks to his crucially characteristic *irony*, and notwithstanding certain temporary setbacks – to preserve himself in a position that is always viable, if only just. The situations of the protagonists at the end of the two novels exemplify the point with great force: whereas Oskar at the end is not only at the mercy of the 'Schwarze Köchin' but also on the verge of being expelled even from the asylum limbo that is his slender refuge, Amsel-Brauchsel is sovereign master to the last of his own subterranean realm, a capitalist among capitalists, an entrepreneur who in his art-cum-business is thoroughly involved in the society and existence that is Germany's. But I shall come back to this.

CHAPTER III

The Symbol of the Dog

We turn now to the most important and recurrent single motif in the novel: the eponymous dog – an image that Grass uses so persistently from title to closing pages that it swiftly becomes symbolic, and the baleful, open-fanged Grass-drawing on the dust-jacket rapidly fulfils its emblematic promise. The basic pattern is one we immediately recognise from *Cat and Mouse*: in both books Grass expresses something baneful through the animal of the dust-jacket's picture and words, and in both books he subsequently identifies the animal with the principal persecutors of the fiction. The graphics of the two dust-jackets show a hall-mark of Grass's style in general: the design is not merely symbolic in its effect, but also in itself. He could easily have created a symbolic effect with more or less straight representations of a cat and a dog – but both drawings are strongly figurative: the cat is wearing a Knight's Cross and has large malevolent eyes that transfix the reader, while the *Dog Years* image is not only black, open-fanged and wolf-like, but is also a representation, not of a dog as such, but of a skeletal human hand in a dog-like, wolf-like shape. The reader is thus made aware before he even opens the book that its dog motif is meant entirely symbolically; and he soon realises that it is in fact a means – like the cat of the novella – for conveying certain patterns of *human* behaviour.[13]

Like the vile crows, like the masks of Amsel's attackers, and like the 'temple' that is the setting of Jenny's persecution, Grass's symbolic dog is emphatically black: after the point has been made visually on the dust-jacket, the motif is reiterated with remarkable frequency throughout the narrative, the blackness of the various dogs being echoed almost two hundred times in all. In the majority of cases there is no special emphasis, but just a steady cumulative effect. In certain cases the context gives the motif extra force: Grandmother Matern's attack on Lorchen, for instance (68; 55), the opening page of the 'Love Letters' (139; 117), Hitler's visit to Zoppot with his hound Prinz (303, 304, 305; 252, 253, 254). Sometimes, though, there is a resonant emphasis on blackness, as for instance in the prelude to Harras's third and most savage attack on Felsner-Imbs, where Harras and the caged wolves are expressively depicted together, and their colouring is insistently compared (240; 200-1). But a much more important case in point is the first extensive reference to Harras in the Second Book, where an already powerful evocation of the animal's blackness suddenly intensifies even further in an extraordinary associative run of words:

überall ... glänzte sein Haar schwarz, regenschirmschwarz, priesterschwarz, witwenschwarz, schutzstaffelschwarz, schul-tafelschwarz, falangeschwarz, amselschwarz, othelloschwarz, ruhrschwarz, veilchenschwarz, tomatenschwarz, zitronen-schwarz, mehlschwarz, milchschwarz, schneeschwarz. (148)

all over him ... his hair glistened black, umbrella-black, priest-black, widow-black, SS-black, blackboard-black, Falange-black, blackbird-black, Othello-black, Ruhr-black, violet-black, tomato-black, lemon-black, flour-black, milk-black, snow-black. (124)

It is fascinating to see how those stalwart critics of Grass, Günter Blöcker and Walter Jens, both betray the inadequacy of their attitude in their responses to this passage, with Blöcker deriding it as typical of Grass's supposed orgiastic excesses,[14] and Jens complaining of 'indiscriminate associations – first thirty variations then an oxymoron to cap it all'.[15] On the contrary, this associative run is not at all undisciplined or self-indulgent. It is a conceit, certainly – but a highly functional one: it sharply emphasises the general motif of blackness; it points up the violent historical reality behind the fiction, with its references to the SS and the Falange (the 'fists' passage is to follow only a page later); and most significant of all, its gradual shift from black through violet-red-lemon-white to the final 'snow-black' oxy-moron brings together through one arresting word both the central symbolism of the black hound and the savage attacks on Amsel and Jenny in the 'pure' white snow. A tendentious inter-
206

pretation, perhaps? – after all, the passage comes a full hundred pages before the Passion sequence itself. But for one thing, a snow-blackness motif has by this time been long since established in the novel ('Crows in the snow – what a subject!'; 67; 54); for another, and much more importantly, the whole page-long depiction of Harras that culminates in this passage is repeated almost verbatim in the 'radio discussion', the crucial function of which is, after all, to confront the posturing Matern with his true past, and in particular the critical assault on his 'friend'. And this Harras passage is not repeated just anywhere in the 'discussion', but as its emphatic, rhythmic, ritual conclusion, so that the 'snow-black' oxymoron is in effect its final dramatic word (612-13; 505-6).

Something that goes together very closely with the motif of the dog's blackness is the strong wolf motif in the novel. This begins with the depiction of the dogs' ancestry, for just as Walter Matern is represented as descending from inveterately violent stock ('from the medieval robber Materna, by way of Grandma, who was a genuine Matern'; 28; 21 and *passim*[16]), so the novel's dynasty of dogs is described as having a wolf as their savage forbear. The first intimation of this comes typically in the opening episode of Matern and the knife: 'Senta has no intention of going back to the wolves, but instead will remain a gooddog gooddog gooddog ...' (15; 9) – and at once we have not only the wolf notion in itself, but also the notion of an atavistic return to wolfishness which will turn out to be a cardinal theme of the book. The second wolf allusion, however, is even more pointed than the first, for it makes the vital connection between primitive wolf and Adolf Hitler (even though the pattern established through these resonant, quasi-Biblical words does not acquire its full meaning for the reader until much later on):

Pawel ... hatte Perkun aus dem Litauischen mitgebracht und zeigte auf Verlangen eine Art Stammbaum vor, dem jedermann entnehmen konnte, dass Perkuns Grossmutter väterlicherseits eine litauische, russische oder polnische Wölfin gewesen war.

Und Perkun zeugte Senta; und Senta warf Harras; und Harras zeugte Prinz; und Prinz machte Geschichte ... (22)

Pawel ... had brought Perkun with him from Lithuania and

207

*on request exhibited a kind of pedigree, which made it clear
to whom it may concern that Perkun's grandmother on her
father's side had been a Lithuanian, Russian or Polish she-wolf.
And Perkun begat Senta; and Senta whelped Harras; and
Harras begat Prinz; and Prinz made history ... (15)*

The prefigurative impact of these words is greatly increased by
the fact that Grass repeats them in modified form on two further
occasions in the First Book (45, 70; 35-6, 57 – indeed they recur
as a leitmotif in the Second Book too, though without specific
mention of the ancestral wolf). But it is typically in the 'radio
discussion', the forceful recapitulation of the novel's main
events, that the leitmotif with its wolf-to-National-Socialism
implication is most demonstratively used:

Matern: Oh, ihr einander in den Schwanz beissenden Hundejahre! Am Anfang gab es eine litauische Wölfin. Diese
wurde mit einem Schäferhundrüden gekreuzt. Dieser Untat
entsprang ein Rüde, dessen Namen kein Stammbaum nennt.
Und er, der Namenlose, zeugte Perkun. Und Perkun zeugte
Senta ...
Diskutantenchor: Und Senta warf Harras ...
Matern: Und Harras zeugte Prinz, der heute als Pluto an
meiner Seite sein Gnadenbrot kauen darf. Oh, ihr heiser
geheulten Hundejahre! (608)

*Matern: O ye dog years, biting each other's tails! In the be-
ginning there was a Lithuanian she-wolf. She was crossed
with a male sheep-dog. The outcome of this vile deed was
a male whose name does not figure in any pedigree. And he,
the nameless one, begat Perkun, and Perkun begat Senta ...
Chorus: And Senta whelped Harras ...
Matern: And Harras begat Prinz, who may graciously spend
his retirement at my side. O ye dog years hoarse from
howling! (502-3)*

And the symbolical reference of the wolf-dog image becomes
particularly clear in the lines that follow on from this passage,
for Grass has Matern allude – however obliquely and histrionic-
ally – to the concentration camp exterminations: 'Have you
fathomed the parable? Do you realise the seven-figured reckon-
208

ing of accursed dog years?' And within a page the savaging of Amsel begins to be re-narrated.

As we have seen, Senta, the novel's first representative of the dynasty of dogs, is described at a very early stage as 'not wanting to return to the wolves' – but it is for just such an atavistic throwback that this same dog later has to be destroyed : ' – she tore a sheep limb from limb like a wolf and attacked an agent from the fire insurance company – ' (84; 69). In the case of Senta's offspring, Harras, there is just the same process, but it is much more emphatically conveyed. Not only is there Harras's mounting savagery in itself – foreshadowed quite early in the Second Book through the warnings of Police Lieutenant Mirchau (166-7; *139-40*), and manifested in the successive attacks on Felsner-Imbs – but Grass also makes Harras part of the most tense and pointed wolf evocation in the novel : the depiction of the three caged wolves tracking impatiently to and fro in the Freudental menagerie, waiting for the chance to escape and kill, as the first reference immediately establishes : 'And the wolves? Who gave the wolves? Wolves that later broke out of the enclosure, tore a berry-picking child to pieces, and, once shot, had their pictures in the papers?' (239; *200*). Harras is shown responding strongly to these savage cousins : he stands stock still outside their pen, gives out a hoarse whining sound ('kujiehnt heiser') and has to be whistled at to rejoin the Liebenaus and Pokriefkes. This linking of Harras and the wolves is pointed enough in itself – but it becomes even more pointed when we realise what it serves to prelude : one has not turned the page before Harras breaks loose on his third and most savage attack on Felsner-Imbs – and before the Passion sequence duly commences.

The whole imagery of the dogs, I have suggested, is meant above all as a metaphor for savage modes of *human* behaviour, and the various hounds are accordingly closely identified with the book's chief persecutors – the fictional Tulla and Matern, and the historical Hitler. This identification is certainly most memorable in the case of Tulla Pokriefke. Not only does she use Harras to intimidate Jenny, set him on Felsner-Imbs, and generally bend him to her purpose, untaming him in the process (166-7; *140*; Amsel 'corrupts' Harras in an opposite sense : he makes him excessively tame! 193 f., 199; *162, 167*), not only is there all this, but there is also the unforgettable episode in which Tulla, after the drowning of her beloved Konrad, takes

209

animal refuge in Harras's kennel and eats, sleeps, excretes and exists as he does on all fours for a week on end: nowhere is the brute pattern of her existence more manifest than in this strange and haunting sequence (168-80; *141-51*). It is then immediately followed by the introduction of the novel's most significant combination of dog-wolf and human: the linking up of Harras's offspring, Prinz, and Adolf Hitler (again, Tulla is prominent here: it is she who chiefly appears in the press photographs alongside the sire of the Führer's new hound, 185; *155*). Later, in the Third Book, the motif comes full circle in that the wolfish lineage comes back into the keeping of Walter Matern: after having been identified with Senta in his childhood, he duly becomes the inheritor of Prinz, Senta's Hitlerite descendant. One of the most important functions of the dog symbolism becomes apparent here: by closely associating different persons with what is in effect a single archetype – 'a dog by the name of Perkun Senta Harras Prinz Pluto' (621-2; *514*) – Grass plainly identifies them as all belonging together, as being in other words all exponents of the same destructive, lupine spirit, and in the same period of 'dog years' (whether he does this convincingly is another matter, as we shall see later on).

The fact that Grass brings the historical German Führer into his fiction, and links him directly to its central symbol, shows more clearly than perhaps any other single factor how the book is concerned with a specifically *German* process. This is indicated, too, by a leitmotif representation of the dog as both black *and* German ('schwarzer deutscher Schäferhund') – the contrast in this respect between the 'black' symbolism of *The Tin Drum* (the 'Schwarze Köchin') and *Dog Years* being a characteristic one indeed. Grass even has Harras regarded by people *within* the story as symbolic of Hitler's German regime: Matern in his drunken distress after Amsel's disappearance curses the dog as 'Nazi Nazi Nazi Nazi!' (290, cf. 293; *242, 244*); and a hundred pages later Harry Liebenau's father, after hearing among other things of Oswald Brunies's extermination and his own son's volunteering for war service, goes out on the twentieth of April 1944, and smashes the now dead Harras's kennel to splinters with an axe. His behaviour is eloquent of itself, but Grass makes the point quite explicit:

Weil aber am zwanzigsten April der fünfundfünfzigste

Geburtstag desselben Führers und Reichskanzlers gefeiert wurde, dem zehn Jahre zuvor der junge Schäferhund Prinz, aus Harras Stamm, geschenkt worden war, begriff alle Welt in den Fenstern des Mietshauses und hinter den Hobelbänken der Tischlerei, dass mehr zerschlagen wurde als morsches Holz und löchrige Teerpappe. (392)

But because the fifty-fifth birthday of the selfsame Führer and Chancellor to whom the young shepherd dog Prinz of Harras' line had been presented ten years before, was celebrated on April 20th, everybody at the apartment house windows and at the workbenches in the shop understood that more had been smashed than rotting wood and torn tar-paper. (324)

In the Third Book, the main function of the dog image remains that of symbolising a destructive spirit amidst the Germans, and demonstrating that it lives on, in Grass's view, into post-war Germany. Grass himself confirmed this in an interview with Heinrich Vormweg in 1964; Vormweg asked whether the dog had been included in the Third Book to represent the inner *Schweinehund* that had perhaps remained with the Germans into the post-war period – 'Of course, said Günter Grass. But he had tried not simply to state it as a fact, but to make it become graphically apparent.'[17] The point is strongly conveyed during the sequence of Prinz's flight from Hitler to Matern. Grass has Hitler indissolubly link the dog-wolf and Germany with remarks like 'Berlin is still German. Vienna will be German again. And never will the dog be negated.' (421; 348). He sends Dönitz the papers authorising him to become his successor – and includes Prinz's pedigree. And in his last will and testament, so Grass's fiction goes, he bequeaths the dog as his 'gift to the German people' (423; 349). Then, in the eight-line closing letter of the Second Book, the connection between Hitler's dog and post-war Germany is programmatically established:

Es war einmal ein Hund,
    der verliess seinen Herrn und brachte einen langen Weg hinter sich. Nur Kaninchen rümpfen die Nase; doch niemand, der lesen kann, möge glauben, der Hund sei nicht angekommen. (427)

There was once a dog,

who left his Master and travelled a long way. Only rabbits pucker up their noses; but let no one who can read suppose that the dog did not arrive. (353)

Needless to say, Prinz-Pluto remains emphatically Hitlerite in the final Book. When Matern (in a typical empty gesture) spits on Hitler's face shown in the posters stacked in the mine, Prinz-Pluto licks it clean, and when Matern begins crumpling the posters the dog becomes so threatening that he has to stop (443-4; 367). The pattern is the same in the 'radio discussion': Prinz-Pluto remains indifferent to Mozart's *Kleine Nachtmusik*, but wags his tail on hearing the German National Anthem and howls on hearing the Wagner so beloved by his erstwhile Master; then, as a final indication, Grass has the dog lick the portrait of Hitler that is put before him (597-9; 493-5). Most importantly, too, the earlier theme of Hitler's having bequeathed his black dog-wolf to the German people is repeated here (601; 496) – and Walter Matern, the principal persecutor of the story, is specifically defined as the trustee of this lupine patrimony; whereupon the 'discussion' turns to establishing his fitness for the task, and retraces the novel's main thread of persecution through to the murderous attack on Eduard Amsel, before finally returning to the dog metaphor and closing, as we have seen, on the highly-charged 'snow-black' oxymoron.

It must be clear what kind of historical view lies behind this treatment of the dog image. Grass does not see the events and the era depicted in his novel as a separate, autonomous phenomenon with its own particular logic. On the contrary, he has a strong sense of a continuous historical process, as we have often observed before. Thus the continuation of the dog metaphor in the Third Book reflects Grass's conviction that the collapse of Hitler's Reich did not mean that Germany suddenly stopped being Germany: in his view, the old wolfish strain survived as before, recessive, yes, but still capable of being made dominant through a wrong conjunction of influences. But Grass wanted to do much more in the Third Book than simply attest the survival of the strain: he wanted to challenge the contrary and dangerously false notion that the Federal Republic is a separate and new culture, and that all remembrance of the savage past is an irrelevant, constricting burden that must be shed as rapidly as possible. I shall argue that it is indeed the central purpose of the Third Book to hold up an image of the inner reality of Germany, and in particular of its recent past, against its smooth mask of comfort, opulence and above all of would-be newness. Thus the emphasis with Matern in the Third Book is no longer on his savagery but on his falseness and role-playing; he is representative of all those Germans who 'want to forget', as the last page of the 'Love Letters' expressly has it; or in the words of the opening lines of the 'First Materniad': 'He has a spoon but no memory.' (431; 357). But Hitler's black and German dog, a 'walking piece of the past' (557; 460) prevents him from forgetting: the dog-wolf pattern is central to him and his culture, as the Third Book's opening words convey – 'The dog stands central', and this knowledge is forced on him, despite all his 'lies' and 'play-acting', in the shape of Prinz-Pluto, who proves impossible to chase away – 'There aren't that many stones in the world.' And so Matern will as it were be force-fed on the dog-food leftovers of his and Germany's past: 'For there are scraps everywhere – dog food: the twenty-nine potato years. Memory soup. Remembrance dumplings. . . . Gritty guilt: that's the salt.'

From this opening page of the Third Book right through to its closing paragraphs, Grass firmly maintains his dog metaphor along the lines I have described. Sooner or later, though, we shall have to ask the question whether Grass's resolute symbolic intent does not perhaps, with the dog image as in other respects, bring about a fiction that is schematic and contrived instead of having the suppleness and vitality that elsewhere mark his narrative. But meanwhile, let us take a closer look at the novel's richest configuration: Eduard Amsel and Walter Matern, and the relationship between them. For although we have considered the two protagonists in terms of the theme of persecution and suffering, there is clearly a great deal more to them than that.

CHAPTER IV

The Two 'Friends':
'Weak' Master, 'Mighty' Servant

A dialectic of physical power and unphysical power: this, I have suggested, is one of the key elements in the relationship between the novel's two protagonists.

So far as sheer physical power and brute force are concerned, the narrative from its first beginnings leaves no room for doubt as to which of the two 'friends' is on top: Walter Matern is not merely the stronger of the two, but is projected as the very embodiment of naked strength − hence the fists motif, his various onslaughts against and on behalf of Eddi Amsel, his participation in the SA pogroms against Jews, Poles and Leftists, his part in the beer-hall brawl, his treatment of Tulla after the 'Knochenberg' episode. Another insistent mark of his violent being is his treatment of animals, as typified in the opening episode through the description of the symbolic penknife as

[ein Taschenmesser,] das im letzten Sommer an Folcherts Schuppentor einen Schmetterling genagelt, unter der Anlege-brücke von Kriwes Fähre innerhalb eines Tages vier Ratten, in den Dünen beinahe ein Kaninchen und vor zwei Wochen einen Maulwurf getroffen hatte, bevor Senta ihn erwischen konnte. (15-16)

[a penknife] which last summer had pinned a butterfly to Folchert's barn door, which under the wharf of Kriwe's ferry had in one day speared four rats, had almost speared a rabbit in the dunes, and two weeks ago had pegged a mole before Senta could catch it. (10)

And we learn subsequently of Matern hunting with Senta in

the dunes, yearning to snatch the eels from the cows' udders, clubbing rats in the sewer (then using the same club to batter Amsel with), killing other rats and slitting open seagulls, using countless frogs for batting practice, shooting at hares and crows, and dismembering and squashing flies – and it is of course Matern who kills Harras and later stones Prinz and beats him with a club.

The clear fiction is that Eduard Amsel in his flabby fatness is in the same degree physically impotent as Matern is physically powerful, a pattern that is vividly expressed in the passage describing Amsel's ludicrous fists, or rather absence of fists (200-1; *168*) – a passage that also sharply epitomises his vulnerability: 'Faustrecht sprach ihn schuldig; Faustkämpfe machten ihn zum Punching-Ball' ('*The law of the fist pronounced him guilty; fist fights made him into a punching bag*'). But it is the context of this very same fists passage that also illuminates the reverse side of the situation, namely Amsel's absolute power and supremacy where brain is involved and not brawn. For Grass has him join Matern's sports club – and become part of a volley-ball team 'that soon came to be feared and was to become first in the league. For Eddi Amsel directed, he was the heart and centre of the team: a born creative player' (204; *171*). The quite different roles played within the team by the two 'friends' are characteristic ones: while Matern is the physical power-house of the team – 'der Schmetterer' ('*the smasher*'), Amsel is its creative spirit and tactician, its 'Hertz und Zentrale', and all the other team-members are in effect the subordinate functionaries of his purpose.

Matern, then, is dominant wherever brute strength is concerned, while Amsel is supreme in all other situations – and it is precisely this dialectic of power that is clearly established in the initial symbolic episode: the reader is presented with the comically fat, squat Eduard Amsel and the tough, fist-swinging Walter Matern – but the latter is defeated at the very climax of his muscular caper when a mere 'brief stare' from the other boy suffices to knock him wildly off balance and make him lose sight of the knife as it flies through the air (17; *11*). Even in the image of the boys' departure from the scene, Grass precisely conveys Eddi Amsel's unphysical command of the relationship: 'Now they get going ... Half a pace ahead: Amsel. Half a pace behind: Walter Matern. He is dragging Amsel's bits and pieces.'

215

(19; 13). The symbol is one that Grass has used to effect before: Pilenz, too, was described as trailing along behind his 'friend' (154; 167); and we find it used again and again in *Dog Years* to express the changing relationship between Tulla Pokriefke and Jenny Brunies.[18] We also find it recurring in connection with the protagonists, in the remark at the close of the 'Eighteenth Morning Shift': 'Amsel ... was always ahead of him', etc. – but the context of this remark is an astonishing one, for what Grass does here is to figure the two boys explicitly in terms of master and hopelessly subordinate servant, of 'Herr' and 'Paslack':[19]

Nicht Amsel kassierte. Walter Matern hatte ... den Kaufpreis zu nennen ... und die Münzen einzustreichen. Zudem war Walter Matern für den Transport der verkauften wie der ausgeliehenen Scheuchen zuständig. Er geriet in Abhängigkeit. Amsel machte ihn zum Paslack. In kurzatmigen Revolten versuchte er auszubrechen. Die Geschichte mit dem Taschenmesser war solch ein ohnmächtiger Versuch; denn Amsel blieb ihm, so kurzbeinig dicklich er durch die Welt kugelte, immer voraus. Wenn die Beiden über den Deich liefen, hielt sich der Müllerssohn, nach Art der Paslacken, einen halben Schritt hinter dem Erbauer immer neuer Vogelscheuchen. Auch schleppte der Paslack dem Herrn die Materialien: Bohnenstangen und nasse Lumpen, was alles die Weichsel angeschwemmt hatte. (72)

Amsel did not take in the money.... Walter Matern had to state the price ... and pocket the coins. In addition Walter Matern was responsible for the transportation of sold or rented scarecrows. He lost his independence. Amsel made him his flunkey. Now and then he rebelled and tried to regain his freedom, but never for very long. The incident with the pocketknife was a futile attempt of this kind; for Amsel, though he rolled fat and shortlegged through the world, was always ahead of him. When the two went along the dike, the miller's son, after the manner of flunkeys, remained half a step behind the untiring builder of scarecrows. The flunkey also carried his master's materials: beanpoles and wet rags, whatever the Vistula had washed ashore. (59)

This passage is certainly one of the most illuminating in the novel. For one thing, it greatly clarifies the opening knife event by defining it beyond doubt as an impotent attempt by the 'Paslack' to escape the other's strange hold over him. But more generally and more importantly, the passage offers us insight into the whole dynamic of the two boys' relationship: the six-year-old Matern is drawn *nolens volens* into a subservient attachment to the other boy; he lashes out from time to time in his subservience, and thereby often inflicts suffering through his superior physical strength, as when he clubs his 'friend' in the shaft beneath the church, or when he brutalises him in the snow; and finally, for all his spasmodic recalcitrance, he remains for ever bound by Amsel's spell.

CHAPTER V

The Two 'Friends': Walter Matern

The Aggressor Confounded

Matern's thraldom to Amsel is clearly enough conveyed at beginning and end of the novel through the symbolic episodes with the knife – but it is equally strongly, if less explicitly, indicated through the critical sequence of the snow attack. For this is essentially a further act of futile rebellion, and one that backfires just as surely as Heini Pilenz's did in *Cat and Mouse*: Matern does get rid of Amsel in a sheerly physical sense, but becomes as a result more than ever a victim of his subservient fixation on his 'friend', to the point of becoming totally disoriented. This is part, as we shall see, of one of the novel's most striking motifs: Amsel, Jenny, Matern, and to a certain extent Tulla, are all metamorphosed by the two critical acts of persecution – but it is the would-be victims who are beneficially metamorphosed in Grass's fiction, while the persecutors paradoxically suffer, albeit in a non-physical sense. The net result with Matern is that he simply goes to pieces. The particular mark of this is his slide into drunkenness (280-1, 283, etc.; *234, 236*); he is then expelled from the SA for theft while drunk, gains a job at the civic theatre in Schwerin but is sacked without notice 'for incessant drunkenness', goes off to Düsseldorf for a job in children's radio, gets engaged but not for long, and lands after a while in the police cells, where he is beaten up and allowed to secure his release only by volunteering for armed service.

Matern being the very embodiment of falseness and lack of integrity, it is characteristic that in his outward postures he turns on 'the system', on other people and things, and abusively blames them for everything, without seemingly recognising any fault in himself. Hence his killing of Harras after violently cursing him as a 'Nazi Nazi Nazi Nazi' (290; 242) and as a 'Nazi pig' (293; 244); hence too, for instance, his drunken inculpation of Martin Heidegger as a 'pre-Socratic Nazi dog' (393-4; 325). But beneath this outward show of contumely, Matern's real and devouring preoccupation is with the disappearance of his 'friend'-cum-victim-cum-master Eduard Amsel. Grass has this driving concern of Matern's show itself most plainly when he first brings him back into the narrative after the critical attack sequence, as in the episode of Matern's drunken vision of the Virgin Mary, when he implores her over and over again to reveal Amsel's whereabouts (287-8; 239-40), and likewise in the immediately ensuing depiction of Matern's repeated visits to Felsner-Imbs in search of the same information. Some ten pages later, after the poisoning of Harras, Matern disappears from the narrative once more and is only transiently mentioned in the remaining half of the Second Book; but even on his last fleeting appearance, when we find him pouring abuse on Heidegger, the real nub proves yet again to be Eduard Amsel: 'What have you done with Tubby Amsel? You pre-Socratic Nazi dog!' (393-4; 325).

When it comes to the Third Book, however, the pattern is not just intermittently figured, but is made paramount: Matern in his 'Materniads' is seemingly engaged upon a grand, heroical campaign to root out and punish connivers and exponents of National Socialism who have managed to carve themselves a niche in post-war Germany; in truth, though, these grandiose activities are sheer posturings – and what drives him along willy-nilly in these posturings, thus making him a classic outsider with a railway-station lavatory as his one real centre-point, is the motor of his fixation on Amsel. Matern's first visitation in his supposed avenger role is typical: his very first words in direct speech to Jochen Sawatzki both suppress his own decisive part in the snow attack *and* betray his enduring preoccupation with its victim, however casual the words might appear: 'Say, ... whatever became of Amsel? ... what I want to know is this: what did you do with him afterwards, I mean in Steffensweg, after the eight of you had ...?' (449-50; 372). Just the same combination is apparent fifteen pages later, when Matern, again as pseudo-avenger, seeks out Alfred Lüxenich: the music he listens to conjures up remembrance of Amsel's singing, and his response signals both his fixation and his falseness:

'Ja, ich habe ihn geliebt. Und sie haben ihn mir genommen. Schon als Knabe schützte ich ihn mit meinen Fäusten ... Aber die anderen waren stärker, und ich konnte nur ohnmächtig zusehen, wie Terror diese Stimme zerbrach. Eddi, mein Eddi! ...' (465)

'Yes, I loved him. And they took him away from me. Even as a boy, I defended him with my fists ... But the others were stronger, and I could only look on helplessly as terror broke that voice. Eddi, my Eddi! ...' (385)

The motif of Matern's subjection to the memory of Amsel is further reinforced in later contexts in the Third Book. The decisive question, though, is why Matern is so fixated on his erstwhile 'friend' from the snow attack onwards. And there can be little doubt that what we are to recognise is that same ravaging force in Matern that was earlier figured in Heini Pilenz, namely, a dynamic sense of guilt.[20]

This is first made apparent in the Second Book, through Matern's reference (in the drunken scene involving the Virgin Mary) to the Cain and Abel myth — and Grass increases the metaphoric force of this by having the narrator add: 'At that time I only dimly suspected who was meant by Cain and Abel.' (285; 238). Similarly, the act of remembrance that Grass has Matern carry out on his release from the P.O.W. camp towards the start of the Third Book also implies a needling sense of guilt, in that it shows how his awareness is still firmly centred on the brutal snow attack and its consequences:

Erinnere Dich! ... Wieviele Zähne hat der Mensch? ... Acht oder neun Vermummte? Wieviele Namen leben noch? ... Was flüsterten die Mehlwürmer Deines Vaters, als der Sohn den Müller fragte, wie es jemandem gehe und was der treibe? Sie flüsterten, erinnere Dich, jener sei stockheiser und rauche dennoch den lieben langen Tag lang Zigaretten aneinandergereiht. (435)

Remember! ... How many teeth has a man? ... Were there eight or nine muffled figures? How many names are still alive? ... What did your father's mealworms whisper when his son asked him how somebody was getting along and what was *he doing? They whispered, remember, that this somebody was hoarse as a grater and nevertheless chain-smoked all day long. (360-1)*

But these lines include one pointer of special importance: Matern's query about human teeth ('Wieviele Zähne hat der Mensch?') – for this connects with one of the book's most arresting numerical conceits, the leitmotif of Eduard Amsel's thirty-two teeth, a leitmotif that was already firmly established in the Second Book (from the point in the critical attack sequence where Amsel flung his thirty-two knocked-out teeth into the bushes, 262-3; *219*), and which is given great force in the 'Materniads'. It is not frequently used during the Third Book's first three phases (involving Prinz-Pluto, Matern's pose as 'Great Avenger', and the episode around Anton Matern); but once the narrative begins to move towards its climax, that is, once Grass begins to confront his poseur-protagonist increasingly with the latter's own true image, so the 'thirty-two teeth' image becomes steadily more emphatic as a token of the snow attack and Matern's absolute guilt.

The point where the novel shifts most obviously into its climactic phase is the opening of the sixth chapter, 'The Eighty-eighth Sterile Materniad'. And Grass not only has the narrator Matern speak in the first person for the first time, he not only has him delineate his own falseness in exact, graphic detail ('Behold me: Bald-headed inside and out. An empty cupboard full of uniforms for every conviction'; 514; *425*) – he also has him programmatically define the savaging of Amsel as the central issue, and has him do so precisely in terms of the 'thirty-two teeth' motif, for the opening paragraph ends: 'It is a question of teeth, thirty-two of them.... Every tooth counts.'

The motif is twice reinforced in the succeeding paragraph, but then, in the episode of Matern's and the Sawatzkis' visit to the 'Mortuary' restaurant, it is given remarkable emphasis through the use of grotesque visual imagery: Matern at first persists in his Avenger pose (523; *433*) – but the arrival of an ice-cream dessert in the shape of full sets of thirty-two human teeth confounds him utterly by confronting him with the image of his inveterate, most irritant sense of guilt. By a typical device, the severity of this experience for Matern is expressed through a physical response: he vomits, and what comes out is the vomit of years ('er erbricht sich gründlich und jahrelang', 525; 434). Extreme dislocation was signalled in just such a way with Agnes and Oskar, and again with Joachim Mahlke.

From this point through to the end of the novel, the motif is used repeatedly and emphatically. Thus the number thirty-two recurs no less than ten times on one page in the Osterhues episode (545; 450). It figures in Walli Sawatzki's vision of the snow attack (555; 458). Above all, it is given a predominant role in the crucial 'radio discussion' (570ff., 470ff.): there are thirty-two young people ranged against Matern; the 'first series of test questions' centres entirely on 'thirty-two'; and towards the end of the 'discussion' when the snow attack is again recited, the number thirty-two is ranked alongside the emblematic black hound as a specific 'fixed point' of the proceedings. Then again, the motif is included in Amsel's 'excrement' monologue preceding the strange inferno in Jenny's Berlin bar (638; 527), and it is insistently incorporated into the final panorama of Amsel's scarecrow factory, with its thirty-two chambers and thirty-two tubs in the first of these chambers, etc., etc. (652ff.; 538ff.).

One other instance of the motif deserves special mention, for it is a particularly revealing one. It occurs in the episode describing Matern's flight from Düsseldorf. Matern is horrified by the scarecrows he sees running along by the train, which he identifies with those of his erstwhile 'friend'. Already in flight, he flees yet again, this time to the would-be refuge of the train's toilet, but there too he finds himself confronted by an image reflecting both the lupine strain in general and the snow attack in particular: the intense drawing of a dog on the wall: ' – the black-sketched dog Perkun Senta Harras Prinz Pluto leaping over a garden fence –' (620; 512). Doubly in flight now, he flees yet again, but only to find the scarecrows by the train being joined by a three-dimensional version of the dog scribbled on the wall – and it is here that the tell-tale motif occurs, for Grass has Matern describe the dog as 'Eight – twenty-four – thirty-two-legged'. We come back here to our previous theme: there can be little doubt that what is being conveyed is a consuming, uncontrollable sense of guilt in the 'hero', the fiction clearly being that the Amsel scarecrows and the thirty-two-legged dog are just projections of Matern's now severely disturbed consciousness.

222

This whole motif of Walter Matern's sense of guilt, however, does have its paradoxical side when considered in terms of the persona's general role within the novel. For as I have argued, Matern is essentially analogous to the symbolic black and German hound in that both, in their different ways, are meant as representations of 'Germanness' – but this appears to be no longer the case when it comes to Matern's over-riding sense of guilt. At the close of the Second Book, Grass depicts the mass of Germans as wanting only to forget their past and their share of guilt, and whilst Matern would dearly like to do the same ('He has a spoon but no memory.'), he is never able to escape his guilty conscience. Thus he seems in the event to be the very opposite of the 'typical German' of post-war years, the representatives of which are such figures as Osterhues, Hufnagel and, above all, Jochen Sawatzki, people who *have* succeeded in shutting off their past and have in consequence managed to build up a stable, 'normal' existence. The question inevitably presents itself: why did Grass choose to invest Matern with such a dynamic sense of guilt, and thus make his archetype untypical?

At a sheer mechanical level, the question finds a ready answer: it was a considerable part of Grass's purpose to lay bare the all too carefully hidden reality of things, and Matern's ineluctable sense of guilt was an expedient device to serve this purpose, along with the similar – though in my view far less convincing – devices of the 'truth spectacles' and the 'radio discussion'. But this is not of itself a sufficient explanation. Had he been so minded, Grass could easily have achieved the same effect by relying exclusively on such mechanisms as the 'truth spectacles', or the interrogation principle that operates in the opening episode of the Third Book and again in the 'radio discussion'; or else he could have used, say, Amsel-Brauxel himself, or some different, detective-type figure, to unmask the truth.

But an ample explanation is soon forthcoming when we look beyond these purely technical considerations: it is surely Grass's fundamental humanist sense of morality that brought him to introduce the historically atypical factor of Matern's disruptive sense of guilt. Grass certainly does not see the destructive processes of the National Socialist era as morally neutral; unlike an earthquake, say, or the attack of a wild animal, they are blameworthy and entail guilt (in this respect, the eponymous dog-wolf image could mislead the unwary reader). Now *Dog*

223

Years is not a *Haupt- und Staatsaktion*. It is concerned not with the political leaders and their acts, but with the mass of ordinary people who would be scandalised by the harming of cats (see 'Faith Hope Love'!), but who connived at – or even, in their small, local way, contributed to – the grotesque savagery symbolised in the book by the 'mound of bones', and who later, in the novel's present-day, still ignore the savage reality of which they were a part. As Amsel says towards the end: 'Ah, how mysterious they are [the Germans], how full of blessed forgetfulness! They cook their soup on blue gas flames, and give it not a thought.' (646; 533). One purpose of the novel, then, is to hold up a mirror to the reader, that is, the ordinary mass of Germans, and thus confront them with their corporately blameworthy past. But this must have entailed the problem of how the moral dimension could most cogently be expressed. It would surely have been inadequate if the guilt of Matern, and therefore of the *hypocrite lecteur*, had been conveyed exclusively from without, by figures such as Liebenau (too young to count as having been tarred by the Nazi brush[21]) or the post-war generation of Walli Sawatzki and the 'radio discussion' participants. Grass's actual fiction is much more telling, whereby the moral dimension is incorporated within Matern himself, the reader's *alter ego*.

This brings us to something perhaps even more important: while Matern's dynamic sense of guilt is clearly unrepresentative, it is so only in degree and not in kind. There appears to be a conviction underlying the novel that feelings of guilt do lurk behind the blithe façade of the Sawatzkis and Osterhues and their would-be 'New Germany', and in these terms the guilt-ridden Matern of the Third Book is only a larger-than-life reflection of what is latently there already. This pattern is well illustrated in the episode of Walli Sawatzki's 'truth spectacles' insight into the savage past of her 'father' and her 'uncle', for they do both experience feelings of guilt – even though they promptly bury them beneath a spate of pretence and misrepresentation (555-6; 458-9).

And at this point we touch on what is, I think, one of the crucial areas of ambiguity in Grass's work – crucial, because it connects ultimately with the whole problem of individual action and its effectiveness. That Grass's treatment of the guilt theme has a moralist-humanist base, so much is clear. What

224

is not so clear is its *intention*: was Grass entirely certain in his own mind whether he chiefly meant it actively or passively, didactically or mimetically? On the one hand, it often seems as though his emphasis on the latent sense of shared guilt among the 'New' Germans – his readers – were part of a challenge to the *status quo*, part of an essentially educative onslaught on falseness. But at the same time there is no lack of evidence to suggest that it is in fact the mimetic aim that is, and has to be, paramount, the aim of doing no more nor less than reflect the true nature of the novel's 'dog years'. We shall look at this in more detail when discussing Amsel-Brauxel later on; but it may fairly be suggested meanwhile that this aphoristic assessment by Liebenau of the scarecrow-builder's creativity is in truth a description of Grass's own inescapably limited objective: 'At most he wished to demonstrate to a dangerously productive environment a productiveness of his own.' (218; *182*).

Role-playing and False Postures

We have dealt in all sorts of ways with the 'teeth-grinding violence' part of Walter Matern. It now remains for us to explore that other key element of 'histrionics' that was signalled years before in *The Tin Drum* (662; *532*), and then confirmed within the opening lines of *Dog Years* itself, by the use of the term 'the Actor'. The reader of *Dog Years* does not of course know at first who is meant by 'the Actor', but it is not long before things become more explicit – thanks to an explanation that establishes not only that histrionic posturing is endemic in the whole Matern dynasty, but also that it goes together with their trait of violence: 'The Materns, especially the teeth-grinding branch of the family, descended from the medieval robber Materna, by way of Grandma ... down to the baptizand Walter Matern, had an innate feeling for grandiose, nay operatic scenes' (28; *21*).

The first occasion when Matern is strongly projected in theatrical terms, is the episode of the two boys' discovery of the skeleton in the underground shaft – an episode whose particular function is to highlight the quite contrary temperaments and responses of the two 'friends': whereas Amsel is calm, detached and soberly observant, Matern responds with intense histrionics (the distinction is pointed with great deliberateness in the first paragraph of the relevant 'Morning Shift', page 88; 73; see also the similar formulation on page 91; 75). As the Grinder stands gazing at the skeleton, Hamletesque posturings take him over completely, his face twists into a grimace, his eyes – instead of looking 'dozy' or 'stupid' as usual – assume a piercing, grim and hateful aspect, and there is a whole rigmarole of forehead-banging and grandiose dark reflection (94; 78); 'Theaterluft weht' (*a theatrical wind is blowing*), as the narrator interjects – thus bringing in the ironic 'Theaterluft' for the fourth time in the 'Shift'. Meanwhile, we are told, Amsel is quietly setting about an activity that is the very epitome of ungrandioseness: he squats down and defecates. And there follows a passage which, with its rhythmic questions relating alternatively to Amsel and his 'friend', points up yet again the absolute difference between them ('Who is squatting there, obliged to relieve himself? Who is standing there, holding a stranger's skull far out in front of him?', etc.)

The contrast conveyed throughout the whole 'Shift' is a crucial one, with Amsel carefully seeking to discover the specific nature and meaning of the phenomena before him, whilst these same phenomena serve in Matern's case only to set off pre-formed, automatic responses, namely the stage responses of the Tragick Hero. Even on its own, Matern's behaviour with the skull would inevitably recall *Hamlet* – but what do we find in the opening lines of the 'Shift': 'Why always ogle at light and shiny skulls? Theatrical wind, Hamletlike maunderings, histrionic gestures!' (88; 73). These formulations plainly call in question the tragical response – and it is vital to realise that Grass's *own* view, and the view informing the whole novel, is being voiced here through the persona of Amsel-Brauxel. Amsel's open-minded, careful and – relative to the other boy's attitude – *ironic* response is at once both genuine and fruitful; Matern's received, automaton-like, pseudo-Hamlet response is not only ungenuine but baneful too: it leads to Amsel's being violently clubbed to the ground just because he offends against Matern's grandiose, false vision of things when he tries to take the skull.

It will be remembered, too, that Grass had already parodied

the same 'Hamlet' response and its 'so superficial marks of beauty' in the arrestingly similar 'Fortuna North' chapter of *The Tin Drum*. But the issue is a much more decisive one in *Dog Years*, for it is one of the novel's driving themes that the horrors of the National Socialist years were made possible at any rate partly because the mass of Germans were predisposed not to see reality as it substantively was, but to register it in terms of some received and false notion that rendered them effectively blind. We have already noted elsewhere the programmatic admission that Grass puts in Liebenau's mouth at the close of the 'Knochenberg' sequence, the admission that he kept the vile truth of the mounds of human bones at bay by means of 'medieval allegories' and Heideggerian verbiage (375-6; *311*; but see also the sequence itself, where reality and abstraction are precisely confronted in the exchanges between Tulla and Störtebeker, 370-1; *306-7*). Needless to say, Matern indulges in the same received Heideggerian abstractions (see for instance 285, 556; *237, 459*), and when it comes to his leaving the P.O.W. camp and entering the post-war world for the first time, a 'complete edition of *Being and Time*' accompanies him along with various cheap-edition plays as the source books of his false responses (436; *361* – and compare 639; *528*). A passage later in the Third Book that dwells at length on Matern's wartime absorption in Heidegger (474; *392*) is also striking for its leitmotif use of the word 'Vernunft' ('*reason*', '*mind*'): Amsel, we are told, thought 'mit Vernunft' ('*using his mind*'), but Matern's dog, we are told three times over, thinks 'ohne Vernunft' ('*mindlessly*') – which underlines yet again the fundamental difference between the two protagonists, with genuine reflection contrasted to a total lack of personal, considered thought. The pattern is clear: Heidegger's writings reinforced such mindlessness as Matern's by supplying a blanket set of preconceived attitudes and notions able to fit – and disguise – every situation. As Matern is explicitly given to say in the same passage: 'His words could be swallowed like butter. He was good against headaches and helped to stave off thought.' It might well be noted here that it is only for this matter of contributing to the false 'transcendance' and disguising of reality that Grass has Heidegger play so considerable a part in the novel. It would be wrong to assume, as some critics have, that Matern's histrionic verbal onslaughts against his mentor are the author's own.

227

When Matern reviles Heidegger in the same context as Hitler and the concentration camps, and lays the fates of Husserl and Amsel at his door (393-4; 325), and when he specifically assimilates Heidegger to Hitler (474; 392) and blames him, not only for 'murdering' Husserl, but also for the attack on Amsel and for the concentration camp exterminations (477; 394), we are not being offered statements of Grass's own view, but simply further tokens of Matern's persona, further indications of his driving sense of guilt, his frustration and impotence, the falseness of his histrionic Avenger role.

After the skeleton episode of the First Book, and various other pointers to Matern's theatrical tendencies, it comes as no surprise to find that instead of entering upon the study of economics, as he is supposed to do, he takes up the stage as a career – though without very much professional success, since bit-parts become his mediocre lot (219; 183), and when he does get his first sizeable role, it is merely that of 'talking reindeer' (in the same production in which Jenny Brunies makes her impressive ballet début as the 'Ice Queen'). Throughout the rest of the novel, the realm of theatre and acting remains the one place in society to which Matern can repeatedly resort – as a member of the Schwerin civic theatre, as children's radio announcer, as moving spirit of a P.O.W. camp drama group, as radio actor yet again, and then, in the narrative present, as 'the Actor' *tout court*, as even the opening lines of the novel present him. (It is indeed remarkable that Grass figured *all* the protagonists of the 'trilogy' – drummer Oskar, clown Mahlke, and *maître de ballet* Amsel-Haseloff, in addition to actor Matern – as belonging within the extra-social society of the performing arts.)

One crucial fact that the early skeleton episode serves to establish is that Matern's role-playing bent is entirely tragical. There is a straightforward sense in which this is true: as an actual performer in the theatre, his most keenly desired roles are such as Othello (281; 234) or Franz or Karl Moor in Schiller's *Die Räuber* (cf. 201; 169), and we hear that he takes special lessons only in comedy and not in tragedy – 'for Matern was convinced that a talent for tragedy was innate in him anyway and that it was only in comedy that he still had his difficulties' (219; 184). But the real significance of this runs deeper, for it is not just Matern's professional aspirations that are tragical, but his whole disposition – whereas Amsel's is ironic and

228

humoristic; and in this contrast we have perhaps the most decisive antithesis of the novel. What this means in practice is that Matern is naturally given to role-empathy; to foresaking his own identity (assuming for a moment that he has such a thing); to assimilating without question to the attitudes and actions of a role, whatever they may be; to approving of a role not according to whether it is true, appropriate, fruitful, but to the scope it offers for grandiose display, noble, glib, received sentiments, buskined, blinkered posturings, the purely histrionic.

Matern is strongly presented in this image in the introductory pages of the 'Materniads' – this title itself serving to ironise his would-be avenger's odyssey. Thus the squalid mess of leftovers which is all that Matern has to live off in the aftermath of the war includes, so we gather in the Third Book's second paragraph, the bits and scraps of 'All those dreary lies. Theatrical roles and life. Matern's dried-up vegetables.' The meaning of this becomes plain towards the beginning of the second 'Materniad': when Matern journeys into post-war life on the train to Cologne, he does so not as someone with a clear and stable identity of his own, but as a poseur, as someone with a 'head full of theatrical parts' (445; 368) – and with his arrival at Cologne station the principal pose of 'Heroic Avenger' is immediately established: 'Ich komme, zu richten mit schwarzem Hund und einer Liste Namen in Herz, Milz und Nieren geschnitten, DIE WOLLEN ABGEZINKT WERDEN.' (446; *I come to judge with a black dog and a list of names incised in my heart, spleen and kidneys. THEY DEMAND TO BE CROSSED OFF.'*, 369. This motto subsequently recurs some forty times in one form or another). He wonders at the time of the currency reform whether he should not perhaps transfer his furious teeth-grinding from its fringe existence in real life back to the stage – and the parts he visualises for himself are all tragical ones: Franz Moor, Danton, Faust, Beckmann in Borchert's *Draussen vor der Tür*, Hamlet (484; 400). Later, too, Grass has him spell out his role-playing reality: 'What else can you do, Matern? ... Speak loudly and distinctly on the stage. Well, then, slip into roles, brush your teeth, knock three times, and get yourself hired: as a character-actor, phenotype, Franz or Karl Moor depending on your mood – ' (546; 451). 'Franz Moor' is prominent in both these instances, and it is indeed on Schiller's *Die Räuber* that his whole posture as Heroic Avenger is modelled.

The Third Book's first mention of the play is in the initial interrogation of Matern, and there are repeated and emphatic references thereafter, many of them complete with characteristic quotations from Schiller's text itself (451, 457, 527, 561-2; 374, 378, 436, 463). But as with so many other things, it is the 'radio discussion' that sees the motif come to its expressive culmination, with the sham theatricality of Matern's behaviour being finally displayed beyond all doubt:

Denn ich, als Schauspieler und Phänotyp, als Karl Moor und Franz Moor: 'Pöbelweisheit, Pöbelfurcht!' verlange nach Gängen hin und her, nach Auftritten plötzlich und unerwartet, nach Worten, von der Rampe zu schleudern, und nach Abgängen, die neuen schrecklichen Auftritt erwarten lassen: 'Aber ich will nächstens unter Euch treten und fürchterlich Musterung halten!' (593)

For I, as actor and phenotype, as Karl Moor and Franz Moor: 'slavish wisdom, slavish fears!' hunger for pacings back and forth, for entrances sudden and unexpected, for phrases to hurl across footlights, exits that give promise of new and terrible entrances: 'But soon I will come among you and hold terrible muster!' (490)

The ungenuineness of Matern's Avenger's crusade is also shown up in other ways. For one thing, he betrays himself on occasion by abruptly casting his role to the winds. Thus he arrives at the Sawatzkis' steaming with vengefulness, but this steam is rapidly lost ('Der Dampfkessel Matern ist entleert', 451; 373), and he becomes the contented guest of his supposed victims, first in their armchair and then in their bed. Likewise with the Hufnagels: he arrives to take vengeance on Hauptmann Hufnagel, but in the event spends a happy Christmas in the bosom of the family.[22] There are also two other elements here that prove to be characteristic. One is the comment, concerning the night spent with Elke Hufnagel: 'Only God in his heaven looked on' (461; 381), which emphasises how even the token vengeance which is all Matern can muster, is a secretive, hole-in-the-corner affair, not an open act of witness; and we repeatedly find this device being used elsewhere to the same effect. The other characteristic element is that, instead of acting out his

230

'vengeance' on the person who is supposed to be its object, in this case Hufnagel, Matern diverts instead to some irrelevant and harmless substitute: he breaks young Elke's Christmas-present pen (and even then goes back on his actions by buying her another to replace it). Again, he does nothing to Hufnagel himself but only to his daughter Elke, whom – at her instigation and to her great delight – he deflowers, imagining this to be fit revenge on her father (461; 381). This is not the first time in the novel that Matern is so depicted: when, after the Amsel attack, he shifted all blame on to the 'system', on to National Socialism in general, he took his spurious revenge by surreptitiously poisoning the dog Harras. And later, on his release from prisoner-of-war camp, he personally dealt with Hitler – that is, he spat on his printed portrait and crushed his printed face (443; 367). Now, after the Hufnagels, Matern proceeds to visit his grand wrath on a certain Leblich, on one Paul Wesseling, on ex-judge Dimke – the results of these visitations being one assassinated canary, five stolen chickens and a burnt-up stamp collection. The pattern is particularly marked when Grass's 'hero' vainly seeks out Martin Heidegger: a letter box is made the recipient of his false rage – 'revenge, hatred and rage try to piss into a letter box' (476; 394), and he attacks the absent Heidegger with words alone, using his brute force only to heave the garden gate from its hinges and hurl it away – after which futile actions he exults: 'The avenger savours the after-taste of accomplished revenge: "He's got his. Now we're quits!"' (477-8; 395).[23]

Matern's whole 'avenger's odyssey', then, is false and futile – and could never be anything else considering that it is founded on one great lie: Matern's pretence that he is in a different category from those against whom his pseudo-vengeance is directed. As Matern himself is given to say:

Was tut ein Rächer, wenn ihm seine Opfer vertraulich die Schulter klopfen: 'Ist ja gut, Junge. Schon kapiert ... Jadoch, jadoch! Hast vollkommen recht: Du bist ein prima Antifa-schist und wir sind allesamt böse kleine Nazis. Einverstanden? Also, warste nich mal, und haste nich mal, und irgend jemand hat mir erzählt ...' (527-8)

What does an avenger do when his victims pat him famili-

arly on the back: 'It's all right, boy. We get you ... Sure, sure,
you're perfectly right. You're an A1 antifascist and we're
lousy little Nazis, the whole lot of us. O.K.? But weren't you
once and didn't you once, and somebody told me ... (436)

This is the big lie in the Third Book – but there is a whole
background of lesser lies as well. The first 'Materniad' plainly
indicates this: 'All those dreary lies', and then demonstrates it:
in the interview with 'Braux', Matern gives his birthday as
19 April 1917, but it becomes clear in the 'radio discussion' later
on that his real birthdate is 20 April – Adolf Hitler's birthday
(cf. 588; 485-6); he misrepresents his involvement in the SA –
'A few months in the SA, for a joke, sort of snooping around
just to see what was going on' (432; 358), claiming, too, that
it was all to protect 'a friend' from the 'mob'; Matern was
thrown out of the SA for petty theft, but he claims that it was
because he refused to carry out orders, and he also pretends at
first that he has forgotten the particulars of his SA unit; he
denies (in front of 'Braux'!) all knowledge of what happened
to Amsel; he claims to have been sacked from the Schwerin
theatre for 'insulting the *Führer* and so on', whereas the truth,
as we later gather from Zander, 'did not lie in the political
sphere, as you now maintain, but ... in the banal sphere of
alcohol.' (560; 462). Matern even lies to himself, when he laments: 'They've hounded me along with all the rest.' (437; 362).
And this goes hand in hand with the specific and fundamental
lie that he had nothing at all to do with the savaging of Amsel,
a lie that is voiced with full tragical posturing and sobbing in
the Lüxenich episode ('And I could only look on helplessly
as terror broke that voice. Eddi, my Eddi!' etc.; 465; 385), but
which is rapidly laid bare when Matern tries it on his erstwhile
co-persecutor, Jochen Sawatzki, by asking him what became
of Amsel and saying that it was Sawatzki and seven others that
had 'done him over':

Der erstaunte Sawatzki ... 'Nä Mänsch, da musst doch nech
miä fragen. War doch Daine Idee, der klaine Besuch.... Un
waas frägst ieberhaupt, wo wiä nech acht Mann hoch sondern
neune, mit Diä neun Mann hoch warrn jewesen. Un Du häst
ihm aijenhändich so fertich jemacht, dass nuscht nischt mäh
iebrig blieb....' (450)

The astonished Sawatzki ... 'Well man, whatcha asking me for? That little visit was your idea.... And whatcha asking questions for anyway, when there wasn't eight of us but nine, nine of us including you. And yer roughed him up so much with yer own two fists that there wasn't nothing left of him any more....' (372)

Even in the 'radio discussion', Matern tries to maintain his deceptions: he lies about his birthday again; about the fate of the knife; and, of course, about the attack on Amsel: 'For instance, my friend Eddi Amsel was beaten up one cold day in January by nine SA men, and I was powerless to help him.' (609; 503). But, as we have seen, the whole nature of the 'truth spectacles' and 'radio discussion' sequences is that they show up the past in all its blackness despite Matern's prevarications. And yet for all this, despite the fact that Matern is tormented from within by his own sense of guilt, and repeatedly confronted from without by the reality of his past, he remains true to his falseness to the very end. He flees from the exposure entailed by the 'radio discussion'; he refuses to be reminded even by Amsel himself of the snow attack ('he doesn't want to remember: "What am I supposed to? You must be pulling my? ..."'; 627; 518); and he flees the subterranean 'pandemonium' that is the mimesis of his world. As the novel indicates in its opening, and stresses repeatedly thereafter, Matern's existence in the narrative present is still entirely that of 'the Actor', of a putter-on of false masks.

A Lack of Identity

That violence and histrionics are constant, stable elements within Walter Matern is beyond any doubt. But it is equally beyond doubt that these two elements could not by any stretch of the imagination be said to constitute a stable and whole personality. Indeed we could say that one of the things that identifies Matern most clearly of all is his *lack* of an identity, inasmuch as 'identity' means something full and integrated. He is 'full of chaos' (558; 461), 'systematically muddled' (281; 234),

233

'ruled by confusion' (670; 552), a persona devoid of wholeness
and an own sense of being. The opening of the 'Eighty-eighth
Sterile Materniad' expresses this programmatically in a passage
that not only identifies Matern as 'empty' and 'inwardly
hollow', and indicates both his general turncoat nature and –
twice – his particular *volte-faces* from communism to fascism
to catholicism to socialism, but also relates him, if implicitly,
to Amsel-Brauchsel's scarecrows (in the phrase 'aussen mit
Stoffresten behängt'):

Schaut mich an: glatzköpfig auch innen. Ein leerer Schrank
voller Uniformen jeder Gesinnung. Ich war rot, trug braun,
ging in Schwarz, verfärbte mich: rot. Spuckt mich an:
Allwetterkleidung, verstellbare Hosenträger, Stehaufmännchen läuft auf Bleisohlen, oben kahl, innen hohl, aussen mit
Stoffresten behängt, roten braunen schwarzen – anspucken!
(514)

*Behold me: bald-headed inside and out. An empty cupboard
full of uniforms for every conviction. I was red, put on
brown, wore black, dyed myself red. Spit on me: clothing
for every kind of weather, adjustable braces, bounceback
man on leaden soles, bald on top, hollow within, outside bedecked with remnants: red brown black – spit on me! (425)*

(The depiction is echoed in the 'chamber of opportunists' part
of the scarecrow sequence later on – and Matern is specifically
identified with it; 674-5; 555-6.)

One of the clearest marks of Matern's instability is the motif
of his wanderings (a motif, incidentally, that recurs over and
over again in German writing of the last two centuries, and
one that could well do with investigation). We have already
seen how, in the aftermath of the snow attacks, he gyrates from
job to job, and from Danzig to Schwerin, to Düsseldorf, to the
battle front. Then in the 'Materniads' he scarcely makes even
token gestures to settle down, but journeys ceaselessly around,
with the Cologne station lavatory as the symbolic centre of
his existence. He is even explicitly typed as 'the Railway-
traveller Walter Matern' (467; 386), 'the travelling avenger' (480;
397), 'the traveller Walter Matern' (651; 537; *passim*).

Something that belongs together with Matern's urinal-centred

234

wanderings is his inability to form any stable human relationships – an inability already grossly manifest in the earlier two
Books in his ambivalent dealings with his 'friend' Amsel. Elke
Hufnagel begs him to be hers (461; 381), but he goes away.
He establishes a kind of home with Fräulein Oelling in her bed-
sitter, but after only six weeks it is all over: 'Cologne calls
him and he responds' (467; 386). But it is above all with Inge
Sawatzki (one of Grass's most finely drawn characters) that he
repeatedly fails to establish a relationship. After his first three-
week sojourn with the Sawatzkis, Inge implores him to take
her away with him, but he refuses. Later, when he is a balding,
gonorrhoeal wreck of a man, she finds him again in Cologne
station as he goes hobbling down to his urinal base, and offers
him a home (481; 398). Before long, however, the driving urge
within him re-asserts itself and destroys the seeming new-found
stability ('Matern wants to settle his scores in the old currency,
that's why he raises hell in Sawatzki's two-and-a-half-room flat';
484; 400) – with the result that Jochen Sawatzki throws him
out. Inge opts to go with him, and a week is spent in a hotel
bedroom. She tries to persuade him to get a job, and a home
for them both, but 'Matern doesn't feel like working; he wants
to wander.' (485; 401). Another night in another hotel, and they
wander on desultorily to a cold night spent in an empty church,
the whole episode ending with Matern violently crushing his
lover's face against the confessional grille and setting off once
more on his futile 'crusade', while Inge gives up and goes back
to Sawatzki. Later, Matern resorts to the Sawatzkis yet again
(though not before 'a last try at the men's toilet'; 515; 425). They
give him a home, and he and Inge – 'das grosse klassische Lie-
bespaar' (538; 'the classical great lovers', 444) – resume their
sex-centred relationship. In due course Matern even seems to
be settling down when he gets his job in radio and sets up a
home of his own at last, with Inge as his 'weekend wife' (565;
466). But then in the end, of course, he flees, and leaves Inge
behind yet again – even partly blaming his flight on her (614;
507). Thus, what with this and the Berlin encounter between
Matern and Brauchsel-Amsel, the human relationships of the
'hero' are even more dismally failed at the close of the fiction
than they were during its course.

As the Inge relationship itself suggests, one compulsion in
Walter Matern that we must recognise along with all the others

is his compulsive sexuality. Although already apparent in the Second Book (see especially the splendid episode involving the prostitutes, 192-3; *161*), it is in the Third Book that it becomes a central motif, beginning with the depiction of Matern's first cavortings with Inge – and her husband – in the Sawatzkis' marriage bed. And the discrepancy between this gratification and Matern's alleged purpose in seeking out the Sawatzkis is plainly underlined: 'Matern, who came with black dog to judge, explores Ingehole with gentle finger', etc. (452; *374*). The whole sporadic relationship of the couple remains thereafter centred on Matern's phallus, as typified when Matern is thrown out after the second *ménage à trois*, and he and Inge go off on their desultory and shortlived wanderings, for Matern's chief activity is to lay his lover at every conceivable opportunity – he even 'does her' in a church confessional (485-6; *402*). After the next abysmal failure in his solitary campaign he returns again to the Sawatzkis – but not before having stocked up with ten packets of contraceptives; and when he goes running to Inge after the sports club débâcle, the narrative dwells for a page on how 'the pair of them, the classic great lovers – Walter and Inge – do what they still can't stop doing.' (538; *444*). Then later the narrative speaks of them getting down to it again in the fields after Matern's futile hunt for Osterhues, and of their weekends spent on the double-bed in Matern's new flat.

Inge Sawatzki, however, is by no means the only woman with whom Matern promiscuously lodges his phallus. After his first cavortings with Inge he moves on to the teenaged Elke Hufnagel, deflowers her *en passant*, regretfully fails to possess himself of either Leblich's wife or Leblich's daughter, and has it with joyous Fräulein Oelling laid over a dustbin. There is later the business of Matern's gonorrhoea, and the typical image of the 'hero' discharging his lust in the guise of vengeance: 'Matern ... journeyed through the land to cross off names with gonococcus-loaded injections and to de-nazify a large circle of acquaintances.', etc. (469; *388*). This part of his 'campaign' is as false as any other, of course: what are supposedly punitive visitations in fact thrill and enthrall their recipients, who in turn besiege him in search of renewed visitations, as is described in a whole page and a half of the narrative (478-9; *395-6*). The outcome of this is that Matern himself goes utterly to the dogs (to use the novel's own image, 479; *396*), for he is turned into a decrepit

236

wreck by his autonomous phallus, his 'mindless stand-up-man' ('Stehaufmännchen ohne Vernunft', 480; 397. The phrases 'mit Vernunft' and 'ohne Vernunft' are used only a few pages earlier to differentiate Amsel and Matern).[24]

It is in the closing sequence down the mine that the whole theme of sexuality is given its final point, in the full-page depiction of the three scarecrow chambers devoted by Amsel-Brauchsel to 'Eros unleashed, Eros inhibited, and phallic narcissism' (667; 549), with the first of these chambers reflecting just that kind of frenetic, insatiable promiscuity which Matern represents throughout his adulthood in the story – and which, of course, was writ so large in *The Tin Drum*, particularly in the Jan Bronski-Agnes Matzerath relationship.[25] What is particularly interesting in this scarecrow passage is that Grass – and this is undoubtedly Grass stepping out from behind the fiction of Matern as narrator – supplies a vivid gloss on promiscuity which, above all in the phrase 'der dennoch niemanden sättigt' (*'but which satisfies no one'*), clearly implies that humanist ethic which, as I have so often argued, informs his work:

Denn hier wird hohngesprochen aller uniformen Zucht und zivilen Würde, weil Hass, Wut und umhergehende Rache ... aufs neue erblühen ... Weil alle entfesselten, gehemmten und selbstherrlichen Scheuchen an einunddemselben Kuchen knabbern, dessen Rezept alle Lüste zum Teig mengt, der dennoch niemanden sättigt, so sehr sich die nacktärschige Bagage, stössig und aller Stellungen mächtig, vögelt und vollspritzt. (667)

For here all uniform discipline and civic dignity are mocked, because hate, rage and roving revenge ... bloom afresh ... Because all unleashed, inhibited and narcissistic scarecrows nibble at the same cake, the recipe for which makes dough of all lusts but satisfies no one, regardless of how strenuously and in what positions the bare-arsed mob fucks and squirts. (549-550)

Needless to say, this is no philippic against sexuality as such, any more than its standpoint is that of 'all uniform discipline and civic dignity'; such things would run counter to the current of Grass's work. What he does seem to be concerned with is

237

that kind of excessive, autonomous, dehumanised sexuality which precludes such things as fulness, integrity, genuineness, both in respect of the individual himself and of his relationships with others. And as I have tried to show in much of this chapter, what the Matern persona with all its parts – autonomous fists, autonomous phallus, compulsive tragical posturing, itinerancy and the rest – fundamentally expresses, is precisely that lack of humane integrity and genuineness implied by these lines towards the close of the novel.

CHAPTER VI

The Two 'Friends': Eduard Amsel

We turn back again now from the one main character to the other, from Matern to his 'friend', master, victim and opposite, Amsel-Brauchsel, the figure who, as Grass's fiction has it, is head of the 'collective of authors' and thus the novel's moving spirit, who is also billed at an early stage as the book's chief protagonist (38; 29), and whose works – his scarecrow mimesis of a society and culture – are celebrated by the whole novel, inasmuch as it is proffered as a *Festschrift* for the tenth anniversary of his subterranean factory (32; 24). But Amsel-Brauchsel is paramount in a much more crucial and subtle sense, too: he is not only a profoundly conceived artist figure, and not only the notional moving spirit of the book as well as its chief protagonist, but he is also an embodiment of those very attitudes which inform the novel as a whole. To put it another way: in Amsel-Brauchsel *qua* scarecrow mimetist Grass crystallises, isolates, objectivises his *own* stance as writer of the novel. Grass is 'der Vergangenheit hinterdrein' (88; *'chasing the past'*, 73) – so is Brauchsel; Grass is concerned to illuminate the reality behind the façade – so is Brauchsel, the fictive manufacturer of the 'truth spectacles'; Grass figures, above all in Walter Matern, a shabby, self-deluding, automaton-like society – so does Brauchsel in his methodically filthied scarecrow robots. This is not to say that there is a simple equation 'Amsel-Brauchsel = Grass' – it would be ludicrously inept to imagine any such thing, for *Dog Years* is not an autobiography; but there can be no doubt at all that Grass's protagonist mirrors more lucidly and precisely than any other of his characters to date his understanding of the artist's function and scope within that particular society that he deliberately opted to stay in – the Federal Republic of Germany.

Amsel and Reality

In discussing the episode of the boys' discovery of the skeleton beneath the church, we saw how sharply, even schematically, Grass differentiated the responses of his two characters: on the one hand, Matern's automatic, tragical posturing; on the other, Amsel's careful, detached, ironic watchfulness. And this watchfulness of Amsel's is emphasised throughout the episode. It is he who, within seconds of first entering the classroom at their new school, discovers that there must be passageways beneath (Matern is characteristically slow on the uptake, 89; 73), and it is Amsel who spies the trapdoor in the changing-room floor – a trapdoor that was well disguised by the accretions of decades, but still not proof, we hear, against Amsel's gaze. Once they are down below, it is again Amsel who notices a branch leading off their passageway ('Amsel's flashlight discovered it.'; 90; 75), and it is Amsel who notices the hole opening into the shaft beneath the church ('They might almost have missed it if Amsel hadn't.'; 91; 75). In typical contrast to this, Matern's contribution to things is not one of mind or eye, but of muscle: it is he who lifts the trapdoor, who opens a rusty iron door below-ground, who goes first, club in hand – and who eventually clubs his 'friend' to the ground. (There was the same polarity in the symbolic knife episode of the novel's beginning: the power of Matern's fist, and the ultimately greater power of Amsel's gaze.)

As for Amsel's response to the skeleton itself, his attitude is as cool and precise as the other boy's is grandiose and extravagant. He is 'sober' and 'matter of fact' (88, 92; 73, 76), he carefully applies his artist's eye and mind to acquiring a firm impression of the specific shape and nature of something that is to Matern thoroughly general and unspecific.[26] This pattern is continued in the later part of the 'Shift': Walter Matern 'loudly declaims high-sounding words into the void', but such postures are not for Amsel: he quietly hunts for precise evidence, his approach is careful and analytical – and as a result he succeeds in establishing the exact history of the skeleton by his unearthing and dating of a Napoleonic military button (94-5; 78).

Amsel's penetrating gaze, then, and the whole attitude to

reality of which it is a part, are crucially characteristic of the novel. So for instance in the 'Twentieth Morning Shift', which depicts the young Amsel and his artist's vision of the twelve nuns and twelve knights cavorting in the Materns' mill as it begins to catch fire – for it is stressed over and over again here that Amsel is aglow with insight (while his 'friend' is dozy and unseeing; 76 ff.; 62 ff.). Or there is the later context, after the skeleton episode, when we hear of the apocalyptic destruction of the hero's final childhood creation, the 'Piepmatz' scarecrow, along with all his store of 'props' and bits and pieces – and in this case, the alliance of observant eye and creative mind is especially clearly conveyed:

Eduard Amsel ... verkneift die Äugelchen und sieht etwas. ... der vielzüngig brennende Vogel [beschenkt ihn] mit quicken Ideen und ähnlichen Rosinen. Denn wie das entzündete Tier ... stiebend in sich zusammenfällt, hat Amsel bei sich und in seinem Diarium beschlossen, später, wenn er mal gross ist, die Idee des Vogel Piepmatz wieder aufzunehmen ... (102-3)

Eduard Amsel screws up his eyes and sees something. ... the bird, spouting innumerable tongues of flame ... makes him a present of vibrant ideas and such choice things. For when the burning beast ... collapses in a cloud of dust, Amsel has already resolved in his heart and diary that later, one day when he is big, he will revive the idea of the Great Small Bird ... (85)

Just the same kind of artistic perception by Amsel is classically figured in the Second Book when we hear of the artist's response to the discarded SA uniforms brought along by his 'friend' – uniforms that had gone through many a beer-house brawl, we are told, and were thick with beer and blood etc.:

Er sortierte, zählte, stapelte, nahm Abstand ..., sah mit verkniffenen Augen: Saalschlachten, Bewegung, Durcheinander, Menschen gegen Menschen, Knochen und Tischkanten, Augen und Daumen, Bierflaschen und Zähne, Schreie, stürzende Klaviere, Zierpflanzen, Kronleuchter und über zweihundertfünfzig tiefgekühlte Messerchen; dabei befand sich, ausser den gestapelten Klamotten, nur Walter Matern zwischen der

241

Eichentäfelung. Der trank eine Flasche Selterswasser und sah nicht, was Eddi Amsel sah. (227)

He sorted, counted, piled, stood back ..., looked on with screwed-up eyes: beer-hall brawls, movement, tumult, men against men, bones and table edges, eyes and thumbs, beer bottles and teeth, screams, crashing pianos, potted plants, chandeliers and more than two hundred and fifty ice-cold knives; and yet, apart from the piled-up clobber there was no one between the oak panels but Walter Matern. He was drinking a bottle of Seltzer and didn't see what Eddi Amsel saw. (190)

Amsel as a Mimetist

It is clear from these instances alone that the eye for reality with which Grass endows his hero is of a special kind. Amsel is emphatically not presented as being all-seeing, like a camera lens that indiscriminately picks up every detail that happens to fall within its depth of field. His penetrating gaze is that of an *artist*; and it is the gaze of a *mimetic* artist, that kind of creator whose works are meant, not as renderings of some inward, imaginary world, but as images of outward, objective reality. This is made quite remarkably explicit in what is in fact the novel's first explanation of the power of Amsel's earliest scarecrows:

Wenn all diese vergänglichen Bauwerke immer wieder Fleiss und Anteil der Phantasie des Baumeisters verrieten, war es dennoch Eduard Amsels *wacher Sinn für die vielgestaltete Realität*, war es sein über feisten Wangen *neugieriges Auge*, das seine Produkte mit *gutbeobachteten* Details ausstattete, funktionieren liess und zu vogelscheuchenden Produkten machte. (40; emphasis added)

Though all these transitory edifices revealed industry and imagination on the part of their architect, it was Eduard Amsel's keen sense of reality in all its innumerable forms, the curious eye surmounting his plump cheek, which provided his

242

products with closely observed detail, *which enabled them to fulfil their crow-scaring function.* (*31; emphasis added*)

Any serious reader of Grass's work will need little prompting to recognise that Grass is in fact describing his own, as well as his persona's, art in these lines. And if this connection is doubted, we only have to remember Grass's observation (of November 1959) that he was concerned with 'a reality that needed to be exactly pinned down and described'; or there is above all this statement of Grass's in late 1960, which amounts to a remarkable echo of the novel:

> I work with the imagination, and in doing so make no experiments. I have a lot of ideas, some usable, some not. I test this very carefully, and trying things out in words soon serves to show whether some idea born of pure imagination is capable or not of being realised in words. And the test of this whole imaginative thing is precisely what we call reality, and is in most cases actual, concrete objects. And the asceticism that I impose upon myself today resides simply in the fact that I am mistrustful from the outset of anything laden with abstract thought, and the fact that I do not write about such things either, unless they spark my imagination.[27]

'Imagination', then, is indispensable – but on its own it is inadequate and even treacherous, as is particularly emphasised in Grass's little piece 'Der Inhalt als Widerstand', first published more than two years before *The Tin Drum* and without doubt the most cogent expression of his aesthetic credo that has yet appeared. Here, Grass forcefully condemns the unreality of unbridled fantasy when, apropos of an imaginary poem called 'Engmaschige Drahtzäune' ('*Narrow-mesh Fences*'), he describes the treacherous whisperings of the poet's 'Tischgenossen, der Phantasie' ('*table-companion, Imagination*'):

> Der Kosmos müsse unbedingt eingezogen werden, die motorischen Elemente des geflochtenen Drahtes müssten zum überzeitlichen, übersinnlichen, völlig aufgelösten und zu neuen Werten verschmolzenen Staccato anschwellen. Auch könne man ohne weiteres vom engmaschigen zum elektrisch geladenen Draht übergehen, sinnbildlich den Stacheldraht streifend,

243

und so zu kühnen Bildern, gewagtesten Assoziationen und einem mit Tod und Schwermut behangenen Ausklang kommen.[28]

The cosmos would absolutely have to be brought into it, the dynamic elements in the woven wire-strands would have to swell into a staccato that was beyond time and senses, that was totally dissolved and remoulded into new values. One could also pass on without further ado from narrow-mesh fences to electrified fences, touching symbolically on barbed-wire fences, thus moving on to bold images, to the most daring associations and to a final resonant conclusion laden with death and melancholy.

Grass's point is that the works of an imagination detached from the given, solid realities of existence are false, a sheer lie – the character Krudewil is explicitly given to call his airy-fairy companion Pempelfort a 'liar' in the second section of the piece. And depicted in *Dog Years* are all kinds of what might usefully be termed 'Pempelfortism'. Matern is an inveterate liar and distant cousin of Pempelfort; the Heideggerian abstractions of Störtebeker are similarly false; most lucidly of all, Harry Liebenau's grandiose disguising of the mound of human bones is of much the same order as the falsification of the 'Narrow-mesh Fences'. Amsel-Brauchsel, on the other hand, is a first cousin, a brother even, to Krudewil, the clear exponent of Grass's standpoint, and described characteristically as 'a mistrustful being'. Amsel-Brauchsel is presented as being always out to cast his artist's vision in the shape of *reality*. Hence his characteristic constant watchfulness for 'props', for the tokens of Reality that make his art effective – and it is significantly this activity that is conveyed in the novel's very first depiction of Amsel: 'there's a funny round something, bending over, wanting no doubt to take something from the Vistula. That's Amsel, looking for bits and pieces. What are the bits and pieces for? Everybody knows that.' (13; 8). It is for the same reason that he wants the discarded SA uniforms, and the skull from the skeleton beneath the church – for 'Amsel ... is always short of characteristic props and decor, and therefore of what is most indispensable' (93; 77).

This creative process which Amsel stands for is epitomised with great clarity at an early point in the novel, only two pages

244

after the key passage on his 'keen sense of reality in all its innumerable forms' (that it should be the particular reality of violence and persecution that sets the process going, is also crucial, but I shall come on to this in a moment); the narrative describes how his fatness and freckles made him the local whipping-boy, but then continues:

Zwar weinte Klein-Amsel, wenn ihn die Horde ... schmerzhaft marterte; aber durch Tränen hindurch ... wollten seine in Fett verpackten grüngrauen Äugelchen das Beobachten, Abschätzen, das sachliche Wahrnehmen typischer Bewegungen nicht aufgeben. Zwei drei Tage nach solch einer Prügelei ... fand sich ... dieselbe Prügelszene in einer einzigen vielarmigen Vogelscheuche abgebildet. (42)

Of course young Amsel cried when the gang ... painfully tortured him; but through the tears ... his greenish-grey, fat-encased little eyes never ceased to observe, to appraise, to take careful note of typical movements. Two or three days after one of these beatings ... the very same torture scene would be reproduced in the form of a single many-armed scarecrow. (33)

Much later in the novel, with Amsel now a young adult, this same creative process is illuminated, but from a quite different angle. After a pause of several years Amsel reverts at last to creating scarecrows (217; 182); his imagination is powerful, fired as it is by Weininger's *Sex and Character* (more of this in a while), and he creates a new array of scarecrows – but these new figures are failures, lacking all power and substance, as Amsel himself is the first to realise (223; 187). Why is it that for all the skilfulness behind them, for all their 'Perfektion', these new creations are so void of power that the birds, instead of being routed in panic as they were by Amsel's childhood contraptions, even come to roost on them (224; 187-8)? It is because they are false, contrived constructs of the mind, it is because they bear no significant relationship to the firm, true reality of the external world. And the remedy is quick: instead of staying in the inward realm of his studio, and instead of deriving his creations from his imagination and from the printed word of Weininger, Amsel goes out to the objective world outside, he is offered the spectacle of a violent fight between Matern and a Nazi *Jungvolk* leader, he carefully watches this episode of raw, typical reality – and transmutes it into artistic shapes that again have all the power of his childhood creations. Grass depicts these new successful models – and then adds a gloss of remarkable explicitness:

> Amsel war es gelungen, den Zugang zur Realität wiederzufinden; fortan bastelte er keine modischen Schablonen mehr, Atelierpflanzen und Zimmerlinden, sondern ging auf die Strasse, neugierig und ausgehungert. (225)

> Amsel had found his way back to reality; from that day on his works were no longer modish clichés, studio contraptions, decorative banalities; instead he went out on to the street, sharp-set and curious. (188)

'Reality' and Human Violence

The last quotation (and the new manifestation of Amsel's art to which it refers) implies perhaps more distinctly than any other an answer to the decisive question as to what precisely is meant in *Dog Years* by the notion of 'reality'. For it clearly does not mean the undifferentiated totality of phenomena: the focus is always selective – entailing thereby a particular attitude of mind, in effect a philosophy. Where does Grass have his artist-hero go to rediscover reality? – out on to the street; and the area of reality that his new and cogent art reflects is the *(violent) order of things in human society* – more specifically, the (violent) order of things in that part of human society that is Germany and its culture. Needless to say, National Socialism was the most savage manifestation of this; and it is characteristically the violence of National Socialism, as epitomised by the *Jungvolk* battle, that is mimetised in Amsel's new models (224-5; 188).

It is this notion of reality that is meant by the motto-like declaration that comes early in the novel and in an emphatic end-of-chapter position: 'Die Vogelscheuche wird nach dem Bild

246

des Menschen erschaffen.' (38; *'The scarecrow is created in man's image'*, 30) – a statement that is repeated verbatim three pages later, and which is echoed repeatedly in the closing sequences in Berlin and the mine (638 etc.; 527 etc.). It is surely in terms of this same notion, too, that we must understand 'Amsel's artistic theories' as Grass summarises them in the 'Fourteenth Morning Shift' : ' "Models should preferably be taken from nature." ' (52; *41*). Read in isolation, the word 'Natur' could conceivably be taken to imply bucolic fields and burbling streams and suchlike; but that would be to make Grass a 'Pempelfortian' ('Pempelfort bückt sich und pflückt mit ausgemachtesten Bewegungen eine Blume. Pempelfort: Oh, ich habe eine Metapher gefunden.';[29] *'Pempelfort bends down and, with the most fastidious of movements, picks a flower. Pempelfort: Oh, I have found a metaphor.'*) – and Grass is emphatically a 'Krudewilian', aiming to serve a muse that is 'grey, mistrustful, devoid of knowledge about botany, heaven and death'.[30] In the words of the severe and programmatic poem 'Askese' (*'Asceticism'*), published in 1960 :

> Und an die Wand, wo früher pausenlos
> das grüne Bild das Grüne wiederkäute,
> sollst du mit deinem spitzen Blei
> Askese schreiben, schreib: Askese.[31]

> *And on the wall, where earlier without pause*
> *the ruminant green picture chewed its green,*
> *thou shalt write with thy sharp pencil*
> *this: Askesis; write Askesis.*[32]

A few pages after the enunciation of 'Amsel's artistic theories', Grass again stresses the word 'nature', and this time its un-Pempelfortian meaning is clear beyond doubt. The occasion is Amsel's creation of the scarecrow of Grandmother Matern wielding her cooking-spoon – a scarecrow so effective that mad Lorchen is driven even further out of her wits, so that it has to be dismantled; the episode is then glossed as follows :

> Es hatte also ein Künstler zum erstenmal begreifen müssen, dass seine Werke, *wenn sie nur intensiv genug der Natur entnommen waren*, nicht nur Macht über die Vögel unter dem

247

Himmel hatten, sondern auch Pferden und Kühen, desgleichen dem armen Lorchen, also dem Menschen, die ländlich ruhige Gangart stören konnten. (60; emphasis added)[33]

Thus it was brought home to an artist for the first time that his works had only to be drawn intensely enough from nature to be able not only to dominate the birds of heaven but also to disrupt the tranquil country gait of horses and cows and of poor Lorchen too – in other words, of humans. (48)

Amsel's earliest scarecrows, it is true, are figured in the novel as reflections of a neutral human reality, in the sense that the models are portrayed simply as 'being', not as 'doing' – either *con*structively or *de*structively (cf. 40; *31*). But this phase is short-lived: within two pages of the remark about Amsel's 'keen sense of reality in all its innumerable forms', we hear of his nine-fold representation of Walter Matern swinging his fists in blind rage (42; *33*) – and this scarecrow proves to be exemplary of all his subsequent work in the way it expresses the reality of human antagonism and violence. Hence the later and all too effective scarecrow of Grandmother Matern swinging her giant spoon. Much later still, it is characteristically Harras's first Tulla-inspired attack on Felsner-Imbs that suddenly triggers off in Amsel his first bout of scarecrow activity for years (a bout that sees the first real maturing of his art, and which leads directly to the crisis of the snow attack); as the narrative forcefully puts it, the violent episode 'had released catches deep within Eddi Amsel, opened up wells, let pennies drop, and fostered the growth of a whole crop of ideas, which, sowed during Amsel's childhood, gave promise of a barnbursting harvest' (216; *181*).

Again, it is the reality of human antagonism and violence that is reflected throughout in Amsel's unending fascination for military uniforms and all 'props' that betoken soldiery and war. It is with the First World War helmet on his head that he is first presented in the opening episode (booty that he has fished from the Vistula), and his fondness for collecting military débris and using it for his scarecrows is repeatedly conveyed during his childhood; the description at one point of his diary-cum-sketch book is typical: 'To come right out with it: Amsel's diary teems with uniformed scarecrows' (58; *46*; the rest of the paragraph then illustrates the point with graphic detail). However, it is not

248

until the 'Love Letters', the Book centring on the National Socialist era and hence on the worst of the 'dog years', that the motif is brought to its climax – a climax that links it directly with the crisis of the snow attacks.

We have seen how Amsel is said to abandon his effete and modish studio abstractions and 'find his way back to reality' by going out on to the street (225; *188*). And how do we find this new concern for reality projected in the very next lines?

He showed a mania for uniforms, especially black and brown ones, which were becoming increasingly part of the street scene.... Only with considerable effort did he restrain himself from putting an ad in the *Vorposten* under his own name: 'Wanted: old SA uniforms.'

It is in the train of this revived passion for military paraphernalia that Amsel persuades his 'friend' to join the SA (an action that Matern is outwardly not keen to take, but which precisely suits his inner reality), and thus he acquires his first large batch of torn and filthy uniforms – the violent symbolism of which is clearly conveyed in his *Saalschlacht* vision (227; *190*). After the vicious brawl at the Nazi Party meeting which follows soon after (229 ff.; *192* ff.), and which bears out the truth of Amsel's vision, he receives yet another batch of beer- and blood-stained uniforms – and it is at this point that Grass has Amsel start work on a series of figures that prove to be the most critically important of all his creations. What his first set of new scarecrows does is in effect to subsume two hundred years of German culture – from Goethe and Schiller through Hauptmann to Horst Wessel – under the 'shit brown', 'dung-heap brown', 'indescribable brown' (235; *196-7*) of the dagger-torn and blood-caked Nazi uniforms. But there is a first sign of trouble here, too: Amsel ironises National Socialism both by dressing his own grossly fat and half-Jewish self in Party uniform, and by building a model of himself that is not only clad in the same 'ghastly brown' but also apes the Party salute by means of a built-in mechanism – and this spectacle inevitably offends Matern, now comfortably at home in his Jew-, Pole- and Socialist-beating SA role, just as anything offends him that runs counter to his false and grandiose posturing. Matern turns on his 'friend' in words at first (237; *198*), but when Amsel appears at a Party rally in his home-made

249

uniform and imitates the mob's enthusiasm, there is already the threat of physical violence: 'There [Matern] gave him hell and we thought in another minute he was going to hit him.' (238; 199). Amsel's mimetic will, however, is not to be repressed: with the sequence of the snow attacks already well under way, indeed in the 'letter' preceding Tulla Pokriefke's first persecution of Jenny Brunies, the narrator describes how Amsel is in the middle of making 'SA men who could march and salute, because they had a mechanism in their bellies.' (246; 205-6). Three pages later, this new group of foul brown figures is finished, and with Jenny being led off the while to the black 'temple' and her final persecution, two full 'letters' are devoted to describing first how Amsel gaily arranges his Germanic contraptions in the garden in military rank and file, and then how he sets their clockwork mechanisms going, so that with their pig's bladder heads adorned with the faces of the Nibelungs and Wagner, Hebbel and von Carolsfeld, with their SA caps and blood-stained patchwork uniforms, with their goose-stepping legs, with their club-swinging arms thrown up 'to the regulation height for the German salute' – Amsel this time parodistically playing the part of Hitler himself – they are a sharp, ironic unmasking and debunking of a whole culture. For what Amsel does through his robots, and Grass with him, is to contrast the grandiose, mythic, cultural façade maintained by National Socialism with its sordid, brutal and, above all, ungenuine, automaton-like reality. And it is accordingly thoroughly apt that Walter Matern, the novel's embodiment of this great lie, should return to the centre of the action at this precise point, and bring about the novel's crisis with his savage fists.

'Reality' and the Victims' Metamorphosis

I have earlier tried to show the paradoxical way in which the crisis of the snow attacks is truly critical for Walter Matern, in that he ends up the totally disoriented victim of his own aggression. But what are we to make of the contrary but equally paradoxical outcome for the would-be victims, whose 'visible metamorphosis' (272; 227) in the 'snow miracle' (260; 217) turns them

250

from fat and wobbly mountains of flesh into lithe and slender beings – a beauteous wisp of a ballet-dancer, and a graceful young man of classic proportions? This is potentially a crux; for the imagery is accompanied by no authorial explanations or glosses. To my mind, however, there is little doubt as to how we should see it. What Amsel and Jenny experience at last in their ultimate suffering is the full savage reality of which Matern, Tulla and the 'Knochenberg'-crows are symbolic – and in this ardent crucible they are seared to the point where their inward *artist's* being takes on its true and final form.[34]

That Grass conceived the violence-induced metamorphoses in terms of art is clear beyond question in the case of Jenny Brunies: it was long since made explicit in the narrative that Jenny's mass of fat disguised the makings of a ballet star ('ein nüsschengrosser Balletthimmelstern', 207; *173*); and whereas at the actual moment of her persecution she was still rotundly clumsy and incompetent (253-4; *211-12*), the effect of her metamorphosis is that she suddenly turns into a lissom and gifted ballerina. Liebenau watches her, in the moonlit forest clearing, start on a strict routine of exercises, watches her movements become softer and softer and ever more fluid (261-2; *218-19*), then sees her dance a whole ballet in the snow (which Grass conveys with astonishing poetic power, 263-4; *220*). A few pages later, after recovering from the illness provoked by her persecution, Jenny is depicted as devoting herself totally to ballet training – 'Jenny stands at the exercise rail and starts on her fine career.' (268; *224*) – and only a dozen pages ensue before we hear of her first success as a soloist (in her symbolic role as 'Ice Queen', 279-80; *233-4*).

With Amsel, on the other hand, the position is less clear-cut: while his metamorphosis is just as distinct and absolute as Jenny's in the physical sense, its metaphoric significance is less patent. Whereas Jenny's artistic talent was uncovered for the first time through her ritual suffering, Amsel's creativity had already flourished from his very earliest years by the Vistula. But what his metamorphosis does represent, I would suggest, is the last critical stage in a long process: after the many years through which his *art* was shaped and animated by the reality that is violence and aggression, his ultimate suffering in the crucible of that violence is such that his *whole* relationship to reality is reshaped and retempered. What this seems to entail is a decisive shift in Amsel's stance: Grass has him simultaneously devote himself entirely to his artistic, mimetic purpose (by immediately joining the German Ballet and rapidly becoming its chief *maître de ballet*), and also opt out just as completely from all personal, private involvement in that vicious social reality which has so persecuted him. *The Tin Drum* and *Cat and Mouse*, it might be remembered, both hinged on more or less similar metamorphoses (Oskar's arrest of growth, and later renewal of growth; Mahlke's transformation from anonymous weakling into renowned hero). But it is deeply characteristic of the changed perspective in *Dog Years* that whereas the protagonists of the earlier books lost severely by being transmuted, for all their interim illusions of freedom, Amsel-Brauchsel effectively gains. Oskar Matzerath and Joachim Mahlke both made the fundamental mistake of trying to beat reality at its own game: both try to re-integrate themselves into an alien society, the one by pursuing the norm of ordinary social relationships (Maria, Dorothea Köngetter, etc.), the other by pursuing the norm of destruction (the Knight's Cross) – and they both fail catastrophically. In sharp contrast to this, Eduard Amsel achieves safety and a kind of freedom by deliberately *standing back* from reality, by taking up the stance of a *detached ironist*. And it is Amsel's final and total assumption of this stance that is represented in his metamorphosis through suffering.

It is in this concept of *irony*, I believe, that we find the very essence of Amsel-Brauchsel as Grass has created him. Just as Matern is representative of tragical posturing and falseness, so Amsel is representative of ironic detachment and genuineness[35] – a contrast that we have already seen expressed with great acuity in the skeleton episode of the First Book. In all that we have said about Amsel's 'keen sense of reality in all its innumerable forms' and about his 'Krudewilism', we have in fact been analysing his ironic approach. And the more one examines the figure of Amsel, the more one is struck by the part that irony plays – not only in his artist's mimesis of reality, but in his whole response to that reality. The classic description of his fists (cf. above, p. 195) is typical: his pink, puddingy fists are useless for beating and hitting – but just right for laughing into ('gut zum Hineinlachen', 200; *168*). Tulla baits him as he sketches Harras in the joinery yard, but his answer is a laugh (196; *164*),

252

and when the prancing, frenzied Tulla later drives him out with her 'Itzich!' chorus, he manages, even in his trembling, sweating state, to preserve something of his ironic detachment: 'A smile refused to fade' (199; *167*); and it was Amsel's caustic ironisation of the Hitler cult vis-à-vis August Pokriefke that led to Tulla's onslaught in the first place ('this was the first time he had heard of the man – what was his name again?', etc.; 197; *165*). Amsel's reaction on being clubbed to the ground in the skeleton episode is another typical case in point: he cries abundant tears – but at the same time, we are told, he manages a mocking though good-natured grin, and he also comes out with a typical spoof:

'Walter is a very silly boy.' Mehrmals wiederholt er den Sex-tanersatz und imitiert dabei den Englischlehrer; denn immer, auch während Tränen fliessen, muss er jemanden, notfalls sich selber imitieren: 'Walter is a very silly boy.' (93)

'Walter is a very silly boy.' *Imitating the teacher's voice, he several times repeats this sentence from his first-year English book; for always, even when tears are flowing, he has to imitate somebody, himself if need be: 'Walter is a very silly boy'. (77)*

And his response is much the same (though it avails him nothing on this occasion) when he is encircled years later by his nine masked attackers in the wintry garden of his house:

He gives a high-pitched laugh and wonders with nervous tongue between his lips: 'What can I do for you gentlemen?' Pitiful ideas come to him: 'Would you like me to make you some coffee? There may well be some cake in the house.' (254; *212*)

There is one part of *Dog Years* that is of unparalleled importance in this respect, and that is the strange colloquy that Amsel holds with his assembled scarecrows on pages 220-3 (*184-6*). Grass's simple but trenchant device here is to make his hero reproduce in shortened form whole tracts of Chapter XIII, 'Das Judentum' ('Jewishness'), from Otto Weininger's notorious *Sex and Character* – and there is scarcely a single sentence throughout that is not a direct paraphrase of Weininger's monstrous argument. The reader was told much earlier in the novel how important Weininger's book was to Amsel-Brauchsel (38, and see also 202-3; 29-30, 169-70), but it is only here, in this three-page paraphrase, that we are shown the nature of that importance – and what we find is a brilliant illumination of the cardinal contrast of sock and buskin, irony and the grandiose.

For Weininger in his analysis of types distinguished two opposite categories: a 'good' and 'positive' one, conceived as 'Aryan' and, more specifically, 'Germanic'; and a 'bad' and 'negative' one, conceived as 'Jewish'. The attributes with which Weininger identifies his 'positive' 'Aryan' category, and which are cited by Grass, are such things as 'greatness', 'soul', 'the Faustian', 'the daemonic', etc., etc., or again, in the novel's own Weininger-paraphrase, 'der Glaube, der Eichbaum, das Siegfried-Motiv, die Trompete, das unmittelbare Sein' (223; '*faith, the oak tree, the Siegfried motif, the trumpet, immediate being*', 186; and cf. 203; *170*) – and the dramatic point here is that it is precisely this kind of attitude and this kind of image of Germanness which the novel persistently shows up, above all through Walter Matern, as a hollow mask disguising a savage reality. Weininger's characteristic 'positive' definition, 'to take oneself seriously',[36] though not specifically quoted by Grass, exactly applies to the figure of Matern. Amsel, on the other hand – and through Amsel, Grass himself! – is precisely the opposite, is 'Jewish' indeed in the central Weininger sense that, in his artist's reading and mimesis of reality at least, he *is* 'never anything but ironic' (222; *186*), that he *is* unheroical, irreverent, empirical, detached, 'witzig spottlustig' ('*witty and mocking*'), that he *does* refuse to be swept off his feet by grandiose enthusiasms, by 'oak tree', 'Siegfried motif' and 'immediate being'. In his artist's treatment of reality, Amsel (and Grass with him) might well be defined with Weininger's would-be vituperative phrase as an 'absoluter Ironiker'.[37] And it is notably in just such terms that Grass has Matern condemn his 'friend', as in his drunken explanations to the Virgin Mary after the other's disappearance: 'it was that cynical streak I couldn't stomach: nothing was sacred to him. That's why ... To him everything was laughable, and always Weininger, that's why we.' (287; *239-40*). And then again, in Matern's impenitent thoughts when faced with Amsel-'Goldmäulchen' ('*Goldmouth*'): 'There he goes again with his cynical talk, cynically smoking cigarettes that call everything into ques-

254

tion ... To him nothing is pure. Always standing values on their heads so that their trousers slip down to their knees.' (645; 533).[38] Needless to say, the reader must not make the mistake of taking Matern's strictures at their face value: Amsel is *not* a cynic, an irreverent mocker of everything under the sun. As with his creator, Amsel's irony is always and without exception founded in humanist values; it is always aimed at illuminating false masks and the gross, inhumane reality they conceal. And this is one chief reason why Matern attacks him in the garden, just as it is the reason why he hits Tulla when she brings back the skull from the monstrous 'Knochenberg'.

Returning now to the matter of Amsel's change of stance in the train of violence and the 'snow miracle', we come upon one of the most particular features of the novel. Oskar Matzerath and Joachim Mahlke both tried, if in different degrees, to flee their predicament by playing along with the reality that beset them – but they failed, and were driven in the end to an even more desperate flight. Eduard Amsel flees in a similar way (by going to Berlin, the very capital of National Socialism, and becoming a high personage in the official German Ballet Company) – but in marked contrast to the pattern of the previous books, he does not end up worse off than before. This is where his new stance reveals its effectiveness: Amsel manages to escape the vicious order that has always afflicted him by detaching himself from all personal and direct involvement in it, and by confronting it henceforth only from behind the safety of a carefully maintained ironic mask.[39] His first such mask is that of 'Hermann Haseloff', and the disguise is so complete that he can openly return to Danzig itself (in his new capacity as *maître de ballet*) without risk of discovery – even Jenny Brunies seems not to be aware of the true identity of her mentor, and there are only the merest hints that Oswald Brunies and Felsner-Imbs are in the know (Brunies: 307; 255-6; Imbs: 289, 344; 241, 285). In the years that follow, Amsel shifts through a whole series of roles – as a 'great impresario' (353; 293), as the interrogator 'Mister Brooks' at the start of the Second Book, as an official of the occupying forces (492; 407), as the moving spirit behind Anton Matern, as a powerful black-market baron. In the explicit words of a passus very early in the book:

Eduard Amsel oder Eddi Amsel, Haseloff, Goldmäulchen und so
weiter, ist unter allen Personen, die diese Festschrift – Brauch-
sels Bergwerk fördert seit bald zehn Jahren weder Kohle, Erz
noch Kali – beleben sollen, der beweglichste Held, Brauxel
ausgenommen. *(32)*

Among all the characters intended to animate this anniversary
volume – Brauchsel's mine has been producing neither coal,
nor iron ores, nor potash for almost ten years – Eduard Amsel,
or Eddi Amsel, Haseloff, Goldmouth, and so on, is the most
mercurical hero, except for Brauxel. (24)

I say 'explicit' – but this is only partly valid, for the narrator is
also strikingly inexplicit in what he says: he carefully tells
us what the mine does not produce rather than what it does
produce, and he deliberately leads us up the garden path by
implying that he, Brauxel, is a quite different person from Amsel-
Haseloff-Goldmäulchen; whereas this Brauxel-Brauchsel-Brauk-
sel persona is in truth another disguise of Eduard Amsel himself.
And this pattern prevails throughout the whole initial projection
of the narrative: Grass has Amsel's defensive stance of irony and
mask operate throughout his role as narrator. Who are the 'Du',
'Sie' and 'Du' that the narrator tells us about, or fails to tell us
about, in the opening line? and 'the Actor'? and the 'scarecrows'? And when 'Brauxel' first introduces himself in the
second paragraph – 'Der hier die Feder führt, wird zur Zeit
Brauxel genannt ('*The present writer bears at the moment the*
name of Brauxel') – the reader is at once forewarned by the
words 'zur Zeit' ('*at the moment*') that there is much he is not
being told; it will be a long time before he knows for certain
'Brauxel's' true identity.

Behind the Mask: Present and Past

Eduard Amsel may adopt a variety of roles from his metamorphosis onwards – but I need scarcely labour the point that his
role-playing is of quite a different order from Oskar's or Walter
Matern's, in the sense that it has nothing whatsoever to do with

any loss of identity, fragmentation of personality, etc. Unlike Matern, Amsel-Brauchsel is not 'inwardly hollow', unlike Oskar, he is never driven to ask himself: 'Who are you? What is your real name? What are you after?' He may present himself to the reader – and with much mysteriousness – as a factory-owning capitalist, as 'ein nüchterner Mann der freien Marktwirtschaft' (28; *a sober-minded man at home in a free-market economy*, 21); but behind this expedient disguise he remains possessed of a clear sense of his identity, his values, his function (see above, pp. 203-4). In both his activities in the narrative present – as mass-producer of scarecrows, and above all as begetter, controller and chief narrator of the novel itself – he remains exactly as he was in the narrative past: an artist, the mimetist of a violent reality, with an aggrieved humanism as his motivating force. But there is one decisive difference: the young Amsel reflected the reality around him at the time – but the present Amsel-Brauchsel is concerned almost exclusively to mirror the *past*.

This insistent focus on the past is a prime feature of the whole 'trilogy', and there were undoubtedly compulsive private and inward reasons for its being so. But the deliberate and public motives are certainly at least as important: it was Grass's purpose in *Dog Years*, as I have argued before, to hold up a stark image of Germany's violent past – above all through the persona of Walter Matern – in order to combat the illusion that all is thoroughly 'new' and 'changed' in the present. This intent is clearly at work throughout, but the last fifth of the book bears its stamp to a quite remarkable degree, from the 'truth spectacles' episode through to the final dramatic confrontation between the two protagonists. It is of course Brauchsel who invents and markets the 'miracle spectacles' (with their 'magic' additive derived from Oswald Brunies!),[40] and their function is spelt out in no uncertain terms:

[es] wiederholen sich im doppelten Rund der Vatererkennungsbrillen Gewalttaten, verübt geduldet veranlasst vor elf zwölf dreizehn Jahren: Mord, oft hundertfacher. Beihilfe zum. Zigarettenrauchen und Zusehen, während. Bewährte dekorierte umjubelte Mörder.... Jeder Vater hat wenigstens einen [Mord] zu verbergen. Viele bleiben so gut wie ungeschehen, verschüttet verhängt eingemietet, bis im elften Nachkriegsjahr die

Wunderbrillen auf den Markt kommen und Täter zur Schau stellen. *(552)*

The scenes that occur over and over again in the father-recognition glasses are acts of violence performed tolerated instigated eleven twelve thirteen years ago. Murders, often by the hundred. Aiding and abetting. Smoking cigarettes and looking on while. Murderers who have proved their worth and been decorated and adulated.... Every father has at least one [murder] to hide. Many lie buried curtained covered over as if they had never happened, until in the eleventh postwar year miracle glasses appear on the market and expose the people responsible. (455-6)

In this same episode, in the later 'radio discussion' (characteristically entitled 'Discussion With Our Past', 564; 465), and again in the course of his vain attempt to flee the truth, Matern is repeatedly forced to stare his past in the face until, in the closing sequence, he is brought into total confrontation with the past in the shape of his erstwhile victim. And from the very first sentence re-establishing Amsel's presence, the emphasis is on the brutality that he suffered at the other's hands: the narrative immediately particularises his 'smooth-combed hair', his hoarseness and his avid smoking (624; 515) – and all these attributes connote his beating in the snow, especially that of smoking, which has recurred so often by this time that it clearly ranks as a leitmotif (the leitmotif of Amsel's knocked-out teeth is also brought in a few lines later). The smoking metonymy is strongly in evidence in the paragraphs that follow (625, 626; 516, 517), and Grass then uses it to bring the sequence to its first climax, in that he has Amsel refer directly to the snow attack and try to force Matern to face the truth: Matern criticises his companion for smoking when he is already so hoarse, but Amsel points out that it was not smoking but 'etwas, ein Jemand' ('*something, a somebody*') that caused his hoarseness many years earlier – 'Na, Sie erinnern sich gewiss.' (627; '*Hm, you no doubt remember*', 518). It is this prodding half-statement, half-question that is the vital element – and only a page and a half later, with Matern continuing to blame the other's hoarseness on his smoking, the crucial words resound again :

258

Das hört Goldmäulchen gerne, wenn sich Matern mit so vielen Worten besorgt zeigt. Dennoch erinnert es ihn immer wieder daran, dass seine chronische Heiserkeit nicht vom unmässigen Rauchen herrührt, sondern genau zu datieren ist: 'An einem Januarnachmittag, Jahre zurück. Sie erinnern sich gewiss, lieber Matern. Es lag viel Schnee aufeinander.' (629)

Goldmouth is pleased to hear Matern's concern expressed so prolixly. But still he reminds him over and over again that his chronic hoarseness doesn't come from immoderate smoking, but can be dated with precision: 'One January afternoon, years ago. You no doubt remember, my dear Matern. There was a lot of snow on the ground.' (519)

But Grass has his mimetist-victim bring out into the light an even deeper past than the snow attack: Amsel reminds his 'friend' of the symbolic boyhood happening with the knife ('Once upon a time there were two little boys', etc.; 630; 520), thus echoing the very beginning of the novel – and this brings us to the fact that even the opening sequence of the book was itself emphatically an act of remembrance. In the explicit words that begin the 'Fourth Morning Shift': 'Brauxel lays bare the past of a pocket knife'; or again, even earlier still: 'What has long been forgotten rises to memory ... with the help of the Vistula' (10; 5; this passage is echoed in the 'radio discussion', see 605; 500); and the opening of the 'Fifth Morning Shift' makes this perspective even more explicit:

Brauksel hat sich also, wie vorgesehen, über's Papier gebeugt, hat, während die anderen Chronisten sich gleichfalls und termingerecht über die Vergangenheit gebeugt und mit den Niederschriften begonnen haben, die Weichsel fliessen lassen. Noch macht es ihm Spass, sich genau zu erinnern: Vor vielen vielen Jahren ... (19)

And so Brauksel, as planned, sits bent over his paper and, while the other chroniclers bend likewise and punctually over the past and begin recording, has let the Vistula flow. It still amuses him, for the time being, to remember every detail: Many many years ago ...[41] (13)

And in the skeleton episode Amsel-Brauchsel is given to describe himself specifically as 'seeking out the past' ('der Vergangenheit hinterdrein', 88; 73).

The sheer doggedness of this concentration on the past, however, gives the measure of what Grass sees as the contrary inclination: a ubiquitous urge among Germans to deny and suppress the reality of their past (see the trenchant close of the Second Book). Everyone wants to bury his past and live as though nothing had happened; in Grass's words concerning the first winter after the war: 'Snow is falling for reasons of de-Nazification: everybody is putting objects and facts out into the severe wintry countryside for them to be snowed under.' (455; 376). 'Schwamm drüber!', 'wipe the slate clean': that, says Grass, is the constant motto, as typified by Jochen Sawatzki's response when Matern has hunted him out in his supposed campaign of vengeance: 'Iss ja glicklich väbei dä janze Zaubä mit Ändleesung und Ändsieg. Heer bloss auf damit. Schwamm drieber ond nuä kaine Vorwirrfe nech.' (450; *To hell with the final solution and final victory routine. It's finished and good riddance. I don't want to hear no more about it. Forget it ever happened, and just don't start pointing fingers.*', 373). And the attitude is mirrored with careful emphasis in the context of the 'truth spectacles', when Walli Sawatzki returns from hospital metamorphosed by her insight into the brutal reality of the past:

Alle hoffen, das Kind möge vergessen haben, warum es so spitz und ernst geworden, warum es nicht rundlich und drollig geblieben. Denn zu diesem Zwecke war Walli im Krankenhaus: gute Pflege, damit Walli vergisst. Diese Verhaltensweise wird mehr und mehr zur Hauptlebensregel aller Beteiligten: Vergessen! ... Jeder Mensch muss vergessen können. Die Vergesslichkeit ist etwas Natürliches. Das Gedächtnis sollte von angenehmen Erinnerungen bewohnt sein und nicht von quälenden Garstigkeiten. (etc.) (556-7)

All hope that the child has forgotten why she has grown so peaked and solemn, why she isn't plump and jolly any more. Because that's what Walli was in hospital for: to be well looked after so that she would forget. This increasingly becomes the first principle of all concerned: Forget! ... Learn to forget. Forgetfulness is natural. The mind should be occu-

pied by pleasant memories and not by nasty tormenting
thoughts. (etc.) (459)

This brings us back to the crucial confrontation of the two protagonists towards the end of the novel – for it is here that the
theme of the Germans' suppression of their past is most powerfully stressed, not least in the pointed formulation on the
Germans 'blessèd forgetfulness': 'they cook their pea soup on
blue gas flames, and give it not a thought' (646; 533). But there
lies the desperate rub: can anything defeat this infinite forgetfulness? *Dog Years* may confront the *hypocrite lecteur* with the
image of his past – but the novel also consistently implies that
the Germans are quite immune against any attempt to make
them acknowledge the truth and rethink their position accordingly. Thus there is not a single 'ex-persecutor' in the book who
shows any genuine awareness or contrition; there is either suppression – the 'Schwamm drüber' response – or else there is
falsification, as in Sawatzki's and Matern's reaction to Walli's
recognition of their past: 'both are of the opinion that even then
they were against it: "When you come right down to it, our sturm
was kind of a refuge for the inner emigraishun."' (556; 459).
And it is precisely this resistance to truth that is most keenly
demonstrated in the final sequence: Matern remains steadfastly
blinkered and impenitent despite all Amsel's attempts to force
insight upon him, as for instance in the first of the 'You no doubt
remember' passages: 'But strenuously as Matern swirls the
remnant of beer in his glass, he doesn't want to remember:
"What am I supposed to? Are you trying to pull my? ..."' (627;
518); his response is just the same the second time: Amsel
reminds him of the events in the January snow years before, but
Matern refuses to be reminded and again blames the other's
hoarseness on his heavy smoking (629; 519-20); and the point is
driven home a few pages later: 'What good can it do for the
smoker to keep insisting on the true source of his chronic hoarseness, that January frost which suddenly turned to a thaw;
Matern continues to put the blame on cigarettes ...' (632; 522).
Matern may be constantly driven in the Third Book by the thorn
of a guilty conscience – but this goes directly against his conscious will ('Lethe Lethe, how do we get rid of memories?'; 437;
362); he is entirely lacking in that humanist moral sense that
is so fundamental to Amsel, and by the whole buskined nature

261

of his being he is incapable of critical self-appraisal and the will to reform himself. Again, the final sequence of the novel confirms this emphatically – for Grass has Matern re-enact the original symbolic event with the knife, thus demonstrating beyond doubt his utter impenitence and unchangedness.

All this clearly points to an unhopeful view of contemporary Germany on Grass's part – and we find the same unhopeful view implied throughout the novel's mimesis of post-war Germany, for instance in the allegoric depiction of the nation's economic recovery in terms of the idiom 'Da ist der Wurm drin' (literally 'the worm is in it', on the analogy of fruit that may be outwardly perfect, but is inwardly rotten). Again, this same view is strongly conveyed in the final sequence, not only through the fiction of Matern and his incorrigible non-acceptance of truth, but also and above all through the extended metaphor of Amsel-Brauchsel's underground 'Pandemonium' and its depiction of Germany in terms of soulless automata. And it should be clear that this subterranean scarecrow world, though partly universal in its reference, is chiefly intended by Grass as a reflection of things German. Witness for instance the manner in which the scarecrow motif is reintroduced towards the close of the penultimate 'Materniad', where Amsel, only shortly after the 'blessèd forgetfulness' passage, is given to declare : 'Of course you may say that every man is a potential scarecrow ... But among all the nations that stand as arsenals of scarecrows, it is first and foremost the Germans, even more so than the Jews, who have it in them to give the world the archetypal scarecrow someday.' (646-7; 533-4). It will be noted, too, that Brauxel's scarecrows in the final 'Materniad' are 'of German blood' and speak 'scarecrow German' (666, 679; 549, 559), while 'the whole of Germany' splits its sides in the 'laughter chamber' (661; 545). Similarly, the history acted out by the scarecrows on pages 671-3 is Germany's history, and the 'scarecrow state' and its constitution portrayed on pages 665-6 clearly refer to nowhere but Germany. Furthermore, it should not be forgotten that Grass includes in his Pandemonium the novel's central symbolic figure : the black and German hound. In the words ascribed to Hitler in the Second Book : 'The dog ... was-there, is-there and will remain-there.' 421; 349).

The significance of all this for our discussion of Amsel-Brauxel is considerable. For Amsel-Brauxel is chiefly projected as an artist, an ironic, humanist illuminator of a violent reality – and Grass's unhopeful view of contemporary Germany necessarily entails the problem of how such an artist can justify his art and carry it on: what is the point of holding up a mirror to reality if all remain resolutely blind to it and to its reformative implications? It could conceivably be argued that Amsel's scarecrows, and *Dog Years* as a whole, are neutral and gratuitous, 'zwecklos und gegen nichts gebaut' (40; *31*), that the novel is the product purely and simply of an aesthetic *Spieltrieb* ('play urge', cf. 7; *3*) – but I hope I have demonstrated clearly enough that this is not the case: the fictive narrator-in-chief, and through him the real Günter Grass, *are* activated by a profound humanism, and they *do* have a positive moral purpose. Thus the problem is acute: how can such a stance be valid when it meets with no due response? Matern remains unchanged to the end, and as for Amsel-Brauksel's mimetic scarecrows, they are merely consumer goods swallowed up by a consumer society; as Grass himself has remarked: 'Amsels Kunst mündet ja nur in Fabrikation ein.' (*'Amsel's art does end up as just mass production.'*)[42] It is this dilemma, I think, which may be glimpsed behind the grim, sardonic mood that Grass depicts in his hero in the long monologue which recapitulates the novel and prefaces the strange inferno in Jenny's bar, with Amsel-Brauxel speaking of his incessant cigarette stubs as 'Exkremente' (*'excrement'*) – 'Diese da, lieber Freund, stellen sozusagen meinen existentiellen Stuhlgang dar.... Abfälle Abfälle! Sind wir nicht? Oder werden wir nicht? Leben wir etwa nicht von?' (637; *'They, my dear friend, are my existential bowel movements, so to speak.... Waste and rubbish! Aren't we all? Or won't we be? Don't we live on it?', 526*). Considered in this unhopeful light, narrative art diminishes to a sheer means of survival in an alien and infernal world:

Erzählt Kinder, erzählt! ... Lasst den Faden nicht abreissen, Kinder! Denn solange wir noch Geschichten erzählen, leben wir. Solange uns etwas einfällt, mit und ohne Pointe, ... solange uns Geschichten noch zu unterhalten vermögen, vermag keine Hölle uns unterhaltsam sein. Du bist dran, Walter! Erzähle, solang Dir Dein Leben lieb ist! (641)

More stories! More stories! Keep going! As long as we're telling stories, we're alive. As long as stories keep coming, with or without a point, ... as long as stories have power to entertain us, no hell can take us in. Your turn, Walter! Tell stories as long as you love your life! (529)

But however grim all this may appear in its particular context, it certainly needs to be seen in a larger perspective. The mood in *Dog Years* may seem defensive and unconfident enough in itself – but it appears positively sanguine when compared with the black mood of pessimism and disintegration with which *The Tin Drum* ended. And the position in which Grass depicts Amsel-Brauchsel in the closing stages is characteristically very far removed from the bleak predicament of Oskar Matzerath towards the end of the earlier novel: whereas the fiction with Oskar was that he had already told his story and that he finally collapsed into silence, broken and afraid, the quite different fiction with Amsel-Brauxel is that he constantly commands the situation, that he confronts Matern insistently with the image of his scarecrow reality, and that he then goes on to master-mind the telling of the story, the humanist resurrection of the past which is the novel as a whole. It is in this closing sequence, too, that we find Grass perhaps indicating after all an answer to the severe question as to the validity and effectiveness of art such as Amsel's (and Grass's own): although he depicts Matern as impenitent and unwilling to acknowledge the reality held in front of his eyes, he does still depict him as sorely troubled and discomfited by this reality: Matern is already in flight from the probings of the 'radio discussion' when the final sequence begins; he is reduced to a sense of total impotence by the end of the Berlin episode (647-8; 534-5); and he is further routed by the spectacle of the mine in the closing 'Materniad' (669, etc.; 551-2, etc.). This depiction of Matern's discomfiture surely implies the hope that the novel as a whole might have the same effect of being a beneficial irritant working against such dangerous forces as complacency, falseness and deliberate blindness. And it is perhaps chiefly this which is symbolised through the detail of the knife: Amsel-Brauxel has painstakingly dredged up this token of Matern's past from the waters of time and confronted him with its reality, and although Matern tries to commit it to oblivion once more by throwing it into the Spree, he acts in vain: as often as he does so, Amsel-Brauxel will dredge it up again (647; 534). In the programmatic words that accom-
264

pany Brauxel's account of his recovery of the knife some ten pages earlier:

Es ist sinnlos, Taschenmesser in Flüsse zu werfen. Jeder Fluss gibt Taschenmesser bedingungslos zurück. Ja, nicht nur Taschenmesser! Genau so sinnlos war es, den sogenannten Nibelungenhort im Rhein zu versenken. Denn käme einer, der an den gehorteten Schätzen dieses unruhigen Volkes ernsthaft interessiert wäre – wie etwa ich am Schicksal des Taschenmessers Anteil nahm – der Nibelungenhort käme ans Licht ... (635)

It's absurd to throw pocketknives into rivers. Every river gives back pocketknives unconditionally. And not only pocketknives! It was equally absurd to sink the so-called Hoard of the Nibelungs in the Rhine. For if someone were to come along with a serious interest in the treasures hoarded by this restless people – as I for instance am interested in the fate of the pocketknife – the Hoard of the Nibelungs would come to light ... (524)

Or to quote the more trenchant words that Grass puts in Liebenau's mouth concerning Stutthof and its mass exterminations: 'Das wussten alle, und wer es vergessen hat, mag sich erinnern' (325; 'Everybody knew it, and those who have forgotten – may they remember', 270).

If we move outside the novel for a moment, there can be no doubt at all that Grass aspires to have a 'productive irritant' effect in his activities within the social and political sphere. As he himself wrote (in 1967) of his political endeavours:

The aim of my efforts was to set scepticism, criticism and active political commotion against soothing reassurances, promises of security and breaches of the constitution. It was and is my concern to carry this critical, politically active commotion into the German Social-Democratic party, so that criticism might effect change instead of becoming an end in itself and becoming part of the general stagnation.[43]

One does not have to modify the terms of this remark very much to see that it also applies very accurately to Dog Years –

265

which Grass did after all define as 'a political novel' a good three years before it was even published.[44] But what is particularly interesting about the remark is the way it so clearly contrasts the opposites of 'change' and 'stagnation': not only is *Dog Years* of 1963 fraught with this problem of change/non-change, but the problem is at the very heart of both *Local Anaesthetic* and *From the Diary of a Snail*. On the one hand Grass – by his own definition – is a 'born sceptic with inclinations to pessimism',[45] he is a man who feels bound to meet the charge of 'failing to change things' with the 'resigned or, as you might also say, slightly melancholic sentence: "Quite right, changing things is something I cannot manage!" ';[46] on the other hand, Grass is also a committed activist whose necessary premise is that *some* kind of progress can be achieved, however minimal. The risk of becoming yet another 'hero against absurdity' is great, but the risk must be taken. In the magnificent paradoxical words at the close of *From the Diary of a Snail*:

Nur wer den Stillstand im Fortschritt kennt und achtet, wer schon einmal, wer mehrmals aufgegeben hat, wer auf dem leeren Schneckenhaus gesessen und die Schattenseite der Utopie bewohnt hat, kann Fortschritt ermessen.

Only those who know and respect stasis within progress, those who have given up once and those who have given up often, those who have sat on the empty snail's shell and dwelt on the dark side of Utopia, only they are capable of measuring progress.

CHAPTER VII

Conclusion

Mercifully, it is not for us to consider whether Grass's political commitment is 'right' or 'wrong', or whether the notion of progress is valid or absurd. But one question we cannot avoid is the aesthetic one: is the novel itself a success? is *Dog Years* altogether convincing as a work of art? And the answer to this, I think, must be that the book is marred by some fundamental weaknesses and does fail in the end to carry conviction.

It is almost entirely in the last two-fifths of the novel that the weaknesses lie: after the steady, compelling progression of the earlier pages, the narrative line rapidly becomes disjointed and irregular, the whole manner and arrangement of the fiction change. This is not to say that there is a break of *thematic* continuity, for as we have seen, the issues remain constant throughout. What changes is the material fiction by means of which these issues are conveyed. So long as the fiction is detached in time, strongly localised (Schiewenhorst, Nickelswalde and the Vistula, and later Danzig), and clearly structured in terms of characters and plot (Amsel, Matern and the secondary figures, and their inter-action through the years), so long as all this obtains, the novel carries conviction in a masterly way; but this lucid pattern tails off once Grass moves on into the quite different place and time of post-war West Germany – and he finds nothing equivalent to replace it with, contriving instead a fiction that is jerky and laboured and persistently unconvincing. Remarkably enough, the problem is mirrored within the novel itself in the episode of Amsel's failure when, as a young adult, he first starts making scarecrows again; and the point about his failed creations is precisely that they are contrived and unconvincing, that there is a 'loss of substance' ('Substanzschwund') as against his earlier creations. These failed scarecrows, as we have seen, were described in a key passage as 'Atelierpflanzen', as forced and artificial products of the

267

artist's studio (225; *188*) – and one might well see the last two-fifths of *Dog Years* in just such terms.

It is not that Grass completely abandons the lucid pattern of the earlier part of the book: he does try to carry over as much of it as he can into the new situation – and this is just where he comes unstuck. The treatment of the eponymous dog symbolism is altogether symptomatic. The symbol could not be dropped, of course (as for instance the sub-plot of Tulla and Jenny validly could be), so Grass contrived the business of Prinz's escape from Hitler, an episode that is not only improbable as well as unhistorical, but also highly laboured in its fourteen-page execution, above all in the way that it suddenly and without any preparation converts the dog into an allegorical personage complete with intellect and the power of speech (423 f.; *350 f.*). But this is only the first in a succession of hollow contrivances: Grass has the dog deliberately seek out Matern and refuse to part from him; he has the dog recognise Hitler in the poster photograph; he brings in the dog that runs along by Matern's train towards the end, and the dog that Amsel has when he meets his 'friend' in Berlin. One gets the Symbolic Meaning, of course – but how grossly artificial is the manner of it all! The position is much the same with Amsel: his protean presence in the 'Materniads' is inorganic and contrived right from his interrogation of Matern at the beginning to his meeting of the train towards the end. The pattern with Matern is different: his histrionic Avenger's Crusade *is* an organic development of the earlier narrative (though it arguably carries on too long); and yet there is something quite startlingly unconvincing about Matern in the Third Book, and that is the very fact that he is supposed to be its narrator – for it is a total and constant contradiction that Matern should show such insight and awareness as he does, especially since what is most often being revealed is Matern himself, the blind and foolish histrion! Lastly, to name just one more variety of 'Atelierpflanzen' in the Third Book: the basic ideas behind the meal-worm episode and the 'radio discussion' are perhaps perfectly sound and laudable in themselves – but Grass exploits them far beyond what they can bear, and ends up with over-wrought and unattractive contrivances.

Why is it that the fiction in *Dog Years* incontestably changes in nature and arguably deteriorates in effectiveness and the

268

power to carry the reader? (And it might be noted that scarcely any commentator on the novel has yet found in favour of the Third Book.[47]) Many people tend to argue along the lines that Grass's epic talent is rooted in the past and is simply incapable of feeding off the present; thus Kurt Batt for instance, in a stringent critique of the novel, described the past as the 'true source of Grass's narrative power' and spoke of Grass's 'aberration' into the present as being responsible for what he called 'fantastical cyphers and surrealist practices', 'brilliant non-senses', 'an abstract-allegorical tangle'.[48] But then what about *Local Anaesthetic*, a novel of marvellous poise and coherence (*pace* its numerous critics) that is set almost exclusively in the post-war period? There is very probably a degree of truth in the Batt kind of argument – but as it stands, the argument is too facile. What I think we *can* say is that the past reality, the lost world of Danzig and his childhood, increasingly presents itself to Grass in terms quite different from those in which the post-1945 reality presents itself to him, and that he therefore runs considerable risks, aesthetically speaking, in trying to join the two realities consecutively (instead, for instance, of using the kind of interleaving process that he applies so effectively in *Local Anaesthetic*). This can be regarded to some extent as a technical problem – and Grass certainly seems to have faced great technical difficulties in writing *Dog Years*. Thus his first attempt – differently conceived, and with the title *Potato Peelings* – broke down completely after three hundred and fifty pages because, as Grass himself has explained, the narrative mode became 'strained and contrived' ('überanstrengt und künstlich').[49] And even the small number of wall-plans that I have been able to see show quite clearly that the novel as it stands is in fact compounded of designs for several separate novels. This could conceivably turn out to be true of all Grass's works – but in the case of *Dog Years*, at any rate, no single conception ever developed that was powerful enough to unite the parts and make for cogency. Interestingly enough, Grass has said that he is more attached to *Dog Years* than to any of his other prose works – but for the very reason that it did not quite come off ('es ist oft misslungen'), and because it is the 'least rounded' ('das unfertigste') of his books.[50]

Whatever the technical difficulties may have been, though, it may be taken for granted that they were only an outward manifestation of a more fundamental problem – and this problem, I believe, has to do with the vital question of detachment. For it can well be argued that Grass's epic talent functions properly and effectively only when he is sufficiently distanced, emotionally and intellectually, from whatever it is that he is trying to shape. This, surely, is what enabled his rendering of the pre-1945 past in both novels and in *Cat and Mouse* to be so compelling; and as I argued in Part One, Grass's treatment of Catholicism in *The Tin Drum* got out of hand for the very reason that he was still too viscerally involved in it. It is revealing, too, to compare the Third Book of *The Tin Drum* and the Third Book of *Dog Years*: there can be little doubt that Grass's mimesis of post-war Germany was much more substantial and effective in the first novel than in the later one – and there is little doubt in my own mind that the deterioration occurred chiefly because Grass had meanwhile begun to move towards his later intense involvement in the state and future of his country, and therefore found it impossible to establish a due aesthetic perspective. Grass's social-political moralism vented itself too forcefully, and thus infringed the necessary condition of his art. He should have stuck to the practice figured through the artist persona of Amsel: 'gegen niemanden baute er, aus formalen Gründen. Allenfalls hatte er vor, einer gefährlich produktiven Umwelt seinerseits Produktivität zu beweisen.' (218; *'His constructs were directed against no one, on formal grounds. At most he wished to demonstrate to a dangerously productive environment a productiveness of his own.'*, 182). 'Abstand nehmen' – 'standing back', distancing oneself sufficiently from the object in question: this essential creative procedure is one that Amsel is repeatedly said to carry out (cf. 92, 223, 227; *76, 187, 190*) – but it is one that Grass himself seemingly could not manage in the last two-fifths of his novel. It is a pity that the 'Danzig trilogy' should have tailed off in this way. And yet I am sure we need not regret it too much: for one thing, the problems of *Dog Years* were the beginning of a period of readjustment that led in the end to *Local Anaesthetic* – a novel of supreme ironic detachment that will one day be accepted as a masterpiece; for another thing, the local weaknesses in part of one book do little to detract from the greatness of the 'trilogy' as a whole – perhaps the finest body of fiction in modern German literature?

270

Notes

(Bibliographical references are given in abbreviated form throughout these Notes; for full details, see Bibliography.)

Preface

1 Letter to Reddick, June 1970. Cf. also Grass's remark of 1964, as reported by Heinrich Vormweg: 'Incidentally, [he added] the relationship between *The Tin Drum, Cat and Mouse* and *Dog Years* is also mostly overlooked.' Vormweg, 'Der Berühmte', 47.

2 Jens, 'Das Pandämonium des Günter Grass', 17. See also for instance Subiotto, 'Günter Grass', 228.

3 Cf. Grass's own explanation – 'The story *Cat and Mouse*, originally a bit of the new novel, separated out all on its own.', etc. – recorded in: Hartlaub, 'Wir, die wir übriggeblieben sind ... ' Grass has also given this fuller explanation: 'Richtig ist vielmehr, dass mir der gesamte Stoff der Novelle "Katz und Maus" die Erstkonzeption des Romans "Hundejahre" zerschlagen hatte. Ich hatte das Manuskript damals unter dem Titel "Kartoffelschalen" mit einer zwar reizvollen, aber auf die Dauer nicht tragfähigen Konzeption begonnen; und als auf Seite 350 (etwa) der Mahlke-Stoff als Kapitel und Episode dargestellt werden sollte, bemerkte ich die falsche Erzählkonzeption, legte den begonnenen Roman "Kartoffelschalen" zur Seite und schrieb, weil sich der Mahlke-Stoff zur Novelle auswuchs, die Novelle "Katz und Maus".' (Letter to Reddick, January 1971; *What is true is that the whole matter of the novella "Cat and Mouse" destroyed my original conception of the novel "Dog Years". At that time I had started on the manuscript, under the title "Potato Peelings", with a conception which, though certainly appealing, was inadequate in the long run to carry the book; and when at about page 350 the Mahlke business was due*

271

to be done as a chapter and episode, I noticed that the narrative conception was wrong, laid the half-finished novel "Potato Peelings" aside, and, since the Mahlke business was growing into a novella, I wrote the novella "Cat and Mouse".')

4   Kurt Lothar Tank, in his monograph on Grass, alleges that Joachim Mahlke, the hero of *Cat and Mouse*, was also originally part of *The Tin Drum* − but Grass has specifically refuted this (letter to Reddick, January 1971). See Tank, *Günter Grass*, 64.

5   Grass − Reddick interview, June 1971.

6   This plan (together with another) is visible in a photograph reproduced in Loetscher, 'Günter Grass', 17.

Part One: The Tin Drum

1   Although nominally annual, the *Gruppe 47* prize had not in fact been awarded since 1955 (Martin Walser), and was not awarded again until 1962 (Johannes Bobrowski). Cf. Richter, *Almanach der Gruppe 47, 1947-1962*, 449, etc.; see also Lettau, *Die Gruppe 47 − Bericht Kritik Polemik*, 137-42.

2   Translated from Holthusen, *Avantgardismus und die Zukunft der modernen Kunst*, 54, 55.

3   Holthusen, 55.

4   Translated from the official text, as reported in Schwab-Felisch, 'Ein Trauerspiel'.

5   Translated from (anon.) 'Stimmen zum Literatur-Preis-Krach'.

6   See for instance *Die Welt*, 8.10.65; *Die Zeit*, 15.10.65; *Der Spiegel*, 20.10.65.

7   Translated from Höllerer, 'Roman im Kreuzfeuer'.

8   Toynbee, 'A Best-seller from Germany'.

9   (anon.) 'Drum of Neutrality', 776.

10   (anon.) 'Zunge heraus', 64.

11   Holthusen, 55.

12   Holthusen, 56.

13   Cf. Idris Parry: 'André Breton ... might have been thinking of Oskar when he wrote that the art of the insane is the key to freedom'; and 'Oskar ... is free.' 'Aspects of Günter

Grass's Narrative Technique', 105, 107.

14 Holthusen, 54.

15 *Die Vorzüge der Windhühner*, 40.

16 *Gleisdreieck*, 71.

17 In this book, quotations from the 'trilogy' are partly given in translation only, and partly both in German and in English (in which case the English version is printed in italics). In all cases, however, double page references are given: the first, in roman type, refers to the German original, the second, in italics, refers to the English translation (see Bibliography for details of editions). The English versions of quotations from the 'trilogy' are all taken from the official translations by Ralph Manheim, to whom all credit is due, with amendments where appropriate for extra clarity. In the case of other translated quotations, the English is mine unless otherwise indicated.

18 Cf. the 'obscene little men' (10; *16*) that Oskar's visitors scrawl on the white of his bed.

19 *Gleisdreick*, 30-1.

20 Günter Grass, *Selected Poems*, 43, 45.

21 Cf. Genesis 1:23.

22 Hayman, 'Günter Grass', 29.

23 Cf. *Dog Years*, 10 (*5*).

24 Grass's last phrase echoes a fixed idiom in German, which derives in turn from Poland's patriotic 'Dombrovski March'.

25 *Über das Selbstverständliche*, 104.

26 Grass's faintly scurrilous figuration of existence and of the Christian deity has an impressive lineage in German literature, and similar passages may be found in Goethe, 'Bonaventura', Kleist, Büchner, Grabbe, Heine, Rilke, etc. (cf. Reddick, *The Eccentric Narrative World of Günter Grass*, 18 f.). Höllerer has dealt with this tradition in his book *Zwischen Klassik und Moderne*, published in 1958 – a book which Grass avowedly discussed with its author 'for hours and whole nights' whilst writing *The Tin Drum* in Paris. (See also below, 276, note 69.)

27 Forster, 'Günter Grass', 15, 13.

28 Translated from Hartlaub, 'Wir, die wir übriggeblieben sind ...'

29 See 29 ff., 39 ff., 79 f. in this book.

30 Cf. also *The Tin Drum*, 62-3 (*57*)!

31 Blöcker, 'Rückkehr zur Nabelschnur'.

32 The motifs of 'excretion' and 'ominous birds' are characteristic of the 'trilogy' (and are quite absent from *Local Anaesthetic*). The particular combination in these *Tin Drum* incidents has a grim counterpart in *Cat and Mouse*: the boys chew the seagull droppings on the wreck, the slimy muck is spat back into the sea, the gulls devour it, drop fresh droppings on the wreck, and the boys continue the cycle. – See 99 f. in this book.

33 The relationship in *Dog Years* between Walter Matern, Inge Sawatzki and Jochen Sawatzki will be described in almost identical terms: 'Solange schon steht das Dreipersonenstück auf dem Spielplan.' (454; *'That's how long the triangle play has been on the programme.'*, 376).

34 The motifs of 'repulsion' and an 'abyss' are powerful in Grass partly because they have become regular topoi in modern literature since about 1770 – especially German literature; cf. Reddick, *The Eccentric Narrative World of Günter Grass*, 42 f.

35 Cf. Reddick, 'Eine epische Trilogie des Leidens?'

36 Translated from Wieser, 'Fabulierer und Moralist', 1190. Wieser, it might be noted, was a close confidant of Grass's during the writing of *The Tin Drum*.

37 Grass uses a very similar image in relation to Tulla Pokriefke in *Dog Years*. See 186 in this book.

38 Sheer dislocation of the human form is a recurrent motif in Grass. Cf. the severed finger towards the close of *The Tin Drum*; the drawings of the dismembered doll in *Gleisdreieck*, 40, 45; the animated bits of body in *Dog Years*, 675 (556); and cf. also *The Tin Drum*, 257 (214)!

39 Grass has readily confirmed to me that he based himself on Jean Paul's 'Rede' (*Siebenkäs*, 'Erstes Blumenstück'). There is even a verbal echo: the word 'Fackeltanz' occurs in Grass as it did in Jean Paul.

40 This linking of disparates is in fact a recurrent feature of the book; cf. 22, 43, 45, 59, 369, (26, 42, 44, 54, 300); and cf. 31 in this book.

41 'Zunge heraus', 77.

42 Translated from Horst, 'Heimsuche', 1194.

43 See also 332 (271)!

44 Oskar's sexuality betrays him dismally in the coconut-runner episode. Again, the severe effect of this débâcle on Oskar

274

is signalled by tears, ironically presented though they are (639 f.; *514 f.*).

45   See also the autobiographical poem 'Kleckerburg' (*Ausge-fragt*, 91): 'Und aufgewachsen bin ich zwischen/Dem heilgen Geist und Hitlers Bild.' ('*And I grew up, was raised between/the Holy Ghost and Hitler's photograph,*'; Grass, *New Poems*, 65 f.). – See also below, 280, note 26.

46   Hartlaub, 'Wir, die wir übriggeblieben sind ...'

47   Cf. the short but heavily theatrical exchange between Oskar and 'Raskolnikoff' in the Third Book, 586 (*473*).

48   Cf. Kirn, 'Sein Zwerg haut auf die Trommel'; also 'Zunge heraus', 69.

49   Grass in the interview with Kirn.

50   Quoted in 'Zunge heraus', 75.

51   Cf. 54, 599, 603 (*50-1, 483, 486*).

52   Wagenbach, 'Günter Grass', 121.

53   These details were given by Grass in an unpublished radio interview with Horst Bienek in 1962, and are quoted by Tank, *Günter Grass*, 59 f.

54   Kirn, 'Sein Zwerg haut auf die Trommel'.

55   Henri Plard – whom Grass specifically commended to me in 1965 – has some especially interesting things to say on Grass's indebtedness to the Baroque in general and the picaresque tradition in particular: Plard, 'Verteidigung der Blechtrommeln'.

56   'My already keen scepticism' (81; *72*); 'did they think that I clung to tradition, that I let myself be burdened by principles?' (79; *70*).

57   Alter, *Rogue's Progress. Studies in the Picaresque Novel* (Cambridge, Mass., 1964), 71.

58   Cf. 134 and 432 (*114, 348*), where Oskar's observer role is explicitly spelt out.

59   So it seems, at least. But Grass appears to do a Sherlock Holmes with 'Störtebeker', the ringleader, whom he brings back as the 'hero'-narrator of *Local Anaesthetic*.

60   Alter, 41.

61   Forster, 'Günter Grass', 6.

62   Alter, 84.

63   Alter, 66.

64   Alter, 41.

65   Cf. 449 (*362*), after Oskar's return home from his travels

with Bebra: 'The whole world had forsaken me', but 'I still had my drum.'

66 Alter, 3. The quotation is taken from Rowland's translation of 1586, edited and republished by Blackwell, Oxford, 1924.

67 Alter, 110.

68 Höllerer-Reddick interview, January 1966.

69 Oskar's strange laughter is in fact part of one of the novel's most impressive tokens of duality and dislocation: the persistent motif of laughing and crying (cf. Reddick, *The Eccentric Narrative World of Günter Grass*, 141-4). There is an evident connection between this and Grass's long debates with Walter Höllerer on the subject of the latter's book *Zwischen Klassik und Moderne* – subtitled 'Lachen und Weinen in der Dichtung einer Übergangszeit' (*'Laughter and Tears in the Writing of a Transition Period'*); Höllerer made this remark to me about their mutual fascination for the motif: 'Wir sahen darin ein Mittel des Zeigens, das existentiell ist aber nichts mit Philosophie zu tun hat.' (*'We saw in it a means of "showing" that was existential without having anything to do with philosophy.'*)

70 This is finely emphasised through his two solitary friendships: Klepp swaps personalities at the drop of a hat, Vittlar repeatedly indulges in 'theatrical posturing' (347; 282). And it is well worth noting that for Grass these figures – along with Bebra, Schugger Leo, Sabber Willem and the rest – are in some crucial sense *extensions* of Oskar himself. He spontaneously insisted on this when I talked to him in 1966 ('Oskar projiziert sie alle'; *'Oskar projects them all'*), and did so again in 1971, when he categorised them as 'Spiegelungen Matzerathscher Art und Denkungsweise', 'Ergänzungen von der Person Oskars', 'Ausspielmöglichkeiten von Oskars Existenz' (*'reflections of Matzerath's way of being and thinking', 'extensions of Oskar's person', 'alternative possibilities of Oskar's existence'*).

71 This is curiously reminiscent of the opening words of E. T. A. Hoffmann's *Kreisleriana* – themselves reminiscent of the opening of Diderot's *Jacques le Fataliste*. Cf. Reddick, *The Eccentric Narrative World of Günter Grass*, 21.

72 Wieser, 'Fabulierer und Moralist', 1188; Wagenbach, 'Günter Grass', 126.

73 The English translation should read 'And no doubt it all

starts with his brain', not – as printed – 'It's bound to attack his brain in the end.'

74 *Dog Years*, 154 (*129*).

75 As in the case of the two decisive falls, most commentators have taken the linear approach and have unquestioningly accepted Oskar's version of the Dorothea affair. Thus for instance A. Leslie Willson, Idris Parry and L. W. Forster all assure us that Oskar is quite innocent of the murder (Willson, 'The Grotesque Everyman in Günter Grass's "Die Blechtrommel" ', 137; Parry, 'Aspects of Günter Grass's Narrative Technique', 104; Forster, 'Günter Grass', 8). It might also be noted here that an interrogation technique similar to that in the Oskar-Vittlar passage is also used to effect at the beginning of the Third Book of *Dog Years* – and also recurs, albeit in a much modified form, as a central technique in *Local Anaesthetic*.

Part Two: Cat and Mouse

1 Höllerer-Reddick interview, January 1966. The title-page description of the book in the English editions as 'A Novel' is wrong : Grass's own explicit sub-title was 'Eine Novelle'.

2 The dust-jacket designs for all three books in their hardback editions (English as well as German) are by Grass, as are the cover designs for the German paperback editions of *The Tin Drum* and *Dog Years* (but not of *Cat and Mouse*).

3 There is a fascinatingly similar ambiguity over the colour of the cat; compare 5, 116, 142, 149 (*8, 127, 155, 162*).

4 In the exhibition mounted as part of the Kafka Colloquium held by the West Berlin Academy of Arts in Spring 1966, there was a black-draped maze in whose avenues placards with conflicting interpretations of Kafka were hung. The idea for this maze was Grass's.

5 There is a startling echo of this opening paragraph in *Dog Years* (208 f.; *174 f.*) : a tableau depiction of Amsel's and Jenny's persecution not only repeats the sharply ironic 'und einmal' that began *Cat and Mouse*, and not only explicitly refers back to the cat's attack on Mahlke – but also mentions the smoking crema-

torium no less than three times. (Cf. 175 f. in this book).

6 Cf. Franz Magnus Böhme, *Deutsches Kinderlied und Kinderspiel* (Leipzig, 1924; reprint of original edition of 1897).

7 Grass notably describes the new cat in the very same terms as the original one: 'The ... black cat showed a white bib'(5; 8); 'the cat wasn't grey, it was more a black cat, and it showed a white bib' (149; 162).

8 As Grass himself has apparently said: 'Oskar has his drum, and Pilenz, the altar boy, has his guilt complex, that is the motor driving him to recount the story of Mahlke.' Cited by Tank, *Günter Grass*, 77. Cf. also below, 282, note 20.

9 It has been remarked by K. H. Ruhleder that Mahlke's centre parting reflects pre-Gothic representations of the crucified Christ. ('A Pattern of Messianic Thought in Günter Grass's "Katz und Maus"', 604).

10 Letter to Reddick, December 1970, in the aftermath of a dispute in the correspondence columns of the *Times Literary Supplement* (9.10.70, 16.10.70, 30.10.70, 13.11.70).

11 *Über meinen Lehrer Döblin und andere Vorträge*, 8.

12 Gerhard Kaiser, with his recent short monograph on *Cat and Mouse* (*Günter Grass – Katz und Maus*), has given us what must certainly count as one of the most careful and perceptive studies on Grass so far available. None the less, I am convinced that he is too rampantly post-Freudian in his central interpretation – a tendency well exemplified by the way he speaks of the photograph in terms of 'the potency symbol of the locomotive' (23). Kaiser (46) justifiably attacks the interpretational excesses of K. H. Ruhleder – yet his own approach is often not dissimilar in principle to Ruhleder's, in that both rely too heavily on systems of symbolism that are not derived from Grass's own text. Kaiser's evaluation of the train in the photograph as a 'potency symbol' seems to me to be essentially no less wayward than Ruhleder's extraordinary interpretation of it as a vagina, erect penis and castration symbol all rolled into one (Ruhleder, 'A Pattern of Messianic Thought', 607).

13 In the first reference to the sequence (21; 23-4), two lines are quoted from the eighth strophe, followed by three dots, and it is worth noting the words that these three dots stand for: *'Fac me tecum plangere./Fac, ut portem Christi mortem,/ Passionis fac consortem/Et plagas recolere.'*

14 See also 18, 56, 57-8, 113-14 (*21, 63, 64, 124*).

15 Cf. for instance 43, 157 (*48, 169*).

16 The image of Mary's symbolic impregnation is an ancient one, cf. Ruhleder, 'A Pattern of Messianic Thought', 603 (see also 606, where Ruhleder speaks of 'the hero's sexual desire for the Virgin').

17 Translated from Fritz Usinger, *Die geistige Figur des Clowns in unserer Zeit* (Wiesbaden, 1964), 28.

18 Translated from Karl Wolfskehl, 'Gegenspieler (Zur Metaphysik des Clowns)', *Gesammelte Werke* (Hamburg, 1960), vol. II, 434.

19 Friedrichsmeyer, 'Aspects of Myth, Parody and Obscenity in Grass' "Die Blechtrommel" and "Katz und Maus"', 246. See also Bruce, 'The Equivocating Narrator in Günter Grass's "Katz und Maus"', 140. Gerhard Kaiser, too, makes the same fundamental mistake (*Günter Grass –Katz und Maus*, especially 13).

20 Kaiser rightly refers to Goethe's 'unerhörte Begebenheit' ('*singular occurrence*') definition of the novella, but argues that it is Mahlke's winning of the Knight's Cross that constitutes the 'unerhörte Begebenheit' (*op. cit.*, 30). This is much too limiting. It is the *whole* single-but-multiple dynamic of Mahlke's actions and reactions that is the extraordinary occurrence, not just part of it (– as Goethe's definition would itself require : 'was ist eine Novelle anders als eine sich ereignete Begebenheit').

21 It may be tempting to see this episode in terms of the Biblical fall, as it is undoubtedly tempting to think that the book's central motif harks back to the *Genesis* derivation of the term 'Adam's apple' (cf. for instance Horst, 'Ferne Trommelschläge', 1197; Friedrichsmeyer, 'Aspects of Myth, Parody and Obscenity', 248). On the other hand Grass has rejected this outright (interview with Reddick, 1966), and the book itself, taken as a whole, does not seem to invite such an interpretation. Kaiser's treatment of the matter is characteristically ingenious : he does draw on the Biblical reference and the 'fall from grace' notion – but 'de-biblicalises' them completely in terms of his general socio-psychological argument (*op. cit.*, 13 f. and *passim*).

22 *The Tin Drum* includes a description of Alfred Matzerath that strangely anticipates the novella's description of Mahlke : 'Immer wenn ich seinen Nacken sah, tat er mir leid: sein ausladender Hinterkopf und die beiden Angströhren, die ihm aus dem Kragen gegen den Haaransatz wuchsen.' (196; '*I always felt*

*sorry for him when I saw the back of his neck: that jutting
occiput and those two "fear cords" that grew out of his collar
and mounted to his hairline.', 165).*

23 The same might be said of the masturbation episode; but
that episode is not only adequately motivated within its own
context, it also has no precise repercussions within the story.

24 Grass can scarcely have been unaware of the passus in
Kierkegaard's diary concerning his 'Master Thief' figure: 'Such
a master thief will also boldly ... and freely confess his crime
and suffer his punishment as one who remains aware that he
lived for an idea.' (translated from *Samlede Vaerker* I AA12).

25 By the end of the book, this ironic appellation has been
used some twenty times altogether. The echo of Alain-Fournier's
Le grand Meaulnes is not coincidental: in 1966 Grass specifically
mentioned that he had modelled certain formal aspects of his
novella on Alain-Fournier's book, and confirmed this again in
1971 – joking that *Cat and Mouse* was 'sozusagen die deutsche
Antwort drauf' ('*so to speak the German reply to it*'). He
incidentally also confirmed that he had been influenced, though
much less strongly, by Musil's *Die Verwirrungen des Zöglings
Törless*. (*Young Törless*.)

26 This image of physical confrontation resonates throughout the novella, often pointed up by the use of a quite specific
'confrontational' word: 'thin-skinned and vulnerable, we confronted one another betwixt the thorns' (127; *138-9* – the Oliva
Castle Garden encounter); 'I sat opposite Mahlke' (120; *131* –
Pilenz's visit for Sunday tea); 'we were sitting face to face.
Although I have never again to this day set foot in a rowing
boat, we are still sitting face to face' (168; *181-2* – the final
journey out to the wreck). This precise setting-off of Mahlke and
Pilenz is a typical mark of Grass's increasingly dialectic pro-
cedures, and it has a symbolic correlative in the novella: the
portraits of Hitler and Conradi (the founder of the humanistic
Conradinum) confront one another across the school hall (81;
90) – just as the portraits of Hitler and Beethoven confronted
one another across the Matzeraths' living-room. (See 47 and 167
in this book, and note 45 above, 274-5.)

27 Ottinger, 'Zur mehrdimensionalen Erklärung von Straftaten Jugendlicher am Beispiel der Novelle "Katz und Maus"
von Günter Grass', 47.

28 Grass-Reddick interview, 1966. Kaiser puts exactly the opposite interpretation on it, describing Mahlke's response as 'infantile', 'regression instead of progression into maturity'; *Günter Grass – Katz und Maus*, 30; see also 28.

29 There is in fact a whole motif on these lines in the novel; cf. Reddick, *The Eccentric Narrative World of Günter Grass*, 425-6, especially 426, note 1.

30 Cf. the line in the poem 'Drei Vater Unser' : 'Wer oben liegt, hat gewonnen' (*'Whoever is on top has won'*) – a line that occurs in a verse beginning 'Komm, wir spielen Kain und Abel' (*'Come on, we're playing Cain and Abel'*) – *Die Vorzüge der Windhühner*, 50.

31 Grass-Reddick interview, 1966. The context of the remark was such that Grass's word 'Fall' meant 'downfall', not 'case'.

32 *Dog Years*, 109 (*91*).

33 *Dog Years*, 330 (*274*).

34 The phrase 'unwürdiges Verhalten' is likewise used of Oswald Brunies – *Dog Years*, 339 (*281*).

35 See also 86 and 88 (*95, 97*): the submarine commander dons the same 'traditional red gym shorts' for his appearance in the school gym.

Part Three: Dog Years

1 Figures as supplied by Luchterhand Verlag, Fischer Bücherei and Rowohlt Taschenbuch Verlag.

2 Jens, 'Das Pandämonium des Günter Grass', 18.

3 Nagel, 'Günter Grass' "Hundejahre" ', 20. See also Klunker, 'Günter Grass und seine Kritiker'.

4 The clear impression in the book is that Brunies is killed at Stutthof (cf. *Cat and Mouse*, 48-9; *56*). It is thus interesting to note that one of the wall-plans indicates a 'journey to Brunies' at a very late stage in the book. Even more interesting is the evidence of the same plan that Brunies's arrest was to be directly paralleled by the arrest of Amsel himself.

5 Grass-Reddick interview, June 1971.

6 Grass uses the same motif elsewhere as well; see below, note 41.

7 The working title 'Ice-warehouse and Mound of Bones' on

a 1959 wall-plan, mentioned earlier, tends to suggest that the ice-warehouse episode originally figured large in Grass's imagination. On the actual plot-diagram of the wall-plan in question, however, the entry 'In the ice-warehouse' is plainly an afterthought, and a second item 'Ice-warehouse' may well also have been a late addition; furthermore, both entries are in relatively very small writing. A later wall-plan (1960) then duly sketches the episode much as we know it from the book as published: 'With Jenny in the ice-warehouse Tulla shuts them both in, but Jenny protects Harry.'

8   Nothing so clearly displays the triviality of W. J. Schwarz's volume on Grass (*Der Erzähler Günter Grass*) as his breathtaking misunderstanding of Matern, whom he describes as 'the loyal friend and protector of Amsel', 48; 'a character at bottom kindly and honest', 51; etc., etc.

9   Cf. 329-30, 344, 345, and especially 635-6 (273-4, 285, 286, 525).

10   Meyer, *Der Sonderling in der deutschen Dichtung* (Munich, 1963).

11   It is worth remembering here that Grass has specifically remarked that he broke off to write *Cat and Mouse* when his novel had got as far as 'about page 350' (see above, 271, note 3) – i.e. just when he had finished the fifty or so pages in which Brunies's attitude and downfall are chiefly dealt with.

12   Cf. especially note 40 below.

13   The pattern of persecution is also evoked in the novel through other animal images: there is the stuffed eagle with a stuffed lamb in its claws in a Danzig shop-window (96; 80) – and on the next page we hear that it is especially this that inspires Amsel to create his 'Great Little Bird' scarecrow; eagle and wolf images are repeatedly used in connection with Hitler; the verb 'hechten' (from *Hecht*, 'pike') is used of Matern on one aggressive occasion (224; 188); Amsel's pseudonym 'Haseloff' is said to derive from the 'hakenschlagenden Hasen' ('*zigzagging hare*') rather than from the 'zustossenden Habicht' ('*pouncing hawk*'; 282; 235).

14   Blöcker, 'Im Zeichen des Hundes'.

15   Jens, 'Das Pandämonium des Günter Grass', 18.

16   See especially 642 f. (530 f.).

17   Vormweg, 'Der Berühmte', 47.

18 Cf. 250, 273, 274, 279 (209, 228, 229, 233). See also 318 (265).

19 'PASLACKEN umsonst und ohne eigenen Nutzen sich für andere abmühen, andern oft und ohne Dank Gefälligkeiten erweisen ...' H. Frischbier, *Preussisches Wörterbuch* (Berlin, 1883). 'PASLACK Arbeiter für alle andern; gutmütiger Tölpel; Diener.' *Deutsches Wörterbuch*, ed. L. Mackensen (Munich, 1967).

20 Grass (letter to Reddick, December 1970): 'der Erzählmotor Schuld läuft bei Matern besonders hochtourig' (*'the narrative motor of guilt runs at particularly high revs with Matern'*).

21 Cf. Liebenau's response to Matern's attempts to explain away his past: 'Never mind, Matern, I know. If I'd been born a couple of years earlier, they'd have got me to fall for it just like you.' (568; 469). Interestingly, Liebenau (born May 1927) is almost the exact contemporary of Grass himself (born October 1927). What is even more interesting, though, is the fact that all the protagonists of the 'trilogy' without exception are made a decisive amount older than their creator: Oskar, born 1924; Mahlke, born 1925; Amsel and Matern, born 1917.

22 See also 467, 531 ff., 539-40, 558 f. (386-7, 438 ff., 445, 460 f. – Matern and the Dulleck brothers, Matern and the volleyball players, Matern and Semrau, Matern and Zander).

23 See also 559 (461-2), concerning Matern's absurd charade of poisoning Zander's trees; and 566 (467), when he furiously deals with his enemies – by tearing house-flies to pieces.

24 The 'Stehaufmännchen' image, which Grass uses several times, has a double reference: it relates both to Matern's ever-ready phallus, and, through the word's normal meaning of 'kelly doll', to his function as a representative of forces constantly recurrent, despite everything, in the German pattern of things. See 585-6 (483-4), where both meanings are again in evidence.

25 Grass reintroduces the same theme in *Local Anaesthetic*, see especially 116 ff. (91 ff.). Cf. Reddick, 'Action and Impotence. Günter Grass's *örtlich betäubt*', 568.

26 Cf. the striking description of Amsel's kindred spirit, Jenny Brunies: 'Seen from without, her eyes were silly under melancholy lashes; appraised from within, they had the gift of seeing through to the dry substantiality of things, even when they were things that stood on the tips of silver slippers and in

stage lighting signified a dying swan.' (349; 289).

27 Recorded in 'Lyrik heute', *Akzente* IIX (1961), 1, 43.

28 'Der Inhalt als Widerstand', 61.

29 'Der Inhalt als Widerstand', 58.

30 'Der Inhalt als Widerstand', 60.

31 *Gleisdreieck*, 57.

32 Günter Grass, *Selected Poems*, 49.

33 For another striking reference to 'nature', see the beginning of the letter that describes Amsel's recovery of creative power after his lapse into cliché etc.: 'Neither Tulla nor I could help him;/nature helped: in October Walter Matern had a fist fight with a platoon leader of a platoon of Jungvolk' (224; *188*).

34 The image of 'searing' is not mine, but the book's own: we are told some forty pages before the attack sequence even begins, that Amsel could see the gifted ballerina slumbering expectantly beneath Jenny's fat; and 'it would only be necessary to melt away the tallow and lard in a constantly sizzling pan until a balletically slender wisp could execute the famous thirty-two fouettés en tournant in the crackling flame.' (207; *173*). Another analogous image is that of insect metamorphosis: Jenny is repeatedly referred to as a 'Puppe', which means 'pupa' as well as 'little girl', 'child's doll'; and the sloughing image is implicit in the remark 'that a young man slipped out of the corpulent Amsel' (266; 222; cf. 464; *384*). It might be noted, incidentally, that Walli Sawatzki is later also transformed by the same savage reality: what she perceives through the 'truth spectacles' changes her from 'rund und drollig' to 'spitz und ernst' (556; *'plump and jolly', 'peaked and solemn', 459*; see 260 in this book).

35 In this contrasting of sock and buskin, *Dog Years* is astonishingly reminiscent of E. T. A. Hoffmann's *Prinzessin Brambilla*, with its conflict between the ironic and tragical sides of Giglio Fava. We might remember, too, that combined in Oskar Matzerath were the contrary 'tears' and 'brainbox' personas.

36 Otto Weininger, *Geschlecht und Charakter* (Leipzig and Vienna, 1909, 11th edn), 438.

37 Weininger, 441.

38 'calling everything into question' ('alles in Frage stellend'): it will be recalled that exactly the same phrase was used

concerning Oswald Brunies; see 201 and 202 in this book. (Cf. also 568 (469), where Matern curses the adult Liebenau as an 'Infragesteller'.)

39 Oskar achieved a similar kind of safety by joining Bebra's military theatre troupe (which reappears in *Dog Years* as part of Amsel-Haseloff's 'Propagandakompanie', 400; 331) – but Grass then had him return to the lions' den of his own family.

40 The decisive additive in the composition of the lens is mica (548; 453): not only did Brunies specialise in mica (cf. 110 (92) and *passim*), but after his presumed death Amsel-Haseloff had his samples taken away for safe keeping down a mine (353; 292) – presumably Amsel's own mine, and the place where the spectacle lenses are subsequently manufactured. (Cf. also the Berlin episode towards the end: Amsel's special drink at Jenny's bar contains – besides drops of Jenny's urine – a quantum of mica; 637; 526.) This serves to emphasise – in a forced way, I think – the identity of perspective as between Brunies and Amsel.

41 The reminiscent formula 'Vor vielen vielen Jahren' is in fact repeatedly used in the novel – most importantly perhaps in the pram episode towards the beginning of the Second Book (150; 126); but see also e.g. 8, 19, 22, 29, 75 (4, 13, 16, 22, 61).

42 Grass-Reddick interview, June 1971.

43 Translated from 'Zwischenbilanz. Versuch, ein Nachwort zu schreiben', *Über das Selbstverständliche*, 227.

44 Loetscher, 'Günter Grass', 20.

45 'Ich bin von Hause aus ein Skeptiker, neige fast zum Pessimismus'; in: Engert, ' "Ich bin zu realistisch" '.

46 Translated from Klunker, 'Ich und meine Rollen. Günter Grass'.

47 Cf. Klunker, 'Günter Grass und seine Kritiker', 469: 'The critics have almost universally attacked the Third Part, the part most critical of contemporary reality.'

48 Batt, 'Groteske und Parabel', 60.

49 Hartlaub, 'Wir, die wir übriggeblieben sind ...'

50 Grass-Reddick interview, June 1971. Grass added: 'Da bin ich auf das grösste Risiko eingegangen.' ('*It's what I took the greatest risk with.*') – On another occasion, though (letter to Reddick, December 1970), Grass firmly dismissed criticisms of the last part of *Dog Years*, and remarked: 'Ich vertraue hier auf

die Zeit; denn wie Maler beim Setzen der Farben das Nachdun-
keln derselben einkalkulieren, wissen auch Schriftseller, dass die
Zeit Texte, besonders zeitbezogene Texte, zu verändern vermag.'
(*I'm putting my trust in the workings of time; for just as
painters take account of darkening when they put on their
colours, so writers know that time can change literary texts,
especially those of contemporary reference.*')

Bibliography

Works by Grass

The 'Trilogy': editions used
Die Blechtrommel (Neuwied and Berlin, Luchterhand), 11th edn (January 1964). First published: October 1959. The 1st to 11th editions all have the same pagination – but not subsequent editions, which have been entirely reset.
The Tin Drum, trans. Ralph Manheim (New York, Pantheon Books Inc.; London, Secker & Warburg, 1961).
Katz und Maus (Neuwied and Berlin, Luchterhand), 7th edn (January 1964). First published: September 1961.
Cat and Mouse, trans. Ralph Manheim (New York, Harcourt, Brace & World; London, Secker & Warburg, 1963).
Hundejahre (Neuwied and Berlin, Luchterhand), 11th – 16th edns (October 1963). First published: September 1963.
Dog Years, trans. Ralph Manheim (New York, Harcourt, Brace & World; London, Secker & Warburg, 1965).

Other works referred to
Die Vorzüge der Windhühner (Neuwied and Berlin, Luchterhand, 1956).
Gleisdreieck (Darmstadt, Berlin and Neuwied, Luchterhand, 1960).
Ausgefragt (Neuwied and Berlin, Luchterhand, 1967).
Günter Grass, Selected Poems, trans. Michael Hamburger and Christopher Middleton (New York, Harcourt, Brace & World; London, Secker & Warburg, 1966).
Über meinen Lehrer Döblin und andere Vorträge (Berlin, Literarisches Colloquium, 1968). Includes 'Der Inhalt als Widerstand' (originally published in Akzente IV (1957), 229-235).
Über das Selbstverständliche. Reden Aufsätze Offene Briefe Kommentare (Neuwied and Berlin, Luchterhand, 1968).
örtlich betäubt (Neuwied and Berlin, Luchterhand, 1969).

Local Anaesthetic, trans. Ralph Manheim (New York, Harcourt, Brace & World; London, Secker & Warburg, 1970).

Secondary Literature

A comprehensive bibliography was to have been included in this book, but proved too voracious of space. In its stead is a bibliography listing *only* those items referred to in the course of the book. Where a listed item is also to be found in the compendium *Von Buch zu Buch. Günter Grass in der Kritik. Eine Dokumentation*, ed. Gert LOSCHÜTZ (Neuwied and Berlin, 1968), this is indicated by the abbreviation *GGK* (many items appear in reduced form in this compendium). Readers are referred to the Bibliography by Franz Josef Görtz, the fullest available on Grass and his work in general: F. J. GÖRTZ, 'Kommentierte Auswahl-Bibliographie', *Text+Kritik* 1/1a (October 1971), 97-113.

(ANON.) 'Stimmen zum Literatur-Preis-Krach', *Bremer Nachrichten*, 31.12.59.

(ANON.) 'Zunge heraus', *Der Spiegel* 17 (1963), 36, 64-78.

(ANON.) 'Drum of Neutrality', *Times Literary Supplement*, 5.10.62, 776. (Falsely ascribed to Richard Plant by W. V. Blomster; see under TANK below.)

BATT, Kurt, 'Groteske und Parabel. Anmerkungen zu "Hundejahre" von Günter Grass und "Herr Meister" von Walter Jens', *Neue Deutsche Literatur* XII, 7 (July 1964), 57-66.

BLÖCKER, Günter, 'Rückkehr zur Nabelschnur', *Frankfurter Allgemeine Zeitung*, 28.11.59 (*GGK*).

BLÖCKER, Günter, 'Im Zeichen des Hundes', *Frankfurter Allgemeine Zeitung*, 14.9.63.

BRUCE, James C., 'The Equivocating Narrator in Günter Grass's "Katz und Maus"', *Monatshefte* LVIII, 2 (Summer 1966), 139-149.

BUTLER, G. P., MANHEIM, R., REDDICK, J., *et al.* (letters to the Editor on the English translations of Grass), *Times Literary Supplement*, 9.10.70, 16.10.70, 30.10.70, 13.11.70.

ENGERT, Jürgen. '"Ich bin zu realistisch"', *Christ und Welt*, 3.7.70 (Interview).

FORSTER, L. W., 'Günter Grass', *University of Toronto Quarterly* XXXVIII, 1 (October 1968), 1-16.

FRIEDRICHSMEYER, Erhard M., 'Aspects of Myth, Parody and Obscenity in Grass' "Die Blechtrommel" and "Katz und Maus"', *Germanic Review* XL, 3 (May 1965), 240-50.

HAYMAN, Ronald, 'Günter Grass', *Encounter*, September 1970, 26-9 (Interview).

HARTLAUB, Geno, 'Wir, die wir übriggeblieben sind ...', *Sonntagsblatt* (Hamburg), 1.1.67 (Interview) (*GGK*).

HÖLLERER, Walter, 'Roman im Kreuzfeuer', *Der Tagesspiegel* (Berlin), 20.12.59 (*GGK*).

HOLTHUSEN, Hans Egon, *Avantgardismus und die Zukunft der modernen Kunst* (Munich, 1964; Piper Bücherei 196).

HORST, K. A., 'Heimsuche', *Merkur* XIII (1959), 1191-5.

HORST, K. A., 'Ferne Trommelschläge', *Merkur* XV (1961), 1197-8.

JENS, Walter, 'Das Pandämonium des Günter Grass', *Die Zeit*, 6.9.63, 17-18 (*GGK*).

KAISER, Gerhard, *Günter Grass – Katz und Maus* (Munich, 1971; *Literatur im Dialog*, 1).

KIRN, Richard, 'Sein Zwerg haut auf die Trommel', *Frankfurter Neue Presse*, 14.11.59, 11 (Interview).

KLUNKER, Heinz, 'Günter Grass und seine Kritiker. Statt einer verspäteten Rezension der "Hundejahre"', *Europäische Begegnung* 4 (1964), 466-9.

KLUNKER, Heinz, 'Ich und meine Rollen. Günter Grass. Wirklichkeit und Roman, Literatur und Politik – Ein Gespräch', *Deutsches Allgemeines Sonntagsblatt* (Hamburg), 12.10.69, 25.

LETTAU, Reinhard (ed.), *Die Gruppe 47 – Bericht Kritik Polemik* (Neuwied and Berlin, 1967), 137-42.

LOETSCHER, Hugo, 'Günter Grass', *Du* 232 (June 1960), 15-20 (*GGK*, but without photographs).

NAGEL, Ivan, 'Günter Grass' "Hundejahre". Breit ist der Strom der Erinnerung', *Die Zeit*, 27.9.63, 19-20.

OTTINGER, Emil, 'Zur mehrdimensionalen Erklärung von Straftaten Jugendlicher am Beispiel der Novelle "Katz und Maus" von Günter Grass', *Monatsschrift für Kriminologie und Strafrechtsreform* 45 (1962), 175-83 (*GGK*).

PARRY, Idris, 'Aspects of Günter Grass's Narrative Technique', *Forum for Modern Language Studies* III, 2 (April 1967), 99-114.

PLARD, Henri, 'Verteidigung der Blechtrommeln. Über Günter Grass', *Text+Kritik* 1 (1963), 1-8. Republished, with negligible modifications and the title 'Über die "Blechtrommel"', in *Text + Kritik* 1/1a (October 1971), 27-37.

REDDICK, John, *The Eccentric Narrative World of Günter Grass: Aspects of 'Die Blechtrommel', 'Katz und Maus' and 'Hundejahre'* (University of Oxford, unpublished D.Phil. dissertation, 1970).

REDDICK, John, 'Eine epische Trilogie des Leidens? "Die Blechtrommel", "Katz und Maus", "Hundejahre"', *Text + Kritik* 1/1a (October 1971), 38-51.

REDDICK, John, 'Action and Impotence. Günter Grass's *örtlich betäubt*', *Modern Language Review* 67 (1972), 563-78.

RICHTER, Hans Werner (ed., aided by Walter MANNZEN), *Almanach der Gruppe 47, 1947-1962* (Hamburg, 1962) 449, etc.

RUHLEDER, Karl H., 'A Pattern of Messianic Thought in Günter Grass' "Katz und Maus"', *The German Quarterly* XXXIX (1966), 599-612.

SCHWAB-FELISCH, Hans, 'Ein Trauerspiel', *Frankfurter Allgemeine Zeitung*, 29.12.59.

SCHWARZ, Wilhelm Johannes, *Der Erzähler Günter Grass* (Berne and Munich, 1969).

SUBIOTTO, Arrigo V., 'Günter Grass', *Essays on Contemporary German Literature*, ed. Brian Keith-Smith (London, 1966; *German Men of Letters*, IV), 215-35.

TANK, Kurt Lothar, *Günter Grass* (Berlin, 1965; 2nd edn with additional chapter, 1966; *Köpfe des XX. Jahrhunderts*, 38). American edition: *Günter Grass*. Trans. John Conway, with a bibliography compiled by W. V. Blomster (New York, 1969).

TOYNBEE, Philip, 'A Best-seller from Germany', *Observer* (London), 30.9.62.

VORMWEG, Heinrich, 'Der Berühmte. Heinrich Vormweg besucht Günter Grass', *Magnum*, Jahresheft 1964, 46-8 (*GGK*).

WAGENBACH, Klaus, 'Günter Grass', *Schriftsteller der Gegenwart*, ed. Klaus Nonnenmann (Olten and Freiburg-im-Breisgau, 1963), 118-26.

WIESER, Theodor, 'Fabulierer und Moralist', *Merkur* XIII (1959), 1188-91.

WILLSON, A. Leslie, 'The Grotesque Everyman in Günter Grass's "Die Blechtrommel"', *Monatshefte* LVIII, 2 (Summer 1966), 131-8.